THE
SPORTS
DOCTOR'S
FITNESS BOOK
FOR WOMEN

THE SPORTS DOCTOR'S FITNESS BOOK FOR WOMEN

John L. Marshall, M.D.
with
Heather Barbash

DELACORTE PRESS / NEW YORK

Published by
Delacorte Press
1 Dag Hammarskjold Plaza
New York, N.Y. 10017

Manufactured in the United States of America

First printing

Designed by Oksana Kushnir

LIBRARY OF CONGRESS CATALOGING IN PUBLICATION DATA

Marshall, John L
  The sports doctor's fitness book for women.

  Includes index.
  1. Physical fitness for women. 2. Sports for
women—Physiological aspects. I. Barbash, Heather.
II. Title.
GV482.M37   613.7′045   80-25516
  ISBN 0-440-08201-3

Foreword

John Marshall was more a friend than a doctor to his patients, and I think that's why they were always willing to do more for him, to work out longer and train harder. I know that's the way it was for me. I first went to him at the suggestion of the trainers for the New York Apples when I was playing team tennis. My knee wasn't responding to therapy, and the trainers suggested that I see Dr. Marshall, who, they said, was the best orthopedic surgeon in New York and also the best at treating athletes without operating. That's what sold me. So many doctors are quick to cut, but not John. As I soon found out for myself, he always tried first to motivate his patients into training properly so that they could cure themselves. For a professional athlete like me, whose job is on the line, there's a lot of mental anguish that goes along with the very idea of surgery. That's what he understood: he made me believe in myself so I'd work hard and help myself get better.

One of the first things I noticed about John was his terrific enthusiasm, which immediately reassured me. The next thing that impressed me, as funny as it might sound, was his low body fat. It was clear just by looking at him that this guy was active himself, in sports and in life, and of course I responded to that. There are only a few people you meet in your lifetime whom you really hit it off with, and from the first time I saw him in his office, I knew we'd be good friends. We both loved to train hard, we both loved tennis and most sports very much, we both loved to laugh and to have fun while we worked out.

Those of us on the tennis circuit who were his patients, like Rosie Casals, Mary Carillo, and myself, saw John on a regular basis. He stayed with us, checking us out and making sure we kept up with our therapy. What most impressed all of us was that he would go out and train right along with us, pushing himself hard, which in turn made us push ourselves. He was such a rare individual, motivating and inspiring us through his own example.

After working with him for a while, I asked John if I could go around with him and get some understanding of what goes into physical fitness. Here I was, a professional athlete for many years, and yet this was a subject about which I knew very little. I started learning by watching him work with school children, recreational athletes, the ordinary and extraordinary people who were his patients, and afterward he and I would have long talks about sports medicine. He was a great proponent of research, and when I tried out the conclusions that were based on that research, I saw that his ideas really worked. What he'd tell me to do was take my own body type into consideration. He'd profile me and then figure out how I could improve in the areas where I was weakest, how I could make the most of the strengths I had, and how I could work to prevent injuries. It was this kind of profiling that he wanted to make available to everyone—not only his patients—and it was this, together with his belief in individualized training programs, that started him working on his book.

As John and I talked about athletes and fitness we both became aware that those most in need of good clear information are women. Men have been taught that it's character-building to work hard physically while women, on the other hand, have been led to believe that they should not and cannot strain themselves in this

vi

way. Most women have no understanding of how much their bodies can take. I'm in my thirties and so I'm still part of the generation of women who were programmed to think that they weren't as strong as men, that they couldn't train the way men could. John didn't go along with this, and he got the women he worked with to start lifting weights. We all got stronger and we never felt better.

One thing I think not even John realized at first about women was that most don't think they can do anything. It's not simply that we've never been taught how to throw a ball or how to run but that we just don't expect anything from ourselves. I talked to him about this, and when he went to high schools to test girls or when he worked with women skiers and tennis players, he began to understand that before anything else, women had to be taught to believe in themselves. They had to learn to question the myths they'd been programmed into accepting about their limitations, and they had to be encouraged to be more and more active. By directing his book toward women, John wanted to raise their expectations by educating them, giving them the benefit of his research and experience so that their lives, no matter what their age, could be more fulfilling.

The greatest thing about John was that he believed that people could extend themselves and do a lot more than they ever thought they could. He had a wonderful way of getting you to believe this, too, and I think his book ends up helping women do the same thing. Reading it is a step toward changing the quality of your life for the better, and this is what John always thought should be the ultimate goal of the sports medicine doctor.

BILLIE JEAN KING

Acknowledgments

A tremendous amount of enthusiastic teamwork has been involved in creating this book. While this was not only helpful but, in fact, necessary in the early stages, it became absolutely essential after the tragic death of John Marshall in February 1980. The valuable contributions of his colleagues and assistants have been a decisive element in the successful completion of this complex and multifaceted project.

First and most important has been the help of Henry M. Tischler, research associate to the Sports Medicine Department at the Hospital for Special Surgery and a member of the Board of Directors of the John L. Marshall Sports Medicine Research and Education Foundation. From his years of work with John Marshall, Henry had, of all the contributors, the fullest grasp of the material in this book and became most integral to the carrying out and meshing together of all the elements—the initial research and subsequent theories, the collection of pertinent data from a variety of sources, the contacting of experts in many related fields, and the editing of materials. Because he had been so close to Dr. Marshall, Henry was able to offer an invaluable continuity to the evolving book. I am particularly grateful for his encouraging belief in the successful outcome.

Next, I want to express warm gratitude to Nancy M. Andresen, Dr. Marshall's exercise physiology consultant and M.A. from the University of Maryland. Associated for several years with Dr. Marshall, she has shared his belief in the physical potential of women and has been able to give us the benefit of her experience working in fitness and exercise programs with women of all ages and in varying states of health. Nancy has made her expert eye continually available in evaluating programs and has supplied many creative suggestions.

Geraldine Rivero, Dr. Marshall's spirited secretary, has devoted a good deal of time and energy toward getting materials together, meetings set up, and organizing the hectic schedules involved.

I am also, and eternally it seems, indebted to my husband, Joseph Barbash, for his support and wise counsel; to my favorite critic, muse, and friend Joy Gould Boyum; to my French interpreter, my daughter Lisa; to the knowledgeable observations of my tennis-playing son, Tom; and advice from my squash-playing god-children, David and Ingrid Boyum.

Among the doctors who have given not only their time but have evidenced an involvement with the ideas expressed in this book are Dr. Richard S. Rivlin, Chief of Nutrition at Memorial Sloan-Kettering Center and New York Hospital-Cornell Medical Center; Dr. Elizabeth Coryllus, pediatric orthopedic surgeon in Glen Head, Long Island; Dr. Jeffrey Borer, Director of Nuclear Cardiology at New York Hospital and Associate Professor of Medicine at Cornell University Medical College; Dr. Stanley Tischler, Clinical Professor in the department of obstetrics and gynecology at State University of New York, Downstate Medical Center, and attending physician at Jewish Hospital and Medical Center of Brooklyn; and Dr. Marc Weksler, head of the division of geriatrics and gerontology at Cornell University Medical Center.

Other doctors who have shared their thoughts and experience include Dr. Samuel W. Perry III, Assistant Professor of Psychiatry and Dr. Michael Sacks, Associate Professor of Psychiatry, both at

Cornell University Medical College; Dr. Cushman D. Haagensen at Presbyterian Hospital in New York City; Dr. Samuel M. Fox, exercise cardiologist at Georgetown University Medical School; Dr. Sandra Scott of New York State school sports programs; Dr. Sally Short, nutrition consultant to the United States Olympic Teams; and Drs. Parrier and Barrault, sports medicine experts for the French National Sports Institute.

The psychologists who have helped immeasurably are Dr. Marlin M. Mackenzie, Professor of Education at Teacher's College, Columbia University; Dr. Renee McCormick; and Larry Jennings.

Among the non-medical experts who have offered their observations, guidance, and encouragement are Joan Z. Bernstein, general counsel for the Department of Health and Human Resources, and John Dietrich, president of the American International Health Industries.

I am also grateful for those who shared their concern for the improvement of the school sports programs for young women: Margaret Wigiser of the New York Public School Athletic League; D. Kenneth Hafner, retired director of field services for the New York State Public High School Athletic Association; Randee Burke, assistant trainer for the University of Wisconsin football team; and Cathy Heck, head trainer of women's sports at Michigan State.

Among those representing the rapidly growing world of corporate fitness programs and sharing information about it have been Dennis Colacino, Director of Fitness Programs for Pepsico; Gretchen Regan for Remington; and Vicky Olsen.

Insights into community programs for women of all ages and capabilities were offered most generously by Sally Stewart, Physical Education Director of the McBurney "Y" in New York City; Gloria Averbuch of New York Road Runners; and Jiang Rong-Shaun, Head of Mass Sports for the All China Sports Committee in Shanghai.

I also want to thank the many female athletes and participants in fitness programs who have explained their fears and wishes, their ambitions and frustrations, and have offered their own experiences for the benefit of others. The women I've met and talked to from all over the world have included top professionals and amateurs at the height of their careers, young women and girls just starting out in a sport, and older women who have never stopped participating in athletics—and are still enjoying this participation.

Finally, I'm deeply appreciative of the observations supplied to me by those women who only in recent years have begun to lead physically active lives and who are perhaps, above all, the audience John Marshall most wished to reach.

H. B.

Contents

Introduction

John Marshall was an extraordinary man. He loved sports, he loved the practice of sports medicine, he loved life. As his post residency fellows at the Hospital for Special Surgery in New York, we were privileged to be there when he treated many world-class athletes—Billie Jean King, Martina Navratilova, Rosie Casals, Larry Csonka, Julius Erving—and we were even more privileged to be able to learn about sports medicine from a man who had a big hand in creating it.

John's involvement with his patients was always very personal. Julius Erving nicknamed him "Dr. J's Dr. J." It was no surprise to see John running up and down the steps at the Meadowlands with Larry Csonka or hitting tennis balls with Rosie Casals during their recoveries from knee surgery. And he has often been known to take to the slopes skiing down the giant slalom with the racers he was treating.

It was his special empathy with athletes that gave him the idea for new theories of training that turned out to be major innovations in sports medicine. While he was doing his well-known studies on knee surgeries, he began to realize that training played a crucial role in the restoration of the injured joint. If special training methods could help an injured knee function properly again, couldn't these same methods be used on the normal knee to improve performance and decrease the chance of injury?

To test his theory on the importance of proper training, John and the rest of us who were working with him started devising examinations and questionnaires, which have become the core of this book. We tested out theories on teams from Little League through professional, and with athletes from professionals like Arthur Ashe and Billie Jean King to beginners in exercise classes. It was exciting work for all of us, especially when it became clear that John's ideas were right and were working well for athletes and neophytes across the board. Along with refining the tests used on each person he examined, he created what he called a musculoskeletal profile. When this profile was compared with the records of a person's actual injuries, John could then predict what injuries that person would probably be most susceptible to in the future. With this information he could then work out a specific training program for that person, designed to reduce the chance of future injuries. He applied these training concepts to one high school football team, and all neck injuries were actually eliminated, while in another athletic program ankle sprains dramatically decreased. John's ultimate goal, one which he hoped to achieve in this book, was to bring these principles of proper training for one's own body type to the attention of as many people as possible.

John found that most athletes needed more reliable facts about their own body type and potential weaknesses, but he was shocked to learn how little most women athletes knew about their body type and training in general. He had worked with some of the finest women athletes in the world, women who were unmistakably as talented, motivated, and dedicated as any male athlete, and he quickly realized that most of them knew nothing at all about modern training exercise and methods. Despite their willingness to practice, they had never used weights, aerobic training, or specific flexibility exercises in their exercise programs. Most of these women had never been exposed to the kind of training information available to male athletes even on a high school level. John was amazed that an entire group of the best athletes in the world had been so deprived and yet were still able to perform at such high levels. He was excited by the idea of what these women could do if they began to learn more about their own bodies and modern training techniques.

John began working with some of these women athletes and found their response to training similar to that of their male counterparts. Their performances started to improve dramatically, and their injuries were often either prevented or healed. Billie Jean King saw John after previous knee surgery hadn't completely solved her problem. He vetoed further surgery and helped her improve her knee and leg strengths by putting her on a carefully prescribed training program, which has been remarkably successful. She has become an outspoken champion of Dr. John Marshall and his training methods.

John soon realized that while the female athlete who was a serious competitor needs a prescription for training, so too do the constantly increasing number of women and girls just beginning physical activity. The 1970s sports boom had brought with it greater numbers of injuries, many of them a direct reflection of the crucial lack of preparation women had had for sports. Women began to crowd the orthopedic doctor's waiting room. John was convinced that he could help them, and his own patients are the testament to his success. It is this message concerning what total fitness for women is all about that John hoped to bring to as many women as possible through this book.

John was killed in a plane crash on February 12, 1980, on his way to be the consultant to the United States Ski Team at the Winter Olympics at Lake Placid. It is difficult for those of us who worked with him to assess the loss, but we are very grateful for the rich legacy he has left with us. For doctors, he has left behind his landmark innovations in the diagnosis and treatment of knee injuries. For the athlete, the would-be athlete, or the woman who wants to be fit, he has left behind the principles he developed for them in his incredibly dynamic career as a sports doctor.

Marc Sherman, M.D.

W. Hugh Baugher, M.D.

1

The
Changing Scene

Physically active women we've questioned—whether professional competitors, amateur athletes, or just members of fitness programs—have confirmed what many of you may have already observed, that there is a growing acceptance of women as athletes or simply as individuals for whom strenuous exercise is entirely appropriate. And in answering our questions, they almost invariably color this increasingly positive picture with stories from their own experiences.

"About ten years ago I was one of five mothers helping out at a school picnic," a suburban woman in her early forties told us. "Some of the younger children had wandered off, and when the teacher asked if one of us would run after them to bring them back, it was clear none of the other women could manage to move; they seemed riveted to the ground. I was the only one there who could accomplish the feat of running the fraction of a mile to where the children had strayed. Today I still see most of those same women, and it's hard to believe the change. Two of them run

1

around the town reservoir every morning, even in the rain, and another of them recently won a trophy for racquetball."

"At my tennis club, for the past thirty years the women's locker room had been half the size of the men's," another woman reported. "Still, it had never been any problem until the past few years, when more and more women started applying for membership. Now this is a club with no pool, no sauna, no nothing except for the tennis courts, so you really have got to enjoy playing if you want to join. Just last year the board of directors voted to increase our locker room space so we can take in some more women. Our club is extremely tradition-bound, so an alteration like this has got to reflect an acceptance by the board of a genuine change."

A third woman, a dedicated and talented amateur athlete who works as an advertising copywriter, said that she was recently at a meeting with her boss and some clients. She almost jumped when she heard her boss mention to the others that she was a "real jock." "I guess I was so used to that being an insult that at first I didn't register my boss's tone of voice. It was only when I saw everyone smiling and nodding that it occurred to me that he was actually complimenting me and that they were all approving."

As these women went on to point out, the changes they describe are very recent. It's only been since 1972 that the Amateur Athletic Union officially recognized women marathoners in the United States (still, women have no long-distance event in the Olympics, even though Grete Waitz's 2:27:33 in the 1979 New York Marathon would have beaten half the male Olympic marathon winners). And only in this past decade have any women professional athletes begun to earn substantial amounts of money. In 1970 Margaret Court won the Grand Slam in tennis and earned less than $15,000 while Tracy Austin earned $498,749 in 1979. As for golf, the average purse for a women's PGA tournament was $127,000 in 1980 compared to only $20,000 in 1970. These growing figures give an importance and prestige to the sportswoman that carries over to the amateur, particularly to the schoolgirl who now has Title IX to help her develop her skills.

Studies carried out in past years have shown that there was little social acceptance for women who had strong ambitions to succeed in sports or who happened to choose activities like softball and basketball instead of swimming or golf. More recently, however, this seems to be changing. One test conducted in the late 1970s at Arizona State University by Kingsley, Brown, and Seibert was expected to uncover evidence that there was a significant difference in the social acceptability of a woman dancer over a woman softball player. Instead, the nonathletes queried did not rate the dancer as significantly more socially acceptable than the softball player, and athletes who responded indicated they considered the softball player the more socially acceptable of the two.

In another test devised by Professors Sage of the University of Northern Colorado and Loudermilk of Sioux Falls College in South Dakota to see if college female athletes experienced role conflict in being both athlete and woman at the same time, the researchers found instead that not only were their subjects free of such conflict, but these women showed significantly higher self-esteem than did nonathletes. The fact that these two tests have turned up attitudes opposite to those found in past studies points up the change we've all seen around us, the increasingly positive feelings about women in sports and the accompanying surge of female participation.

In high schools all over the country, the growth in girls' interest is phenomenal. According to the National Federation of State High School Associations, basketball has grown from 132,299 participants in 1970–1971 to 449,695 in 1978–1979, cross country from 1,719 in 1970–1971 to 59,005 in 1978–1979, and softball from 9,813 in 1970–1971 to 161,962 in 1978–1979. Coaches of girls' teams have told us about the increased response to notices for tryouts, and several young teen-agers have said when we questioned them that their good performance in sports in no way detracted from their acceptability and, in fact, seemed to add to their status. This is in sharp contrast to the responses we've gotten from women in their thirties, many of whom stopped participating in sports or kept their training as much of a secret as they could in high school years for fear of being thought unfeminine. "There's no question about it, I was considered odd," said a tennis player from Michigan. "It was okay when I was in grammar school, but by high school I was certainly cut out of what was the in-crowd. Luckily I had my tennis friends, so I wasn't lonely. But I couldn't help feeling resentful seeing the guys who were athletes end up the school idols while girls like me were lucky when we were just about tolerated."

With attitudes shifting so quickly, the generation gap can be intensified. One of the top American long-distance runners, a woman in her early twenties, told us that when she started training her mother was horrified. "She's since come around 180 degrees but at that time, only five or six years ago, she was sure I'd end up with big muscular legs and she insisted that I stop. I used to have to wait until she went out shopping so that I could train secretly, running up and down our driveway." This runner's legs, by the way, as well as the rest of her body, remain slender and show no bulging muscles although she runs every day, most often twice a day, and takes fourteen-mile daily trips on her bicycle during the warm weather.

Another young woman who is a physical therapist told us that she finally got her mother to join an exercise group after a long campaign of giving her articles to read and showing her statistics to prove the benefits of physical activity. "Then I nearly ruined it all," the daughter went on to report. "My mother was going off to her first class and I said I hoped she'd work up a good sweat. Well, then and there she almost quit, even before she'd started. She was brought up to believe perspiration was unfeminine and embarrassing. It took a lot of persuading to finally get her to go. Now, though, she's so firmly committed, mainly because she feels so much better, that she's talked some of her friends into joining her."

Coaches and instructors report that while there's an initial self-consciousness about exercising in a class, that doesn't last for more than a session or two. "I've found two things happening," an instructor at a large New York Y told us. "The older women are coming in larger numbers, and the younger women are working harder. We used to have to push the young swimmers into the weight-training room and keep after them to increase the poundage of the weights. Now it's just the opposite. We have to make sure they're progressing slowly and carefully enough so that they won't hurt themselves."

This enthusiasm has its negative side, as this instructor has indicated. Because most of the interest in activity is so recent, too many women are simply not in good enough shape to work out as hard as they would like. While some of the coaches at the larger universities that attract elite athletes or those who work with high-ranking amateurs or professionals report that the women start training in top condition, most others have told us that the first task they have is to get their athletes in good enough shape so that they can begin to train. Many of the injuries we've seen would have been avoided if the women involved had been in better condition, first following and then sticking to a well-balanced training regimen.

With the greater amount of attention that is now being paid to the female athlete and to fitness programs for women, what has to follow is a growing awareness and understanding of what goes into safe and satisfying exercise. We think that this knowledge—of what's true about women and their physical potential and how this potential can best be achieved—is a crucial factor that must accompany today's trend toward more and more physical activity. We know that when properly implemented, it is this knowledge that becomes the essential key to physical fitness.

2

Myths about
Women and Sports

Over the years women who showed an interest in physical activity have been inundated with cautions and told endless tales about their own frailty. They have been informed in detail about their limitations and the dangerous risks they face should they be fool-hardy enough to engage in strenuous activity. Most of these warnings, however, are little more than old wives' tales, based on fiction rather than fact. And while many women have already come to realize this, we think it's still worthwhile to examine some of the most prevalent of these inhibiting myths with the hope of dispelling them once and for all.

*MYTH: *Women who lift weights end up with bulging muscles.*

An increase in the bulk of the muscle, muscular hypertrophy, is not a necessary consequence of gaining strength through weight lifting or any other means. In one experiment, where nationally ranked women athletes were given an intensive six-month program of weight training, muscle girth increase ranged from minor to nonexistent although the gains in strength were appreciable. We think that hormonal differences, specifically the low level of the male hormone testosterone, are what prevent women from getting the bulky muscles that men who lift weights often have. The average program of strength training that we recommend—three times a week, one to two sets each time—will end up toning most women's muscles without developing defined musculature.

*MYTH: *Jogging will cause your face to sag.*
No, in fact it's just the opposite. Jogging will improve the elastic tissue in your skin and your subcutaneous tissue (below the level of the skin) just as it improves the tone of your muscles, the strength of your ligaments, and the strength and density of your bones. All tissues respond to physical stress by becoming stronger, and this has been especially noted in the supporting tissues, such as bones, ligaments, and muscles, of the face as well as elsewhere.

*MYTH: *Exercise, particularly jogging, can cause your breasts to sag.*
Running and most other vigorous activities will improve your muscle tone and so, if anything, give more support to your breasts. As for running without a bra, there is no evidence that this does any damage or in any way changes the shape of the breast, according to breast expert Dr. Cushman D. Haagensen at New York's Presbyterian Hospital. Some women runners, especially those with large, pendulous breasts, may find themselves more comfortable when they are wearing bras.

*MYTH: *Exercise can actually reduce the size of your breasts.*
Exercise cannot spot-reduce the breasts any more than it can spot-reduce your hips, buttocks, abdomen, or any other part of you. Reduction in the size of any subcutaneous or fat tissue comes from burning the fat stores. When you exercise frequently and intensively, you burn calories, which reduces your overall weight, including your breasts. The fact that many female distance runners

7

have small breasts has a lot to do with their more slender proportions compared to the average population. Another factor, pointed out by some of the manufacturers of the new "sports" bras, is that smaller-breasted women may simply have been more comfortable in active sports and so have been more likely to participate over a period of time.

*MYTH: *Women should avoid contact sports because of possible breast injury.*
Even in contact sports, serious injury to the breast is extremely rare. In the two cases where this has been tested, coaches and trainers of women's teams in what would seem to be the high-risk sports, such as field hockey and basketball, report few accidents: only one injury has been recorded in the past six years at Kent State University in Ohio and none at all in the past four years at the University of Hawaii. Dr. Haagensen has found from a study of trauma to the breast that blows to this region, while they can cause you to be black and blue, do little harm. Your breast is about nine tenths fat, which is a cushioning protection in itself, and there is no evidence that any kind of exercise or trauma from exercise either produces cancer or aggravates conditions that are cancer precursors.

*MYTH: *Exercise, particularly jogging, can cause your bladder or uterus to drop.*
None of the gynecologists we've questioned, including members of the Brooklyn Gynecological Society, has ever heard of a uterus or bladder dropping because of exercise. This is clearly another example of a mistaken fragility attributed to women.

*MYTH: *Vigorous exercise can harm a woman's reproductive organs.*
Your uterus is probably your best-protected organ. Even a direct blow to your lower abdomen will probably not be able to harm it because of the sheltering surrounding structure of the pelvis. Female reproductive organs, because they are internal, are far less vulnerable to injury than are male organs.

8

*MYTH: *Exercise can have an unfavorable long-term effect on childbirth.*

The great many studies of female athletes substantiate the fact that these women not only have normal pregnancies but often easier childbirth with shorter delivery time. Here are some of the results from tests that disprove this myth about the unfavorable effect of exercise on childbirth. In one obstetrical study of Hungarian female athletes, complications of pregnancy, especially toxemia, were found in a smaller percentage of these athletes than in the nonathletic control group. Incidence of premature births was lower than for the general population, the necessity for cesarean sections was almost 50 percent less than for the control group, and the duration of labor was shorter than the average in 87 percent of the deliveries.

In another study done of ninety-four Finnish women who had competed in national-level baseball and swimming, similar results were recorded. The mean time of labor duration for the athletes was 17 hours 27 minutes as compared with the 21 hours 26 minutes for the nonathletes. The athletes also had fewer complications, including fewer perineal tears, lower incidence of cesarean section, and less necessity for outlet forceps, manual removal of the placenta, or blood transfusions.

Female Olympic participants who become mothers have been found to have shorter second stages of labor compared to women in general, and it's been thought that the difference is due to the athletes' better muscle tone. Whatever exercise does or does not do for women, it clearly has no adverse effect on childbirth.

*MYTH: *Exercise should cease with pregnancy.*

The human embryo is protected by the skin and muscle of the abdominal wall, the thick uterine muscle, and amniotic fluid to absorb shocks. One vivid way that's been used to show how the fetus is protected from trauma is through the experiment with the egg and the plastic jar. A whole egg is placed in a clear plastic vessel full of fluid; the vessel is capped and then dropped from a height. As long as the egg is not actually touching the very bottom of the jar, it can't be broken by the fall because of the cushioning protec-

9

tion of the surrounding fluid, which acts, as amniotic fluid does, to absorb the trauma of a fall or blow.

Appropriate exercise during pregnancy is generally favored by obstetricians who have come to realize that normal physical activity does not lead to spontaneous abortion. As for what exactly is appropriate, the more exercise you're used to, the more you can continue to do up until the time you no longer feel comfortable exercising. The President's Council on Physical Fitness considers the question of the amount and intensity of exercise for pregnant women an individual matter to be discussed between doctor and patient. The fact that many women—from those who work in offices and factories to others in more strenuous rural occupations, even the women who dive for pearls in the frigid waters off Korea and Japan—keep on going right up to the day or days before delivery, with no ill effects on either mother or child, shows that physical activity is not bad during pregnancy. In fact, doctors usually advise their sedentary patients to get some exercise, particularly for the abdominal muscles, during this period.

*MYTH: *Pregnancy, even in the early stages, has an unfavorable effect on a woman's sports performance.*
A bronze medalist in the 1952 Olympic Games was pregnant, three gold medal winners in the 1956 games in Melbourne were pregnant, and JoAnne Gunderson won the U.S. Women's Amateur Golf Championship in her sixth month. For the ordinary woman as well, sports performance in the first or second trimester need not decline. As for your general physical state, with some effort it can get even better during pregnancy. In an experiment made on a healthy nonathletic woman who underwent a fitness program while in her first pregnancy, her maximal oxygen uptake and endurance performance was significantly improved with no harmful effects on either mother or child.

*MYTH: *Exercise is bad for women who are lactating.*
While it might be difficult for a woman who is training seriously for competition to nurse her baby, an athletic woman is certainly

10

capable of producing sufficient amounts of milk. The ability to nurse is not adversely affected by exercise and, as Dr. Haagensen points out, in more primitive societies where mothers work long hours in the fields with their infants beside them, women continue to be capable of nursing despite strenuous activity.

As for serious competitors, because certain endurance athletes, such as long-distance runners, tend to be extremely thin and are consequently often smaller breasted, there has been some thought that these women are less likely to be able to produce milk. In fact, there is no correlation at all between breast size and milk production, so that smaller-breasted women are at no disadvantage if they choose to nurse their babies.

*MYTH: *A woman's athletic performance is unfavorably affected by childbirth.*
A Dutch track star in the London Olympics won three gold medals after having had two children, Andrea Mead Lawrence won a gold medal after becoming a mother, and a study of German champion women athletes shows that among those continuing in sports after childbirth, most made definite objective improvements. Similar improvement has been reported by other Olympic and intercollegiate athletes who have found their performance at least as good and often better after pregnancy. Pregnancy and childbirth seem to give many women increased strength and endurance, possibly because of the new demands being made on the metabolism and entire cardiovascular system. A young mother who finds herself less fit is probably not exercising as much as she used to. Quite often, with little time or opportunity for a regular game of racquetball or morning jogging, she may see her performance drop, but it is due to this lack of preparation rather than because her pregnancy has left her less fit.

*MYTH: *Hormone pills such as contraceptive pills have an unfavorable effect on athletic performance.*
Most athletes who take birth control pills report a decrease in menstrual cramps, a lessening in the amount of flow, a more regular cycle, less fluid retention, and less breast soreness. For some oth-

11

ers, however, there have been adverse symptoms such as nausea, weight gain, and fatigue, which make this method of contraception a poor choice for these women. And of course there can be serious side effects from oral contraceptives that should be carefully weighed in order to determine whether they are the best means of birth control.

*MYTH: *Exercise will permanently damage the menstrual cycle.*

For many women athletes, training seems to have no effect on the menstrual cycle. In one comprehensive survey of over 700 female athletes, 84 percent of them did not show any changes in menstruation as a result of athletic competition.

Still, intense training necessary for the competitive athlete such as the long-distance runner can result in scant, infrequent menstruation or even a total cessation of periods (amenorrhea). Some theories claim it to be a response to the stress of competition and emotional trauma. Others claim that with serious training, a decreased percentage of body fat leads to a change in the pathways of estrogen metabolism and subsequent amenorrhea. Whatever the cause, the effect has been shown to be temporary. A decrease in the intensity of the exercise will most likely restore ovulatory function.

One athlete, in fact, the wife of a gynecologist, became pregnant during the time she was in training and was amenorrheic (had no menstrual periods)—her fertility was obviously unaffected by exercise. Another woman, a runner who had stopped exercising for a period of time and had begun to miss some periods, found her regular cycle returning only after she resumed training. Her gynecologist theorized that since her normal pattern was to exercise, a break in the pattern disrupted her normal menstrual function while a return to her regular routine helped reestablish it. Certainly, if there is no return to regular menses, the female athlete should have the appropriate endocrine and genetic evaluation.

*MYTH: *Exercise increases the severity of your periods.*

We've found no evidence at all that participation in sports causes any unfavorable changes in the menstrual period. We know that women who exercise show an improvement in the premenstrual tension syndrome, and other studies have concluded that while dysmenorrhea (painful periods) is neither aggravated nor cured by sports participation, it is a far less common condition among women who are athletes. This might be explained in part by the fact that some of the causes of painful menstruation are faulty living habits, such as poor posture and muscle fatigue, conditions less likely to occur among those women who are physically active.

*MYTH: *When women are menstruating, their performance is worse in competitive sports.*
Athletic performances are not altered by the menstrual cycle, and this is vividly illustrated by the fact that women on the United States Olympic teams have won gold medals and established new world records during their menstrual periods. Tests among collegiate women athletes show that menstruation does not affect maximum oxygen uptake, one good measure of the ability to perform well, and other tests report that motor efficiency, speed, and endurance are also not affected. And so, while it is likely that those women with severe dysmenorrhea have already been screened out of the top ranks of competitive athletes (few class athletes can afford to take off a few days each month from training), the woman athlete who has normal menstrual periods is demonstrably capable of doing her best during her menses.

*MYTH: *Women should not swim when they are menstruating.*
The intravaginal tampon has made it convenient and comfortable for women to swim during menstruation. Almost all competitive swimmers train and race during their menstrual periods with no adverse effects.

In the past there was some concern about infection coming from bacteria in the water; we now know that the vagina, even during the menstrual period, will not admit water unless it is forced in under pressure (as it might be in water skiing). There has been no evidence that swimming during the menstrual period increases or

13

causes cramps, and there seems no reason at all why you shouldn't swim during any phase of your menstrual cycle.

*MYTH: *Women are more likely to be injured in sports than are men.*

When a woman first starts participating in sports, she is frequently less well trained compared to men. Because of this she can often end up with a greater number of strains and sprains and partial dislocations. Once a woman gets into good condition, though, her injury rate comes close to that of men. A woman who is an expert skier, for example, is far closer to a male expert skier in numbers and kinds of injuries than a novice female skier is to a novice male skier. At West Point, where the athletic program is rigorous for both men and women, the female cadets in the entering class spend far more time in response to sick call than do the men. After training, however, the injury rates between the sexes even out.

3

The Physiological Differences Between Women and Men

Now that we've swept away the myths, we can start to look at the facts, exploring the actual differences between women and men that can affect performance in sports. Years ago it was generally assumed that all of these differences were physical in origin, but more recently we've begun to discover that a great many of what we thought were physical differences are actually based on cultural factors. Take something like upper arm strength. How many females after childhood throw a ball any distance, much less play basketball, baseball, or football? But many men, at least many young men, do. This makes the difference that will affect the development of strength, agility, and skill of motion in your arms, back, and shoulder area, the places where men show the most superior ability.

Many trainers have told us they believe women runners are slower because they just haven't had any really good instruction. It's only been in recent years, in fact, that women have become involved in running sports, primarily distance racing, and even now very few do sprints or middle-distance running. Men, on the other hand, have traditionally received training, encouragement, and opportunity to compete, and these advantages make true comparisons impossible. When you think of how different school athletic programs have been for boys and for girls, it's easy to see why men often seem more adept at physical activity than do women.

Still, there *are* differences that are genetic, and we think it's crucial for a woman to understand just what special problems she might run into because of these differences—because although she can't really change them, there are ways she can successfully deal with them. There are strength training (which is described in Chapter 7), mechanical devices, even techniques and strategies that can frequently compensate for what seems to be an obstacle. We have found that while the structure and composition of male and female bodies can cause some differences in performance, the magnitude of these differences can be decreased. It's clear that the spread between topflight men and women swimmers is narrowing. In the 1936 Olympics, for example, the difference between male and female winners of the 400-meter freestyle was 41.9 seconds while in 1976 it was 17.96 seconds. As for running, women are closing the gap as well. The best marathon time in 1964 for a man was 2 hours 12 minutes and 11.2 seconds, compared to the women's record of 3 hours 19 minutes and 33 seconds. In the 1979 New York Marathon, the women's record was set by Norway's Grete Waitz at 2 hours 27 minutes and 33 seconds. Compare this to the male marathon record, which still holds and was set in 1969 by Australia's Derek Clayton: 2 hours 8 minutes and 33.6 seconds. The 1964 difference was 1 hour 7 minutes and 12.8 seconds, while the difference between male and female marathon records in 1979 was slightly under 19 minutes.

Something else to keep in mind in comparing male and female performance is that some of the facts and figures might have come out differently had a fairer equation been made. For example, why just compare men and women without taking into consideration their differences in size? With size ignored, the difference in lean muscle mass makes women only half as strong as men. But when men and women of the same size are compared, women come out 80 percent as strong.

Other performance differences can be explained in part by the larger height and greater weight of most men when compared to most women. Examples of this are the long jump and the high jump, where, at first, the differences in the distances between male and female performance seem quite large. However, when the distances are viewed in proportion to body weight, the results are essentially the same (for the high jump the male record is 1.2 inches per kilogram of body weight versus the female record of 1.3; for the long jump the male record is 4.9 inches per kilogram of weight versus the female 4.6).

Some of the physical differences between men and women are not liabilities but actually assets. The areas where women may prove superior is a subject relatively unexplored because women's entrance, at least on any large scale, into the world of physical activity has been a fairly recent development. Still, we can see some of the female traits for flexibility, as well as for having larger fat deposits and lighter bone structure, emerging as great advantages in those sports requiring endurance, such as long-distance swimming. It's been predicted, in fact, that in really long running or swimming races of thirty or more miles, women will end up doing even better than men. This will make sense once you know more about some of the physical traits that go into making up the female body.

Here is a list of those physical differences between men and women that may affect athletic performance or state of physical fitness. More than just acquainting you with the facts, some of which you already know or have observed, we want to interpret the significance of these following statements so you can get a more accurate idea of your potential.

STRUCTURAL DIFFERENCES—SKELETAL

Women are smaller than men. Compared with the average adult male, the average adult female is three to four inches shorter and twenty-five to thirty pounds lighter. Although there's no definite proof, we think that it's the male hormone testosterone that helps increase men's total musculoskeletal structure, making them generally bigger than women. How will this affect your performance in a sport? It's certainly not going to be any help in basketball to be small, although in sports like baseball and hockey, some excellent male players have been only five foot five or less. In tennis the shorter player lacks the reach of a taller one, but skill can make up for this. Rosie Casals is small, but other players are well aware they run a great risk trying to lob a ball over her head. She's compensated for her height by developing one of the best overheads in tennis, and it's a challenge to get any ball past her.

Besides developing skill, there's often the possibility of changing technique to help the shorter athlete compensate. The smaller sprinter, for example, should use a different starting technique from the one generally taught, which evolved with the taller male sprinter in mind. If she places her front block closer to the starting line and keeps her feet wider apart in a broader-based position, she'll probably find her performance improving.

There are other activities in which women's smaller bodies are an advantage. These are the sports that call for balance. The smaller skiers on the United States Olympic ski team—Cindy Nelson and Heidi Preuss—are among the best. Their small frames put their centers of gravity lower, so that during their rapid descents down the mountain, their bodies remain more stable.

Women have a slighter bone structure with more delicate ligaments and tendons. This may account for the injuries some women have in sports involving explosive force and sudden changes in speed and motion. In a recent study we've conducted, it was discovered that far greater numbers of serious knee injuries occur in top-ranked women tennis players than in their male equivalents. Mary Carillo, Greer Stevens, Lynn Epstein, Mimmi Wikstedt, Virginia Ruzici, and Rosemary Casals are among the women professionals who have torn a major ligament in the knee, the anterior cruciate ligament. Although we don't know why, we think that perhaps the cellular structure of the ligaments has something to do with it. Ligaments, tendons, muscle, and bone are to a high degree made up of a substance called collagen. We have circumstantial evidence that the collagen in the connective tissue of women is put together somehow differently from that of men.

18

We don't know the nature of these differences or why they occur, but we suspect they're at least in part responsible for the fact that it can take little trauma to tear this ligament in a woman's knee.

One woman recreational player, someone who plays two to three hours a day, tore her anterior cruciate ligament just by standing up with her knee straightened out and toes turned in after picking up a low-angle shot at the net. And while this position is a vulnerable one for the anterior cruciate ligament, the player's movements didn't seem to involve enough force to cause this much damage. Tears in this ligament have also happened to male athletes, but most often they've been caused by far more violent acceleration or deceleration, for example when coming off a bump at high speed on a ski slope or putting weight down on a straight knee in football. Anterior cruciate tears caused by little force are unusual, even for women, but since it happens—when it happens—almost exclusively to women, it points up a vulnerability women may find to injuries stemming from an application of momentum, force, and rotation on their smaller, finer body structure.

Strength training will help, along with instruction in movement dynamics. In tennis this would involve learning to position your body over your feet, point your toes in the direction of movement, and take short quick steps whenever possible. We found working with world-class tennis player Mary Carillo, teaching her to compensate for her ligament injuries, we were showing her the very techniques that her coach, Rick Elstein, had been advising. Good medicine turned out to be good tennis, and more recently, with Rick Elstein, we've developed this synergistic approach with other players. We've been able to help them not only with specific medical problems but, through an analysis of their game, with improving their movement dynamics.

If your more delicate ligaments are not an advantage, your lighter bones certainly can be. The athlete carrying the lighter load will last longer in an endurance sport such as long-distance swimming or marathon racing. One marathon runner, a man who is also an orthopedic surgeon, compared the difference between women and men's bones to aluminum and steel: both have tensile strength but one is a lot heavier than the other, and therefore far more of a burden. Because of their lighter bones, women have a chance to end up the better marathoners. Certainly their times have improved dramatically, with more than a thirty-five minute improvement in the last decade.

Male and Female Bodies Have Different Proportions.

A woman's trunk is longer in relation to her arms and legs. Coordination of the upper body is something with which many women have trouble. Most of the women we've seen have difficulty doing even simple exercises like V-ups (lying on the floor, pulling knees and chest up simultaneously, and then twisting the body), which require balance controlled by the trunk. Your trunk must be stabilized when your legs are contracted, when you initiate leg movements, and when you have to balance your body over your legs. Even professional female athletes we've treated sometimes have extremely weak trunks. One woman professional tennis player, who had been ranked number-one twelve-year-old, at age eighteen couldn't support her weight holding parallel bars with her arms slightly bent.

A weak trunk, along with weak musculature and stiffness in back and hips, may be responsible for women's predisposition to backache. This was certainly the case for one athlete, a professional tennis player who was told she had to undergo surgery, and another, a world-class skier who was told that her problem was psychosomatic. Both were back at their sport—one on the Olympic ski team and the other regaining her team tennis contract—shortly after starting on a training program that helped them compensate for basically weak trunks.

Women have a lower center of gravity. The center of gravity is the spot where gravity exerts the most force, that is, the heaviest area of your body. For men, it's probably located somewhere between the waist and the chest. For women, it's much lower, usually between the hip bones. The disadvantages that go along with this lower center of gravity are that women will have more inertia and somewhat more resistance to rotary movements in the lower limbs. This can surely slow down speed. And although it's far from a proven fact, we've also observed that people with lower centers of gravity seem to be at a disadvantage in actions involving the arms and the shoulders, such as those in tennis or basketball. In these sports your upper extremity control can be important since you can use the action of your arms and shoulders to maintain the rhythm of movement of your trunk and legs. With the center of gravity lower, women have to work at controlling a greater part of their bodies—that is, the part that lies above it. Still, it's far from an impossible task. Think of the many excellent athletes, both male and female, who have gotten past this obstacle through training and improved technique.

The lower center of gravity isn't always a disadvantage. For the skier it's a distinct help in achieving greater balance. As for the wrestler, the lower the center of gravity, the more stable he or she is and the less likely to be thrown to the mat. In soccer, field hockey, and gymnastics, we think this lower center of gravity may also be an advantage.

Women have different hip and leg structure. The average female has a wider pelvis than the average male, this to allow for childbirth. How does it affect your sports performance? When you run, you must shift your pelvis more in order to keep your center of gravity over your weight-bearing foot. As a result, there is greater hip movement and what might seem to be a decrease in efficiency. However, practically, there doesn't seem to be much of a relationship between the width of the hips and running speed, and so it can't be considered a limiting factor.

The wider pelvis also affects the position of your legs. In the female, the femur or upper bone of the leg has an obliquity when compared to a male's. The femur leans in toward the knees, making a woman more likely to be knock-kneed. If your knees point in this way, when you run you may well be putting unequal stress on your knees, pinching the outsides while stretching the insides.

What can make this even worse is that most women are innately flexible, a characteristic that not only makes their knees more mobile but also seems to go along with flat feet, which keep toes turned out and knees turned in even more. Along with all of this, many women have weak thigh muscles that aren't able to hold the kneecaps in place. It's not surprising, then, that many women run-

21

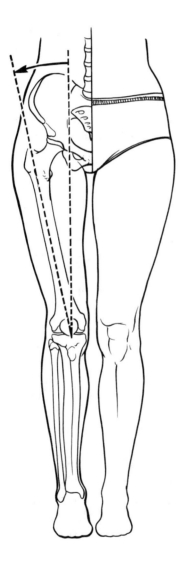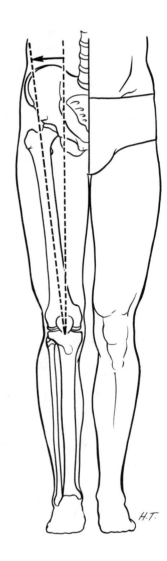

ners end up with sore knees, excessive slipping of the kneecap, and sometimes dislocations. We've noticed this particularly with women in their thirties and forties who have begun participating in an active sport after a decade busy with small children or starting a career. What has happened is that they've had no significant exercise in years and so their muscles are not in condition to control their kneecaps and compensate for the angularity of their knees.

What can you do about all of this? You can shorten your stride and practice running more on your heels. Exercising to strengthen your thigh muscles will help immeasurably. See Chapter 7 for specific thigh exercises. There are also mechanical aids, such as wedges in your running shoes, that will keep your knee from turning in every time you land on your foot or the patella (kneecap) alignment brace we've come up with to help keep the kneecap from slipping. The growth in popularity of running as a sport for women and the increased success of women runners prove that the female hip and leg structures, in the cases where they are disadvantages, are certainly not obstacles that can't be overcome.

Women have narrower shoulders and less chest girth. This narrowness and lack of girth may contribute to the fact that women have less upper body strength than men. We have found that even female world-class athletes can't come close to the average man in doing arm hangs. One twenty-two-year-old woman, a national tennis champion at eighteen, couldn't support her body weight with her arms for even five seconds. Another young woman, ranked among the top ten women squash players in the country, told us that although she had a powerful serve, she couldn't do a single push-up. What she didn't realize was that her strong serve was due to skill, not strength, and that despite her daily exercise on the squash courts, she hadn't really developed her chest and shoulder muscles. In other words, to reach their potential women probably have to make a special effort to develop upper body strength, an effort that will have to come from training and not simply playing a sport.

There's been some thought that the narrower shoulders and chest of a woman are factors in shoulder dislocations, but we think that's not really the case. Among the women we've treated for dislocations and subluxations (a partial slipping in and out, which is a far more frequent problem for a woman than a dislocation), we've seen a high correlation with general body laxity or flexibility. Since women often have the congenital trait for structural laxity or flexible joints, less force is needed to cause subluxation. One high-ranked professional tennis player, a slender and thin-chested woman, has found her shoulder slipping just by serving. For most men it would take far more trauma, such as pitching baseballs at tremendous velocity. Here again, training will help compensate both for the structural laxity and the cultural factor that ball throwing and push-ups and other actions that would develop upper body strength are simply less common activities for females than for males.

Another help is practicing proper technique for throwing, serving, and other upper body motions. For instance, in a tennis serve, it is essential to lead with your shoulder but not with the racket and ball. Then your elbow should follow through, followed by your wrist, racquet, and complete follow-through by your body. If you use the proper technique, this will take the whip of the accelerated force out of your arm, shifting it to your body. When you throw, if you lead with your elbow or hand, the stress will be on your elbow, your forearm, or sometimes on your shoulder. Throw instead in a well-coordinated, synchronized motion of first the complete body, followed by the shoulder, followed by the elbow, and then the hand. This way you'll be much less likely to have concentrated force on your joints. These good mechanics go along with good medicine, improving the strength and power of your throwing while decreasing your potential for injury.

Women have different elbow joints. Put your arms straight out in front of you with your palms turned up. Most men will find their arms forming parallel lines extending from the elbow, but most women will discover their arms forming an X, with their elbows a lot closer to each other. You probably should be more careful to avoid leading with your elbow when you swing a tennis racquet or a golf club, since it's possible that your elbow positioning might give you a greater tendency for elbow trouble. As for throwing sports,

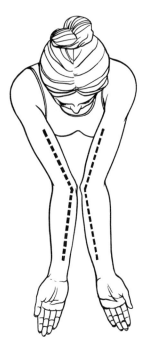
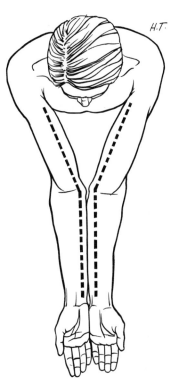

although there is some thought that women are disadvantaged by their elbow joints, we haven't found any correlation to support this.

Women are more flexible. Studies we've done have proven there is a trait for ligamentous laxity. That is, people are born being more tight-jointed or more loose-jointed. Women in general are more loose-jointed than men are in general. What may be surprising to learn is that it's quite common to be flexible and yet have specific joints that are tight. Most often we've found that flexible women have tight heel cords, probably from wearing high heels and running on their toes with hips and legs in a bent position. So even though they have a trait for structural laxity, they may still get the shin splints, ankle sprains, and tendinitis of the calves that tight-jointed males are prone to get. It's a good idea, therefore, even if you think you're supple, to do flexibility exercises, especially of your legs and calves. If you're a runner, stretching your calves should be a frequent routine.

The advantages that go along with being flexible include better performance in pattern movements such as aerobic dance, in gymnastics, and in endurance sports like bicycling and swimming.

On the other hand, you may have more shoulder subluxations (partial dislocations), sprains, or loose kneecaps. Looseness goes along with slowness, but it's a physical handicap you can overcome. An extremely loose-jointed and physically slow tennis player like Chris Evert Lloyd makes up for this by her extraordinary anticipation, reaction, and movement time (all part of movement dynamics). She's been trained to be right where the ball is, and in the end, that's what counts.

It's here that we might mention one kind of athlete who's very rare. This is the athlete who combines great flexibility with great strength. This unusual combination almost always signals an athlete, whether male or female, who has exceptional quality and would be a superior athlete in almost everything he or she did. Heidi Preuss on the United States Olympic ski team, a strong but flexible woman who made the A team at age eighteen, is a good example of this special combination of traits.

STRUCTURAL DIFFERENCES—MUSCLES AND FAT

Women usually have smaller strength (fast-twitch) muscle fiber. Although no muscle is purely one type or the other, the muscle fibers may be predominantly slow- or fast-twitch. This designation refers to their contractile capabilities, which allow some fibers to contract slowly and repetitively while others contract quickly in short strokes of high force. When your brain sends the message for your muscles to move, both fiber types will react together although they'll move in their different ways.

Everyone has varying percentages of each of the muscle types, and we have found that knowing whether you have more fast- or slow-twitch muscle fibers will enable us to make some predictions about your performance in various activities. Most men, for example, with larger fast-twitch fibers, are more likely to excel in sports requiring explosive speed, power, and quickness. Women, however, who have slow-twitch fibers that are equal to men's, compare favorably at endurance sports such as long-distance swimming or running.

We can find out about your fiber type by doing a muscle biopsy, but a simpler way of getting some clues, as we're beginning to discover, is probably by testing how tight or loose you are. Flexibility tests seem to correlate with performance, looser people having better endurance capabilities while tighter people have better strength and speed capabilities. In addition, knowing your predominant fiber type can also give you some idea of what injuries you're probably susceptible to and how you ought to train. For example, we would tell the predominantly loose-jointed types, which include most women, to do strength training, while advising tight-jointed types to concentrate instead on developing endurance and flexibility.

We should point out that there are, of course, exceptions to this, and it is still preferable to actually measure performance when you can, uncovering specific deficits and then training to improve them. Another fact to stress is that as helpful as fiber typing is, we know that the most accurate way to predict performance as well as injury susceptibility is by using multiple factors. That's why we suggest you assess yourself in relation to the general population, with a body fat test, a musculoskeletal profile, and measurement of the other factors that make up the Fitness Self-Portrait. Every one of us is different, and so the more measurements available on each individual, the truer will be the total picture that emerges.

Women have more body fat in relation to total body weight than

27

do men. Women have an average of approximately 20 percent body fat while men have approximately 15 percent. Traditionally, body fat has been the greatest indicator anthropometrically of how you can perform, the theory being that the less body fat, the better. But we would disagree. We've found that the Fitness Self-Portrait (made up of the tests we suggest in Chapter 5) is equally good if not better at telling you about your natural gifts. Of course, if you're fat you carry a lot more around with you that may slow you down. And you may not be very fit. But this just says you need to burn off more calories with diet and a good aerobic program. What we haven't found out is what kind of basic athlete you are. What injuries are you susceptible to? Just what is it that's under that excess bulk? What body traits have you inherited? You want to know what you've got so that you can know what you can do, and we've found that our tests give a truer picture of your potential than does your body fat or any single factor.

Besides, there are advantages to the larger percentage of body fat that women have. For one thing, it gives greater insulation in cold temperatures, including cold waters, perhaps accounting for the excellent record women have had in swimming the English Channel.

Another advantage is that in endurance activities women can use fat as fuel after carbohydrate stores in the body have been depleted. Men, without as much body fat to use for energy, can end up with less endurance.

Women have less potential for building muscle and so are less strong. Although we don't know for sure, it's thought that the male hormone testosterone is the necessary ingredient in producing men's larger muscles. We know that testosterone can increase the protein buildup in the body, favorably influencing the development of muscles. We also know that women do not develop the bulky muscles that men can.

But just how different are male and female muscles? Tests have indicated that strength relative to muscle size is the same in both sexes. It's also true that when men and women are compared in relation to lean body weight, which more accurately reflects muscle mass, the differences are very small and may well be due to the

28

heavier weight of male bones. From the data available, the President's Council on Physical Fitness concludes that the quality of muscles (the contractile properties and the ability to exert force) is quite similar for the two sexes. It's felt that sex strength differences are related to the *use* of muscles in daily life. For example, men and women have similar use of leg muscles, and in lower body strength they are not that far apart. Where the great difference lies is in upper body strength, and that's where daily life comes in. As we've noted, it's the rare girl who really uses her upper body after about the age of twelve. She may run or ski or play tennis, but it's unlikely she'll be doing any hard throwing, as she would playing baseball or basketball, any boxing or weight lifting, any push-ups or chin-ups, which are not at all unusual for boys the same age to be doing. And when a professional athlete like the woman tennis player who couldn't do one push-up or flexed arm hang turns out to be not so unusual at all, we realize just how women have neglected developing upper body strength. Since experience has proven that strength can be greatly increased through the proper activities, and since it's been so recently that women have been physically active in any large numbers, it's probably too soon to make any conclusive statement about women's weaker muscles.

NEUROSTRUCTURAL DIFFERENCES

Women are slower than men in both reaction and movement times. This is a finding gathered from tests made by the President's Council for Physical Fitness. Other tests, however, had more encouraging results. One test from Germany shows that women in general have greater manual skill and dexterity, and we've found that women excel in agility, a combination of strength and flexibility. A test in the United States showed no great differences between the sexes in reaction time to visual stimulus, although men have faster movement times, possibly because of their superior muscle bulk. A general view of recent tests seems to indicate that there is probably no real difference between men and women in regard to either motor learning rate or capacity, unless strength is a factor.

We should also clarify something about reaction time. This term, to a scientist, means a neurological mechanism that cannot be improved, and since men generally do have larger fast-twitch fibers, which react somewhat more quickly to stimulus, then perhaps men are faster. But to the ordinary person, reaction time is something that can get shorter with skill. What most of us are talking about when we say "reaction time" is the actual time when you see a ball coming and you react—it's the movement time, converting what you see into making your body move, and then actually moving. Although the scientist may talk about the one hundredth of a second it may take a muscle to respond, most of us are more concerned with how fast we can get to a ball. And while having larger fast-twitch muscle fibers is still important, we have found that we can take some of the slowest athletes, women tennis players who may have more slow-twitch fibers, and teach them to respond with their racquets more quickly, move more efficiently, increase their reaction time, and end up getting to the ball as fast as someone genetically endowed with many more fast-twitch muscle fibers. So if to a neurologist reaction time is foreordained, to the rest of us it's something we can do something about. After one year of training at the United States Air Force Academy, women cadets were found to have made generally greater improvement in motor fitness than did men. Now we realize they may have started at lower levels, but this finding does underscore our belief that training helps significantly.

CARDIOPULMONARY FUNCTIONS

Women have a lower aerobic (oxygen) capacity than do men. Oxygen is used to break down carbohydrates and fat that supply your muscles with their energy. MaxVO$_2$—max is maximum, V refers to volume and O$_2$ to oxygen—refers to the maximum amount of oxygen you consume per minute during exercise. It is probably the single most valid measure of the functional capacity of your aerobic or oxygen energy system. Statistics show that women in general have a lower maxVO$_2$ than do men, a fact that would seem to judge women as less fit. Still, we know that during the younger years, when the difference in size between sexes is minimal, there is negligible difference in maxVO$_2$. Size is again shown to be a significant factor when we compare men and women of similar dimensions and find the maxVO$_2$ levels narrowing. The smallest difference between the sexes for maximum oxygen consumption is found when men and women are compared relative to their lean body mass.

Women have a lower stroke volume than do men. Your stroke volume is the amount of blood pumped by your heart with each beat. The absolute stroke volume for women is smaller than it is for men, but this is directly related to the fact that women are smaller and consequently have smaller hearts. During exercise your heart can compensate for the lower stroke volume by beating more rapidly so that the amount of blood will be sufficient. As you become more fit, however, your stroke volume will increase and your heart rate will decrease so that your heart can accomplish the same thing with an easier work load. Training has been shown not only to improve heart efficiency in both women and men but even to increase the musculature of the heart itself. The hearts of well-trained young women swimmers, for example, have been found to be better developed than those of sedentary women.

Women have less hemoglobin than do men. Hemoglobin, a compound found in your red blood cells, serves to carry oxygen from your lungs to your muscles. The amount of hemoglobin you have is related to the entire volume of blood in your system. Since women are smaller, with smaller hearts and less blood volume, their hemoglobin supply is also smaller. Training, however, can significantly reduce this difference between men and women, with untrained men having 25 percent more hemoglobin than untrained women while trained men have only 15 percent more than trained women.

Women have a smaller lung capacity than do men. This is again related to the fact that women are smaller, their smaller lungs holding less oxygen. Still, what can be the more important factor is

31

not so much your total lung capacity as how much of that capacity you can actually use. You want to be able to send more oxygen to your muscle cells and get your entire circulatory system to function more rapidly. Again, training makes the difference and can, as has been done with women at the United States service academies, increase your ability to use more of the air in your lungs.

PHYSIOLOGICAL DIFFERENCES—THERMAL

Women's threshold for sweating is two to three degrees centrigrade above men's. In other words, the air has to be hotter for a woman before she starts sweating. And since sweat is a crucial outlet for releasing body heat and salts to regulate body temperature, this fact would seem to show an apparent advantage for men. In the past few years, however, we've found that women are able to regulate their body temperatures effectively, even at this lower sweat rate. It may be that they use their perspiration more efficiently or that they adjust by using some other mechanism. We know that men and women do respond differently to heat stress (in terms of taking in oxygen, for example, or losing weight to evaporation), but the question isn't which sex functions more efficiently in the heat. It's more which mechanisms are being used to help the body adjust. Additional tests will have to be done before this question can be accurately answered. One fact you should know, which has come out of many of these studies, is that fitness, particularly aerobic fitness, makes an enormous difference in being able to exercise under conditions of extreme heat.

Men and women have a different tolerance for cold. While it's only a slight one, this is one case where women do have an advantage because of the insulation from greater fat deposits.

As you can see, the physical capacities of men and women are not all that far apart. Making more equitable comparisons, with the proper adjustments for size, shows that their performances in sports aren't that different either. In distance swimming, for example, where body size difference is reduced by the water and so

32

is much less of a factor, the end results are a lot closer than they are in any other sports event.

As for how much improvement women can make, that's only now begun to be explored. What's ultimately important is not how women compare with men but how they compare with themselves. Measuring yourself against your own previous performance or state of fitness is, of course, the very best kind of competition of all.

4

Your
Medical Profile—
What Your Doctor
Can Tell You

Once you've decided to exercise—to join a fitness program or take up a sport or work out at home—it's time to go to your doctor for a medical profile. You'll be asked some pertinent questions and given a series of examinations to help assure you of fewer aches and pains, injuries, or aggravated conditions. Besides that, with informed guidance from your doctor, it's a lot more likely you'll get the most out of your exercise program.

The medical profile we advise is a physical assessment of your ability to perform in sports safely, not just the usual examination that determines, for example, whether or not you have a normal heart rate or blood pressure. What is most essential, if you want to participate in sports, is how that heart rate or blood pressure responds to the stress of exercise. As for the questions you can be asked, they should be related to your activity—past, current, and future. The information they provide will help your doctor guide you to safe participation.

Who should get this medical profile? We think just about everyone who is going to start in on any new physical regimen. Age may be a factor in determining how extensive some of the testing and evaluation should be, but we think even the youngest would-be athlete should see her doctor for a checkup. We've found incidents of schoolchildren with undetected fractures or heart disease participating in sports programs that have put them in actual jeopardy. Still, this profile is not primarily designed to uncover reasons for restricting sports participation. Instead, it can often advance it. We've encouraged exercising in women with conditions like diabetes who have stayed away from active sports such as running or tennis by convincing them that these activities are basically beneficial and can lower their insulin requirements. And the ordinary woman should be able to learn from the profile about her own physical potential. It's likely she'll find out that she's a lot stronger than she thought she was.

Who should give the medical profile? Unless there's some special problem that might require the attention and advice of a specialist, your own family doctor can be able to evaluate your fitness provided he or she has the interest, training, or experience in the exercise area. While most general practitioners, internists, and family practitioners are expert in giving the basic examination and are well able to assess your cardiorespiratory status in depth, they may prefer to have you be seen by someone who more routinely deals with the musculoskeletal system, if only for that part of the examination.

The procedure outlined in this chapter will provide what we consider a thorough profile. Touching on many crucial areas often overlooked, it provides a more complete picture than the ordinary physical check-up. Find out how fit you are—or could be.

GENERAL MEDICAL HISTORY

This is where you tell your doctor everything that ought to be known about your state of health. The subsequent physical examination, as well as recommendations, will be guided largely by the answers you give to the questions. For example, your description of pain in a joint may point to an undetected fracture. Your doctor's decision to X-ray may end up saving you further injury and discomfort. Or a history of sprains can indicate a loose joint that proper exercise could help stabilize. Your mentioning this history is the only way your doctor will be clued into investigating and then advising you. Some existing conditions may preclude exercise for the time being (coming down hard on a sprained ankle, for example, can cause a break), while certain types of past injuries, such as repeated concussions, can contraindicate certain kinds of sports, such as football.

Here are questions that we ask our patients and that your doctor may ask you, starting with a history of your diseases and illnesses.

YOUR HISTORY OF DISEASE AND ILLNESS

Have you any congenital abnormalities? absent organs? This would include single ovaries or kidneys. Such conditions certainly do not rule out sports participation, but you should weigh the risk factors. If you have an unpaired organ, playing a contact sport can actually become a legal question. Parents have had to sue school boards in order to get their children the medical clearance to be admitted to a football or lacrosse team. We believe that a person with an unpaired organ or eye can participate in most sports as long as she understands the risks involved.

Blood diseases? A lowered hemoglobin rate or hematocrit volume rates in general are especially important to women or girls who have heavy menstrual cycles. There may be times when these women should be advised to curtail their sports participation. Other bleeding disorders, such as abnormalities in the platelets, can keep the blood from clotting, a risk to be weighed in choosing a sport.

For black women another important consideration is the possibility of sickle-cell anemia. Active sports can aggravate this condition, causing sickle crisis with abdominal pains and headaches, and can even lead to heart damage. If your doctor knows you have a trait for sickle-cell anemia, he or she can tell you what symptoms you should look out for when you exercise.

36

Diabetes? Years ago doctors believed that exercise would be harmful to a diabetic, but now we know that just the opposite is true. Exercise not only diminishes the insulin requirements, as we've mentioned, but also has a beneficial stabilizing effect on the cardiovascular disease atherosclerosis, which is associated to a high degree with diabetes.

Sugar, albumin, pus, blood in urine? All or any of these symptoms may point to kidney disease, a condition aggravated by strenuous exercise. Activities such as long-distance running should be avoided. What happens is that with the physical stress of heavy exercise, there is an accompanying muscle breakdown in which protein goes into the blood and from there to the kidneys. Saddle horses, after a weekend of working hard, often suffer from what stable hands call "Monday Morning Stiffness," with muscle breakdown causing stiff joints and swelling. This isn't very different from what happens to the marathoner, who can have severe cramping after running prolonged distances without adequate preparation or training. Still, even for the healthy and well-trained marathoner, this reaction of muscle breakdown can cause the kidneys to shut down temporarily. Since those of you with kidney disease are particularly susceptible, it's important to check out all the above symptoms before you start running.

You should be aware, however, that after heavy exercise the presence of blood in the urine can be a normal response and not an indication of disease.

Coughing up blood? This can be a symptom of tuberculosis or other pulmonary disease, illnesses that go along with special cautions when exercising.

Chronic nosebleeds? This can point up some bleeding abnormality, which can put you at risk in contact sports. Our experience with professional athletes indicates that bleeding problems can be intensified through exercise.

Hepatitis or jaundice? Both can cause an enlarged liver, a special danger in contact sports, where a blow to the belly can rupture the enlarged liver. Even in noncontact sports we advise being cautious. One skier who was practicing freestyle maneuvers developed severe abdominal pains and was rushed to the hospital. There we discovered he had ruptured his spleen, possibly because a recent viral infection had left his spleen enlarged and vulnerable. The pressure in his abdomen, created when he took a large breath before attempting a ski maneuver, could well have been responsible for the rupture. In this case it would have been difficult to anticipate the injury. Still, this incident points up the vulnerability of enlarged abdominal organs even in noncontact sports.

High blood pressure? This can indicate the presence of heart disease and so must be carefully checked out. But don't think high blood pressure necessarily should keep you sedentary. Ask for and then follow your doctor's recommendation. Like diabetes, some types of high blood pressure can respond favorably to exercise. We've seen consistent incidents of lowered resting pulse, even with quality athletes, after they've been put on an endurance training program.

There is usually some difference in the time it takes for someone with high blood pressure or in poor cardiovascular condition to recover normal pulse rate. The person with normal blood pressure will recover to about 50 percent above her resting heart rate within one to two minutes after cessation of exercise, while someone with high blood pressure probably won't reach this point in the same amount of time. This fact, though, should certainly not discourage participating in sports, since, as we've pointed out, exercise will surely improve the picture.

Congenital heart disease, cardiovascular disease, rheumatic fever, murmurs? You should have your history carefully evaluated by an internist or cardiologist who will give you one or more tests—a resting electrocardiogram, an exercise or stress electrocardiogram, or one of the more sophisticated heart scans—to see if exercise might be bad for you. Stress electrocardiography, because of its inaccuracies as well as because some abnormalities do not necessarily point to heart disease, should be correlated very specifically with your history of symptoms. Whatever the final results, it is unlikely that exercise would be completely ruled out. Perhaps, depending on what activities you participate in, you will be asked to modify your routine. Cardiologists have emphasized that the risk of a life-threatening situation is markedly reduced through a graded, sensible program that includes gradual transitions. It's essential for you and for everyone who exercises, even those with no indication of heart disease, to do careful warm-ups before exercising and to cool down afterward.

Chest pains during exercise? Such pains don't have to be an indication of heart disease at all but may point instead to muscular problems, indigestion, ulcers, even gall bladder disorders. Whichever, you should be carefully checked out by your doctor.

Infectious mononucleosis, pneumonia? Mononucleosis, like hepatitis, can give you an enlarged liver, which would be more susceptible to blows. Pneumonia can leave you with shortened breath, a condition that can affect your endurance.

Chronic cough? For those of you with chronic bronchitis, a moderate exercise program could be of great value. It would help you to bring up sputum and expand your lungs, getting their capacity back close to normal. Your doctor should guide you toward the proper modifications and controls.

Epilepsy? Exercise is certainly not contraindicated, although we'd suggest that your coach, instructor, or partner be prepared to help oxygenate you, holding your tongue down during a seizure so that you won't asphyxiate. As you already know, today's medications for epilepsy make seizures less and less likely to occur.

Recurring headaches, blackouts? These symptoms should get checked out. Functional type headaches—those that come from gastrointestinal complaints or menstrual cramps, are often diminished with regular exercise.

Concussion? Unfortunately, once you've had a concussion, your susceptibility to having another is higher. Naturally you'd want to avoid repeated concussions or cerebral irritation. Your doctor may suggest you use moderation in your approach to certain sports, such as skiing or hockey.

Blurred vision, sties, pinkeye? Sties and pinkeye are infectious conditions that are especially likely to spread in situations where people are exercising. These should be checked out, not only for your sake but for others.

Blurred vision may have many causes and should be investigated thoroughly.

Hearing problems? Trouble with your hearing may point up

some underlying congenital problems that you didn't know about, so further investigation is essential. You may find yourself at a disadvantage in some sports where auditory cues help. For example, hearing how a ball comes off a racquet often aids you in preparing for the next move. Still, many hard-of-hearing athletes have learned to compensate.

Skin infections, boils, impetigo? These can be aggravated by the sweating and dirt that often go along with exercise. They can also spread to others. Your doctor may advise you to avoid strenuous workouts where you come in contact with other athletes until these conditions have cleared up.

Allergies? Allergies to medication should be reported to medical personnel or on medical forms at fitness facilities, schools, clubs, etc. Other kinds of allergies, while usually producing less severe reactions, can affect your performance. We've found, for example, that the American players at Wimbledon often have adverse reactions to the English grass courts. It's been essential to control these allergies when they arise.

Frequent indigestion, heartburn? There are too many possibilities for causes and too many areas of your body—gastrointestinal tract, gall bladder, heart, abdominal muscles—that might be involved for your doctor to come up with an easy answer. These symptoms need sorting out and perhaps further testing.

Ulcer? While your diet is the most important factor, exercise can also be helpful. Physical activity cuts down on pH (leaving your stomach less acid), can often help diminish a stressful situation, and will decrease or sublimate spasms by displacing them from the gastrointestinal tract to the muscles.

Appendicitis, hernia? As long as you allow enough time for healing after surgery, these conditions should not cause contraindications for exercise. Occasionally, with some hernia repair, your doctor may suggest modified activity.

Kidney or bladder diseases? Since exercise has a definite effect on changing the content of the urine, kidney and bladder diseases must be carefully monitored and perhaps some modifications of your exercise program will be suggested to you.

Heat exhaustion or heat stress? For some reasons we don't completely understand, those of you who have had heat exhaustion or heat stress are more susceptible the next time around. Plenty of liquids sipped frequently, wearing light cotton clothing, and avoiding as much as possible exercising during the hottest times of the day are cautions you should follow. You should know that it may take your body several days to acclimate itself to warm weather, so if you're coming from the wintery north down to a tropical resort, don't rush from the airport right out onto the tennis courts.

Mental illness? While there are some instances where competitive sports have been considered contraindicated, exercise is often recommended as excellent therapy.

After these more general questions, you will probably be asked to give some specific information about your cardiovascular system since, along with your musculoskeletal system, this system is called upon to perform at high capacity during exercise.

CORONARY HISTORY

Your doctor will ask you about possible symptoms. Do you ever feel light-headed? Do you often faint? Do you have shortness of breath? What has been your tolerance for exercise in the past? Have you had an irregular heartbeat? Rheumatic fever? A viral infection with a prolonged rapid pulse? Frequent sore throats? If you have had none of these symptoms, your doctor will probably just listen to your heart action as part of the general physical examination. If everything is normal, you'll be able to go out and start exercising. Beginning slowly and gradually is in itself a protective device, keeping you from endangering your health.

Of course, your age must be taken into consideration. Women during their childbearing years have a much lower risk of coronary artery disease. We believe this is related to the physiological effect of estrogen and other estrogen-related hormones. After menopause this advantage ceases, and ten years later the risk for women is about the same as it is for men.

What kind of screening should be done for women with normal

menstrual function? For older women, now in the higher risk category? The resting cardiogram is considered by many as a low-yield procedure, insensitive in picking up coronary artery disease. The exercise electrocardiogram or stress test often gives inaccurate readings. There are many incidents of false positives as well as actual cardiac conditions that are overlooked.

Besides, a cardiogram itself can't give the whole answer. We see athletes who are in excellent condition and yet have some bizarre cardiographic recordings. These are basically meaningless in a clinical setting, that is, out on the playing field or in the gym. Your cardiogram, if it turns out to be abnormal, should be further assessed by someone who understands exercise cardiology. It may well be that you're in good enough shape to start an exercise program, despite your cardiogram.

Dr. Samuel M. Fox of Georgetown University, an exercise cardiologist, believes that women with normal weight and menstrual function are rarely at significant risk. If they have no special symptoms, he believes they seldom need to take a stress test before starting an exercise program. Judgments can be better made right in the exercise setting, where problems, should they arise, can be evaluated. A few simple and inexpensive tests might be done —specimens of cholesterol, kidney function chemistries, uric acid specimens, and frequent blood pressure checks. If these are normal and no symptoms arise in a carefully graduated program, no further testing is called for in most cases.

Cardiologist Jeffrey Borer at New York Hospital told us that, for women over forty-five who have never exercised before, he would recommend taking a stress test despite its limitations. A negative history and a negative stress test could give you a 99 percent accurate answer. And since statistically no test is 100 percent accurate, you can't do much better than that.

What if you have had a heart attack? Just about a decade ago someone recovered from a heart attack would be told to remain relatively inactive. But that's all changed now. Two professional athletes, John Hiller of the Detroit Tigers and Dave Stallworth of the New York Knicks, came back and played after heart attacks. For anyone who has had heart disease, some form of exercise is often the best thing for your health. With coronary artery disease, the most common cardiac disease of people in the middle and older age groups, the blocked coronary arteries will prevent a sufficient amount of oxygen from getting in to supply the needs of the heart. Exercise reduces the heart rate and blood pressure response. With the heart rate slower and the blood pressure lower, the amount of oxygen that the heart requires is less for the same amount of exertion.

Exercise offers other benefits as well. An article in the *Journal of the American Medical Association* indicates that high-density lipid or cholesterol level is the most powerful single predictor of coronary artery disease in those over fifty. (Lipids are a group of heterogeneous compounds insoluble in water and soluble in organic solvents like ether or chloroform.) Since exercise is recognized as a factor in lowering cholesterol levels, it should certainly be on the list of recommendations you get from your doctor.

We are including here a questionnaire that we use to assess patients.

CORONARY RISK FACTORS

			points
I. Factors over which you have no control			
A. Age:	10–20 years old		1
	21–30		2
	31–40		3
	41–50		4
	51–60		5
	61 or over		6
B. Sex:	Female under 40		1
	Female 40–50		2
	Female after menopause		3
C. Heredity ("relative" refers to immediate family, i.e., parents, siblings, children)			
No history of heart disease			1
One relative with cardiovascular disease after 60			2

43

Two relatives with cardiovascular disease after 60	3
One relative with cardiovascular disease before 60	4
Two relatives with cardiovascular disease before 60	6
Three relatives with cardiovascular disease before 60	7

II. Factors over which you have control

A. Weight: (see p. 76 for average weight tables)

Greater than 5 pounds below average	0
From 5 pounds below average to 6 pounds above average	1
6–20 pounds overweight	2
21–35 pounds overweight	3
36–50 pounds overweight	5
More than 51 pounds overweight	7

B. Tobacco Smoking:

Don't smoke	0
Smoke less than 10 cigarettes daily	2
10–20 cigarettes daily	4
21–30 cigarettes daily	6
More than 30 cigarettes daily	10

C. Exercise:

Intensive occupational and recreational exertion	1
Moderate occupational and recreational exertion	2
Sedentary work and intense recreational exertion	3
Sedentary work and moderate recreational exertion	5
Sedentary work and light recreational exertion	6
Complete lack of exercise	8

D. Cholesterol or percentage of fat in your diet:

Low blood cholesterol and/or your diet excludes saturated fats and eggs	1
Medium/low cholesterol and/or diet excluding most saturated fats and eggs	2
Borderline cholesterol and/or diet containing	

minimal saturated fats and eggs	3
Mild elevation of cholesterol and/or a diet containing moderate saturated fats and eggs	4
Marked elevation of cholesterol and/or a diet excessive in saturated fats and eggs	5
Extreme elevation of cholesterol and/or a diet excessive in saturated fats and eggs	7

E. Blood Pressure:

Systolic pressure (the upper figure given) of 119 or less	1
Systolic pressure 120–139	2
Systolic pressure 140–159	3
Systolic pressure 160–179	4
Systolic pressure 180–199	6
Systolic pressure 200 or over	8

Add up the results of these eight factors for an overall score.

6–16 is below average
17–24 is average
25–31 is moderate
32–40 is dangerous
Over 41 is urgent and needs immediate medical attention

Recommendations:

If you are in the below average or average risk category, you can begin an exercise program if your doctor tells you that your health continues to be good.

If your risk factor is moderate, you should consult your doctor to determine the proper modification for your program.

If you are in the last two categories, it is essential for you to have all your activities approved first by your doctor.

Additional Notes:

Be sure to bring to your doctor's attention the following:

1—Obesity
2—Diabetes

3—Thyroid disease
4—Chest pains (angina pectoris)
5—High blood pressure (hypertension)
6—Joint pains
7—Heart attack (myocardial infarction)

Do not exercise with the following:

1—Congestive heart failure
2—Heart attack, 3 months previous or less, unless in a physician-directed cardiac rehabilitation program
3—Chest pains with a changing pattern, until checked by a doctor
4—Moderate to severe valvular heart disease—congenital or rheumatic
5—Anemia, with blood hemoglobin less than 10 mg. %
6—Uncontrolled metabolic disease (diabetes, thyrotoxicosis, myxedema)

Next you will be asked about your use of:

MEDICATIONS, STIMULANTS, DRUGS

The following are used for people with heart trouble and should be brought to the attention of your doctor so that he can make the necessary corresponding modifications to your exercise program:

Digitalis. This drug slows down the heart rate and increases its output. It can cause toxicity, resulting in heart rhythm disorders.

Quinidine. This is used to control and prevent heart rhythm disorders. It can have a profound effect on the conduction of electrical impulses through the heart.

Pronestyl. This is another commonly used drug to control heart rhythm disorders.

Inderal (Propranolol). This relatively new drug has multiple effects. It is highly successful in treating angina pectoris (chest pain), in controlling elevated blood pressure, and in steadying certain heart rhythm disorders.

Nitroglycerin. This drug often has an immediate and profoundly effective action in controlling an attack of angina (coronary insufficiency).

Long-acting nitrates (Isosorbide Dinitrate). These have action similar to nitroglycerin but work over a longer period of time. Some are active when applied to the skin as an ointment (Nitrol Ointment).

Diuretics. This is a large group of drugs designed to cause greater loss of urine. These usually work by causing the excretion of salt in the urine, the salt drawing with it an increased amount of fluid. A woman taking a diuretic could become salt-depleted more easily and develop symptoms similar to those of heat exhaustion (weakness, cold clammy skin, and sometimes fainting). She would also lose potassium and so might suffer the severe weakness and fatigue that accompanies an excessive loss of this mineral. Strenuous exercise, especially in hot climates, can be particularly dangerous for someone taking diuretics.

Thyroid Medication. The thyroid is the energy thermostat of the body. Women with overactive thyroids tend to be nervous, tremorous, palpitating, perspiring, and, despite a hardy appetite, they still lose weight. Besides surgery or radioactive treatment, drugs such as propylthiouracil and methimazole are used. Physical activity must be supervised by a doctor, although once the patient reaches a normal level of thyroid activity, she can go back to her usual exercise pattern.

Underactive thyroid glands produce individuals who gain weight easily, are sluggish, and have dry skin. Drugs, including thyroid extract and synthetic preparations such as Proloid, are used for hormone replacement. After several weeks of therapy the patient can exercise as she wishes.

Stimulants and Sedatives. We find very few athletes taking sedatives because they slow you down and decrease your efficiency. As for stimulants, their effect is at best transient. We've found from our experience with professional athletes that the effect of stimulants on athletic performance seems more psychological than anything else.

Nicotine. It is unfortunately true that a good many athletes do continue to smoke. After a long workout, it's not uncommon to see a world-class athlete light up a cigarette. Of course, this differs from sport to sport. Very few swimmers, skiers, and tennis players smoke. But in explosive sports, where endurance capacity is less important, such as football and basketball, there are a great many smokers.

Alcohol. It will depress your concentration, and, because it can also affect your reaction time, alcohol is potentially dangerous in any sport that has hazards. Drinking hasn't been much of a problem among serious athletes, although lately there's been some literature about the incidence of alcoholism among marathon runners. These runners, often intense, competitive, and goal-directed, have similar personality traits to those often found in heavy drinkers.

We've also noticed in recent years an increase in drinking among high school athletes. This reflects the growing problem of excessive drinking and alcoholism in younger and younger age groups.

The medical history will continue with a history of your:

HOSPITALIZATIONS AND OPERATIONS

Since you have already told your doctor that you are about to start on a new regimen of physical exercise, these questions should include any injuries or operations relating to your joints, since these are the areas that will be most affected. The areas include ankles, knees, shoulders, and elbows. Except for such major operations as brain, chest, or cardiovascular surgery, most past operations on the rest of your body, if they are not recent, are relatively unimportant factors as far as physical activity is concerned.

Musculoskeletal surgery, on the other hand, may leave you weaker than you were, with a possible tendency for arthritis. You can end up with less motion and some amount of instability. All this should be taken into consideration when you plan your activities. Your doctor can suggest modifications to help the injured part of your body. For example, if you had knee surgery, it might be advised that you not run on hard pavement but try bicycle riding or swimming instead. If you find you can handle some weight-bearing exercise, your doctor might then recommend you stick to running shorter distances on softer surfaces.

Most doctors' questions concentrate on your heart, liver, your history of childhood diseases, and other areas that, while crucial to your general well-being and a necessary part of your health maintenance program, may not have as much of a direct bearing on your capacity for exercise. Certainly your blood pressure, your history of taking medications, and the state of your lungs are all aspects of you that will influence whether you exercise happily or unhappily or not at all. But 90 percent of the problems that develop from sports come from your musculoskeletal system, and this is the area we've found too often neglected by doctors.

You should inform your doctor of pertinent facts, such as whether or not you wear a brace. You may have bought one in the drugstore, and it might turn out to be the worst thing you could wear for your sore kneecaps. Your doctor has no way of knowing this if you neglect to mention it, and so your kneecaps will continue to be aggravated.

Knee braces these days have almost gotten to be a status symbol, with some athletes wearing them outside their ski pants. For some others we suspect they've become somewhat of a security blanket. There are two specific functions that are helped by the proper open knee brace, such as the Patella Alignment Control Support: controlling knee instability and reducing pain in the kneecap. Other problems are not influenced by any kind of knee support.

More serious physical conditions have also been ignored in the usual medical history. Have you had bone grafts? Spinal plates? Screws? All of these tend to weaken the bone, an important fact for your doctor to know, especially if you want to participate in explosive sports such as skiing, basketball, or soccer. They also may indicate that you had osteomyelitis (inflammation of the bone marrow) when you were younger, a problem in sports if you have to extend your spine, as in horseback riding or jumping straight up in basketball.

49

We don't want to overemphasize the importance of your muscu-loskeletal history, but if you want to exercise, what you really have to know is whether or not you can run on that bad knee or weak ankle, throw with that loose shoulder, hit with that sore elbow. In most cases exercise is good for any of these conditions, but it should be done within certain guidelines. In our training chapter we'll talk more about exercising with an injury.

ORTHOPEDIC HISTORY

Head, neck. One common injury to the neck is the nerve pinch syndrome. It results from direct recurrent trauma to the neck and shoulder and gives you burning pains and stingers (pins and nee-dles) in your neck and sometimes down your arm. The sensation is transient, quickly relieved, and does not cause any permanent damage.

Shoulders. Dislocations can come from tennis, horseback riding, and swimming, not just from contact sports. We had one patient, a sky diver, who kept dislocating her shoulder and was afraid that someday she wouldn't be able to pull the rip cord. Both her shoulders have been repaired surgically but her extreme loose-jointedness makes more dislocations probable. In fact, she has al-ready dislocated one of the repaired shoulders by sky diving again.

Arm, elbow, wrist. Arm problems are common, especially the famous tennis elbow. More women than men seem to have a weakness in the forearm, frequently stemming from such bad habits as hitting the tennis ball late, using a bent wrist, or coming through with the wrist forcefully flexed downward. What hap-pens when you do any of these or when you hit balls that are too hard for you is that you end up straining the muscles on the top of your forearm. These muscles are used to stabilize your wrist, and since they originate at the elbow, when you try to tighten your wrist, you can end up aggravating your elbow. Once the strained muscle is sore and tender, every time you move your wrist up and down—turning doorknobs, picking up packages, even brushing your hair—it can cause pain in your elbow.

Switching from nylon to gut strings and to a less stiff racquet will help. You should also work on changing your technique and start an exercise program that concentrates on increasing strength in your forearm.

Hand. Since most hand injuries come from actual contact sports (such as football), they are less common for women. We do see dislocated thumbs among women skiers, what is called "ski pole thumb."

Spine. Congenital spine defects can cause backaches and poor posture. These are often made worse by the weakness of the abdominal muscles, a weakness many women have. If this is your problem, you should try those exercises that strengthen your abdomen and do not cause you to arch your back outward (lordosis).

Hips, pelvis. Again, these are areas less commonly injured in most sports.

Thigh. Tight thigh muscles can cause pulls. Most women, however, have just the opposite problem, that of loose joints and weak thigh muscles. The weak thigh muscles are a special problem for teen-age girls and older women, both groups starting out in exercise without first going through the essential strengthening exercises. Weak thigh muscles are usually responsible for kneecaps' drifting and ending up painfully sore.

Leg. Women, because of their tight heel cords, can suffer from Achilles tendinitis. Tight heels can be caused by wearing high-heeled shoes, which also often leads to stiffness in the ankles.

Ankle. Ankle problems are not uncommon among women athletes who wear high heels. Besides the stiffness we mentioned, these women have a tendency to walk on their toes, rolling their feet, and so often painfully aggravate their ankles.

Feet. Walking on your toes, as many women do, can also cause pain on the tops of your feet. You should choose your exercise shoes with care, making sure they're wide enough to accommodate your toes without causing the bunions that are another common problem for female athletes.

MENSTRUATION, BIRTH CONTROL, AND PREGNANCY

There are additional questions for women in your medical questionnaire that have to do with your menstrual cycle and your use of birth control devices. Menstrual changes due to exercise are usually transient, as we've said before, but we have to know your pattern before we can judge how your exercise program is affecting you.

Birth control pills can make you more subject to phlebitis, a risk intensified if you have varicose veins. By the way, the swelling of your legs that comes after exercise to those of you with varicose veins should not necessarily keep you from exercising. Being active is a help in circulating your blood out of the legs and into other parts of the body.

Something should be mentioned here about the pooling of blood after exercise. One of the reasons it is important to cool down gradually at the end of an exercise session is because when you neglect to do this, *venous return* to the heart, which is controlled mainly by the muscle pump, drops abruptly and blood pooling can occur in your extremities. This can result in shock or hyperventilation.

As for the IUD, you should take into consideration the abdominal pains that often go along with it as well as increased menstrual flow, both handicaps when exercising.

Unless you have some special problem, you can exercise safely through the first trimester of pregnancy in a sport you are familiar with and have been participating in regularly. As for the second and third trimesters, your obstetrician will probably be guided by how active you've been before. Most of the women athletes we see exercise to some extent right up to the last days of their pregnancies.

TRAINING HISTORY

This last part of your medical history explores an area most often ignored by doctors: just what physical activity have you been doing up to now? And it's not really informative just saying you play tennis twice a week. If you're playing doubles with a group of friends who offer more in the way of conversation than competition, you probably don't exert yourself enough to get your pulse rate up. If you win your matches or have sore muscles after playing or perspire a lot, it doesn't mean you're necessarily working hard. It's important that you learn how to evaluate what you're doing in order to see what you can do. The training history we suggest will force you to examine your past activity in terms of the amount of effort it took. You must be honest both with yourself and with your doctor.

Your past history can give your doctor some important clues as to what kinds of sports you can handle and how hard you can safely work out. If your aerobic level is high, for example, it means you have good endurance and don't have to worry about getting your pulse rate up. However, if it's low, you should be starting on a program of running or bicycling or swimming to build up the capacity of your lungs and increase the efficiency of your circulatory system. You can increase your aerobic capacity in a variety of ways, even as part of your regular sport. If you're a tennis player, for example, practice running from side to side at the base line. Run to the net for several volleys, then back to the base line for some ground strokes, and keep this up until you've elevated your heartbeat to a training level (about 120 to 135 beats per minute for a middle-aged woman). If the weather is bad, you can accomplish good stamina training by riding a stationary bicycle at home. Our chapter on training, Chapter 7, outlines some other ways to maintain or improve your aerobic capacity.

Here are two examples of the training histories we ask for at the Sport Medicine Clinic. The first is for the ordinary person starting some kind of fitness program. For some of the questions you'll be asked to record your pulse rate so that the intensity of your participation can be rated objectively. Your maximum heart rate can be estimated at 220 minus your age; approximately 75 percent of this figure is the rate you should maintain in order to get an effective exercise. Moderate intensity can increase your heart rate slightly, but light activity can have such a minimal effect that you get virtually no cardiopulmonary effect.

The injury questions ask for basic details about the types of injuries you have had, the region of your body they affected, and how they occurred. Your answers can give your doctor a good picture of how you've reacted to sports in the past and how your injuries may affect your future activities.

The second training history is for the professional athlete or serious recreational one. It includes not only the cardiopulmonary training that makes up most of the first questionnaire but also questions about participation in other types of training, including flexibility training, strength training, and power or speed training. The history starts with strength training for the upper body—the neck, shoulders, arms, and hands—and then the lower body—the abdomen, trunk, and legs. Free weights can be used as well as equipment like Universal or Marcy where you can select various amounts of resistance as you work different areas of your body, exercising each part through an entire range of motion; or Cybex or Mini Gym, which are speed controlled, the machine unable to move any faster than the speed that you set. (More descriptions of training equipment are included in Chapter 7.) Nautilus equipment regulates the resistance automatically, providing maximum resistance in all positions. The resistance changes throughout the range of motion, but it feels the same because it is always in proportion to your available strength. Flexibility routines can include yoga, dance, or specific flexibility exercises. Cardiopulmonary activities, as we've mentioned, can vary widely, so that you need not stick to the usual jogging or biking if you prefer to combine vigorous aerobic activity with your regular sport.

ACTIVITY QUESTIONNAIRES

GENERAL PHYSICAL ACTIVITY QUESTIONNAIRE

Give yourself points for each amount of intensity, multiply by the times per week, and add to get your level of activity.

Activity	Intensity	Duration	Points	Times Per Week	Score
calisthenics	light	up to 20 minutes	2	——	——
	moderate	20–40 minutes	3	——	——
	vigorous	40 or more minutes	5	——	——
walking/	slow	up to 3.5 mph	2	——	——
running	moderate	3.5–5 mph	5	——	——
	vigorous	5 mph or faster	7	——	——
	climbing		8	——	——
golf (no motorized	light to moderate	up to 32 holes	2	——	——
cart)	moderate	more than 32 holes	4	——	——
dance	slow	up to 45 minutes	3	——	——
(continuous dance movement)	moderate	more than 45 minutes	5	——	——
bicycling	slow 6–9 mph	30 minutes	3	——	——
	moderate 9–17 mph	30 minutes	4	——	——
	vigorous over 12 mph	30 minutes	6	——	——
swimming	slow	up to 30 yards per minute	3	——	——
	moderate	30–50 yards per minute	5	——	——
	vigorous	more than 50 yards per minute	8	——	——
Ping-Pong	light	up to 45 minutes	2	——	——
	moderate	45 minutes or more	4	——	——
tennis					

doubles	light	up to 45 minutes	2	___	___
	moderate	45–60 minutes	4	___	___
	vigorous	more than 60 minutes	6	___	___
singles	light	up to 30 minutes	3	___	___
	moderate	30–60 minutes	5	___	___
	vigorous	more than 60 minutes	8	___	___
volleyball	light	up to 30 minutes	4	___	___
	moderate	30–60 minutes	6	___	___
	vigorous	more than 60 minutes	8	___	___
skating	light	up to 45 minutes	3	___	___
	moderate	45–90 minutes	5	___	___
	vigorous	more than 90 minutes	7	___	___
skiing (actual ski time) downhill	light	up to 45 minutes	5	___	___
	moderate	45–90 minutes	6	___	___
	vigorous	more than 90 minutes	7	___	___
cross-country	light	30 minutes	7	___	___
	moderate	30–60 minutes	9	___	___
	vigorous	more than 60 minutes	12	___	___
rowing	light	up to 20 minutes	4	___	___
	moderate	20–45 minutes	6	___	___
	vigorous	more than 45 minutes	8	___	___
basketball	light	up to 30 minutes	4	___	___
	moderate	30–60 minutes	6	___	___
	vigorous	more than 60 minutes	8	___	___
soccer	light	up to 30 minutes	4	___	___
	moderate	30–60 minutes	6	___	___
	vigorous	more than 60 minutes	9	___	___
squash, handball, racquetball	light	up to 30 minutes	4	___	___
	moderate	30–60 minutes	6	___	___
	vigorous	more than 60 minutes	9	___	___

TOTAL SCORE

Age:	under 25	25–45	over 45
less than average	less than 20	less than 15	less than 10
average	20 to 30	15 to 25	10 to 20
above average	more than 30	more than 25	more than 20

INJURY HISTORY

Injury Type
0 = unknown
1 = one muscle/tendon injury
2 = two or more muscle/tendon injuries
3 = one ligament injury
4 = two or more ligament injuries
5 = fracture or other type of injury
6 = dislocations, subluxations
Area (examples)
0 = shoulder (dislocation, subluxation)
1 = arm/elbow (tennis elbow)
2 = wrist/hand (sprain/dislocated finger)
3 = spine/neck
4 = pelvis/hip
5 = thigh (bruises, muscle pulls)
6 = knee/kneecap (ligament/kneecap dislocation)
7 = leg (shin splints, muscle pull, tendinitis)
8 = ankle (sprains)
9 = foot (heel pain, arch pain)

	TYPE	AREA	DESCRIBE (Include sport if possible)
1			
2			
3			
4			
5			
6			

SPECIFIC TRAINING HISTORY

NAME: _____ DATE: _____

DATE OF BIRTH: _____

	Type	Duration Each Time	Times Per Week	Additional Description
UPPER BODY	1. Strength *Free Weights Nautilus Universal (Isotonic) Cybex (Isokinetic)			
LOWER BODY	*Free Weights Nautilus Universal (Isotonic) Cybex (Isokinetic)			
	2. Flexibility (describe program)			
	3. Cardiorespiratory Running Bicycle Treadmill Other			
	4. Sports-specific Training (List)			

*Examples of weight training devices

Once the histories have been completed, your doctor will move on to the examinations, starting with the:

GENERAL PHYSICAL EXAM

While this examination should be complete, touching on the entire body and its functions, it should also be kept simple. What your doctor is basically doing is screening out those of you who can move directly into physical activities. A more detailed examination of any particular system or extremity will be done if your history indicates that it's necessary or if your general examination turns up something that requires further attention.

Pulse. Your resting pulse rate can be an indication of what shape you're in, and usually, the lower it is, the more fit you are. But we should emphasize here that there is no fast rule about pulse rate and fitness. We've seen, for example, women in excellent condition with high resting pulse rates as well as others who have inherited lower rates that tell us nothing at all about what shape they're in.

Blood pressure. There's a lot we can learn from your blood pressure. High blood pressure can be an indication of heart disease. These symptoms will tell your doctor to examine the heart itself more closely.

Vision. You should have 20-20 vision, with or without glasses. A great many people are not aware of visual deficiencies, which certainly will prove to be a disadvantage in most sports.

Skin. Your doctor will be looking for infections and rashes, most of which can be irritated during exercise and can spread to others. He or she should also keep an eye out for injection sites—you may be taking medications you haven't mentioned, information crucial for evaluating your capability for strenuous activity.

Scalp. Thin hair can be an indication of thyroid disease. Because the thyroid has a lot to do with the control of your heart and blood pressure, your ability to withstand heavy exercise would be directly affected by an improperly functioning thyroid.

Lymph nodes. An examination of the lymph nodes can uncover blood or lymph disease or the presence of other infections.

Ears and nose. These should be examined for normal structure and function and for the possible presence of infection.

Throat and mouth. Your teeth can give your doctor some valuable clues about your diet, as can the condition of your tongue.

Abdomen. Scars will indicate surgery you may have neglected to report in your history. Some kinds of operations, particularly those involving your veins and arteries, can cause trouble in strenuous activities that produce heavy breathing and excessive stress.

Chest and back. Past chest and back operations—whether on your lungs, spine, or heart—will probably give your doctor reason to limit your activity. Some forms of strength training, including weight lifting for example, may well be ruled out.

You should also have a pelvic examination, which would include internal and external genitalia. Again, we repeat the same cautions about infections and exercise. It's a bad situation for you to have an infection and a bad one as well for those you may be exercising with. It would certainly be wisest to have the proper treatment first.

Nervous system. Weakness on one side of your body when compared to the other can be due to nerve loss. Arms and legs should be equal in reflexes, with ankles and knees symmetrical. Nerve disease in the brain, spinal cord, or peripheral nerves can affect your gait, hindering your running and maneuvering.

LABORATORY TESTS

There are several lab tests that can help your doctor determine your level of fitness. The routine blood counts and chemistries along with a urine analysis are sensible screening for general health, with a sickle-cell test an important addition for blacks.

Electrocardiograms should probably be done for those of you over forty-five who have not had regular exercise in the past, or for anyone with a specific risk factor such as a history of heart attack, high blood pressure, diabetes, obesity, smoking, or with low levels of fitness as shown on the laboratory tests. If an abnormality or further question arises after a resting electrocardiogram, an exercise cardiogram or more sophisticated cardiovascular test will be recommended.

A chest X ray can also be quite helpful in evaluating the condition of your lungs and heart if your physician thinks it's advisable. As a rule other X rays aren't necessary unless you have a specific orthopedic condition or injury.

The muscle tests we suggest in this part of the general examination are just simple comparisons of arm with arm and leg with leg. The muscles on both sides should be roughly the same.

An area that has received attention recently has been the lipid profile, and your doctor may suggest you have this lab test. The high-density lipoproteins in your blood pick up excessive cholesterol and carry it back to the liver for excretion from the body. Low-density lipoproteins, on the other hand, can be deposited in the linings of the coronary arteries, clogging them and perhaps leading to heart attacks. Some experts believe a more fit person would be one with a high level of high-density lipoproteins (HDLs). One of the ways exercise can help you get fit, these experts believe, is by raising your level of HDLs. We know that long-distance runners, for example, have a very much higher level of high-density lipoproteins than the general population.

Your cholesterol level should be on the low side, as should your level of serum triglyceride. Coronary patients, we know, have an increased triglyceride concentration.

FITNESS EXAMINATION

The best tests of your exercise capacity are the specific fitness tests, and we would like to encourage the almost routine use of these in your Medical Profile. Such tests can give a far better picture of the shape you're in than a static test, in which you're sitting still or lying down, since they allow your doctor to see what happens to you in movement, how you respond to stress (that is, any activity from the least to the most strenuous), and how you handle different work loads. There are several of these tests that use simple equipment, and, while not everyone has an exercise bicycle or a treadmill, most people have access to a bench or a short flight of stairs, which is what you need for the Step Test.

In the Masters Step Test, you step on and off a step about sixteen inches high for about five minutes. Your pulse is measured before and after so that it's possible to see just how long your heart rate takes to return to normal. Your recovery rate is then compared to that of others who have taken this test. What can be learned, after some calculations, is how well your heart works, how efficiently it's getting your blood to your muscles, and how much oxygen you've been able to use.

Most doctors don't have a stationary bicycle in their offices; for fitness tests calling for that equipment, your physician may send you instead to a local fitness facility for an assessment. One of these tests is the Astrand bicycle test, in which you ride a stationary bicycle at a fixed resistance for a fixed period of time. A work load is selected that will elicit a heartbeat between 120 and 170 beats per minute. Your heartbeat increases linearly with the work load, along with a proportional increase in oxygen uptake (more oxygen is needed by exercising muscles). Astrand and Rhyming (1954) developed a way of estimating your oxygen uptake for submaximal work loads, so that you do not need to undertake exhaustive exercise in order to find out how you react to physical exertion. From this test you will not only know how you size up and how much work is the right amount for you (because it gets your heart rate up to the proper exercising level) but you'll also be able to see how you improve after you've been working out for a while.

An extremely rough test that we've nevertheless found helpful in telling us something about fitness is the thirty-second pulse rate recovery. We call this test rough because there aren't any exact standards. We have you run in place for thirty seconds, check your pulse rate both before (resting pulse) and after (peak pulse). We then continue to check it each minute to see how long it takes to get down to the level where it was before you started (your resting pulse rate). Most people, we've found, have a recovery index of 80 percent after one minute. The formula to give you your recovery index is: peak pulse minus recovery pulse over peak pulse minus resting pulse, multiplied by one hundred. This test is simple and practical, although, because there is no fixed work load, it isn't acceptable as truly scientific. Still, it can give us clues since we are aware that recovery should be quite rapid. We've also seen a direct correlation among speed of leg movement, the height to which you bring up your knees when running, the pulse rate while exercising, and rate of recovery. The faster you run and the higher you raise your knees, the lower your pulse and the quicker your recovery of a resting pulse rate. And for most normal, healthy people, these simple fitness tests in your doctor's office may be more appropriate than $200 stress tests you take at some specialist's to assess your heart's response to exercise.

MUSCULOSKELETAL EXAMINATION

One of the most important preparticipation evaluations you will need is this one, where the concentration is on your bones, joints, and muscles. Since most injuries and other physical problems that arise in sports are related to the musculoskeletal system, it's essential you be carefully evaluated. Your readiness for participation may be determined as well as the body areas that require remedial therapy and the injuries to which you may be susceptible. Some of this information you yourself can discover with your Fitness Self-Portrait, but we strongly recommend that first your doctor or someone he or she suggests examine your specific joint function, range of motion, stability, presence of pain or discomfort, as well as your ability to execute certain functional tests.

Neck. You may be asked to rotate your head slowly. Any pain in motion or any lack of motion will indicate to your doctor a need for further examination.

Shoulder. You should be able to go through a simple range of motion and maneuvers. You may be asked to hold your arms straight over your head with your elbows back, then rotate both arms in throwing motion and follow them through, and finally to touch your hands to your head. If you can do these simple motions without pain or limitation, then you probably do not have any significant problem with your shoulders.

Elbows. Because most women can hyperextend their forearms

and are loose-jointed, and because their elbows tend to point inward when their arms are outstretched, they can have elbow problems when they take up sports that demand throwing motion, as softball and tennis do. You should be aware of this susceptibility so that you can start strengthening exercises for your arms. (See Chapter 7 for arm exercises.)

Hands. You should be checked for normal finger motion (your fingertips should be able to come into your palms) and for possible swelling, which might indicate old dislocations or arthritis. Swelling in the finger joints closest to the nail indicates a form of arthritis that can give pain and discomfort but is less serious because it doesn't usually occur in other parts of the body. Swelling in the joints closer to the wrists, however, may point to rheumatoid arthritis or gout. If this is the case, exercise can be helpful by preventing stiffness. Still, hard, violent sports or those calling for a strong grip (such as baseball or field hockey) might irritate your condition.

Back and spine. One of the key things you'll be examined for is excessive lordosis or inward curvature of the lower part of the spine. This is often found in people with weak abdominal muscles and excessive weight, which put too much stress on the back. Pregnancy can also produce lordosis so it's a condition women should pay special attention to. Your doctor should warn you against reaching up high or exercising on the belly (for example, doing the Australian crawl or butterfly swimming stroke) if you do have lordosis. Recommended are those exercises that will strengthen your abdomen as well as increase your flexibility, both of which should help considerably.

Your spine will also be examined for anomalies of the spinal cord and for dimples and light brown patches on the skin of the lower back. These may indicate that something is wrong in the bones or spinal cord.

Scoliosis, which is curvature of the spine sideward, isn't a condition that precludes exercise. But because it can relate to other back problems, it should be watched for progression.

You may then be tested by being asked to lean over with your knees straight and your arms dangling in front of you as low toward the floor as possible. Most women can reach down to their ankles, with the most loose-jointed able to touch the floor with their palms. This is a good test for mobility of the spine, a way to spot pain in the spinal cord or nerve routes.

Bending at the waist and moving from side to side is another indication of spinal mobility. If you can't do this easily, you may be susceptible to backaches. An old residual problem in the spine that you never knew you had or that you had simply forgotten about might get worse with some exercises. In this case stretching exercises would be of great help.

MUSCULOSKELETAL FUNCTIONAL TESTS

The following tests will show you and your doctor just how good your knees and ankles are. These joints are where most of the problems arise for athletes, especially those who unknowingly irritate old injuries or ignore weaknesses. The most accurate way to test these joints is by examining them in motion. Any trouble will show up much more clearly in a dynamic situation.

Running in place. We can tell quite a lot about athletic ability simply by watching someone run. Those whose thighs touch and feet turn out have an awkwardness that is likely to extend into their sports performance. But more than this, we can tell if someone has pain, limited motion, or stiffness. You can have a sore knee, for example, and without realizing what you're doing, you may hurry off that bad knee and onto the other one when you exercise. Running in place in the doctor's office will often reveal this problem.

Hopping on each leg. We often find out that patients are incapable of hopping on the involved side. The patients themselves are usually surprised because they have been fooling themselves, compensating with the good leg. We asked one woman who considered herself a good athlete to hop, and she almost collapsed when she attempted it on her injured knee. She could run in place very well, accomplishing this by hurling herself off the injured leg and onto the good one. It was only when all support was taken off the good leg that we could detect the problem. Anyone participating in a sport has to know about the extent of her weakness before she's in a position of having to plant that bad leg, for example, while supporting her body weight as she makes a ski turn. We told the woman who couldn't hop on one side that she had better not attempt to ski at all before her knee problem was taken care of.

Next you may be asked to do a full squat or to squat down as far as you can without discomfort. You'll be questioned about pain in your kneecap or in the cartilage, the small disk inside the knee. Although this doesn't test your ligaments, your doctor can get a good clue as to what's wrong.

Then, if you can, you'll be asked to go down for a full squat and walk that way, in a duck walk. Most people can't even come close to doing this unless they have perfectly normal knees. You'll need some balance and perhaps some skill, but this test is still worthwhile because for those who can do it, it rules out significant knee problems.

In screening large groups of athletes, we have them run in place, hop on each leg, half-squat, full-squat, and duck-walk. If they can do these symmetrically, with no difficulty on either right or left side, we can be pretty sure they're in good shape. We also do these tests with patients recovering from injury. These are part of the simple physical examination we hope your doctor gives you before you start on your new program.

Other tests might include putting your feet and knees together. If your ankles touch and your knees don't, you're bowlegged. And if your knees touch but ankles don't, you're knock-kneed. Each type is susceptible to different kinds of problems. Those who have bowed legs are generally tighter-jointed. They may get pains, have a tendency for arthritis on the inside of the knees, and are also more susceptible to cartilage tears. People with knock-knees—and most women fall into this category—are more susceptible to sore kneecaps and trouble on the outside of the knees. They are also more likely to dislocate kneecaps.

You may also be asked to stand and throw your knees back into extension. Your doctor will look at them sideways to see if you actually are extending or if you are contracting to some extent. If you

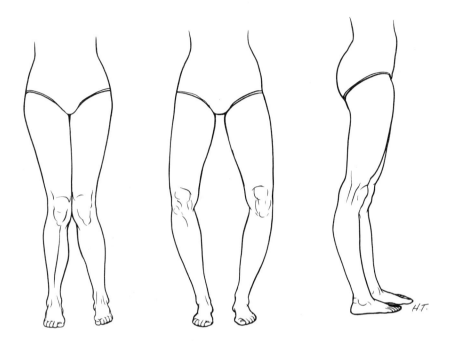

can't extend your knees, you may have something wrong inside them—perhaps cartilage trouble or arthritis or a kneecap problem. On the other hand, if you can hyperextend your knees, that is, straighten them in and out beyond the normal limit, it will suggest to your doctor that you have either a ligament injury or are unusually loose-jointed, with the possibility of loose joints in other parts of your body.

Your doctor should examine your knees in motion, ask you to lie down and straighten and bend your legs. He or she should assess the size of your muscle one hand's breadth above the kneecap. An obvious difference should be measured because any discrepancy of more than one centimeter indicates something is wrong with the knee on the side of the smaller muscle. Leg muscles atrophy with inactivity, whether subtle inactivity or full-blown, as with injury. Your smaller muscle is a clear indicator that something is wrong.

STABILITY TESTS

For anyone planning to take up a contact sport or anyone with a history of injury or with abnormalities in the functional test, stability tests are a must. These diagnostic tests will tell your doctor whether or not your ligaments are performing their specific functions in relation to the joints they restrain. While stability tests may sound simple, they can be subtle, and your doctor may wish to send you to someone who has had experience doing them.

Testing the medial ligament. This is the ligament that starts above the knee on the inside and goes across the knee almost one third of the way down between the knee and ankle. To test stability, you should be lying on your back while your doctor holds up your leg with one hand placed above the ankle, the other hand under your knee. Your doctor will then gently push inward on the thigh while slowly pulling the lower leg away from the body. If there is any difference in the movement of one knee when compared to the other, a serious orthopedic problem is indicated that calls for further diagnosis from a specialist.

The test is repeated with your knee bent at thirty degrees of flexion. Abnormalities found only in this position are of less serious nature, and it's possible surgery can be avoided.

Testing the anterior-posterior cruciate ligaments. The cruciate ligament is an important stabilizer of the knee, and, since we know that early surgery on a damaged cruciate can avoid long-term residual disability and joint deterioration, you can see how important this examination can be. Your doctor will ask you to lie down with your knees flexed at ninety degrees and hips at forty-five degrees. The doctor will then place both hands on the part of your calf below your knee, pulling your lower leg forward and then away,

repeating this with your other leg. If one leg moves forward or backward more than the other, there is a chance of a torn anterior cruciate ligament.

Your doctor will also repeat this procedure, pushing your lower leg away and then pulling it forward. A comparison of the movement of your legs in these directions would point up possible problems with the posterior cruciate. If you were to exercise with an unattended ligament problem, you could aggravate the condition and do yourself considerable unnecessary injury.

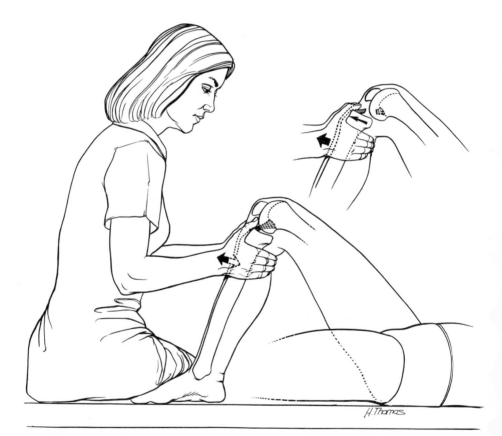

Your doctor can tell a lot from just looking at your knees. Swelling and scars indicate something is or has been wrong beneath the surface. When you are seated at the edge of the examination table, are your kneecaps facing straight ahead or do they point to the inside or outside? If they are not straight when you run, your thigh muscles will have to keep pulling your kneecaps away from the sides. It's important that you be aware of this so that you can strengthen those thigh muscles, avoiding the pain in the front of the knee, aches behind the knee, and the pops and clicks. Women, with generally looser kneecaps and more oblique thigh bones, often end up with these symptoms if they haven't paid special attention to strengthening exercises. And for those of you who run, because you build up the antigravity muscles on the backs of your legs, the muscles on the front of your thighs may get even weaker and less able to control your kneecaps. Your doctor, by looking at your knees, can get a good idea if you are likely to have this problem and can caution you to avoid it through exercise.

Your knees should also be able to go through a full range of motion, should have no fluid in them, not make loud clicks or pops, or slip and slide when going through the stability tests. If you pass all these criteria as well as the functional tests we described earlier, your doctor can safely tell you that your knees are fine and ready for sports.

Your doctor will move your ankles to see if they have limited motion or seem stiff in the heel cords. You may need to work at getting your ankles more flexible before you exercise so that you can avoid those conditions common among women who wear high heels—ankle strains, tendinitis of the heel cord, and soreness at the base of the toes.

How do your feet look? Flattened arches or widened toes will suggest to your doctor that you are susceptible to the kind of ankle sprain that involves the tibia and fibula. Since this sprain is serious and takes a long time to heal properly, you should discuss with your doctor what kind of shoes you should invest in for athletics and what exercises might be of help.

If you have flat feet, your shoes should offer firm support.

Your toes' turning down with your arches high and stiff will in-

71

dicate to your doctor that you may well end up with heel pain and arch problems if you exercise without some accompanying stretching and without using weighted balances for your feet. If you have high arches, your shoes should offer flexible support because you aren't going to change the posture of your foot but, rather, balance it.

Many doctors, not simply sports medicine specialists, will be able to give you this Medical Profile, a thorough series of questions and examinations that have a direct relationship to your participation in physical activity. In addition, your doctor can be especially helpful if he—perhaps because of his own involvement in sports and exercise, his experience with athletes, or his reading in these areas—has a real appreciation of what participating in sports involves. All this information can then be related to you and your specific needs so that you can understand how your body will be functioning when you start on your fitness program.

5

Your Fitness Self-Portrait— Just How Fit Are You?

After your doctor has completed your Medical Profile, the next step will be yours: a Fitness Self-Portrait. In taking it you will discover two crucial facts about yourself: your body type as programmed by your genes and your physical condition as determined by your lifestyle.

Many of you have read or heard about the old way of body typing, dividing people into the tall and thin variety (ectomorph), the short and fat (endomorph), and those in between (mesomorph). These are characteristics that have to do with proficiency in sports and relative ability to attain physical fitness. And while these categories can offer you some insight, the body typing in this Fitness Self-Portrait makes far more subtle distinctions. What we are looking for are not just figures about height and weight—after all, you could be heavy, but what's really significant is what makes up that weight, fat or muscle and bone.

This Fitness Self-Portrait is a far more individualized method of evaluation, allowing you to discover your characteristics in several categories. How do you compare to others in cardiovascular fitness? Upper and lower body strength? How flexible do your ligaments allow you to be? What kind of fiber type is predominant in the makeup of your muscles and what is the significance of this fact?

After completing your Fitness Self-Portrait you are going to be able to figure out, first, your physical capabilities and, second, how you can train in order to increase your performance and level of fitness. Third, you'll be able to know just which injuries you are susceptible to so that you can take the proper steps to avoid them. In most of the following tests you can grade yourself on a point system, giving you an overall fitness score.

Since your immediate goal is to do as well as you can on these tests, allow yourself ample time to relax after each. None of them should be especially fatiguing, but if any seems to be strenuous, or if your time is limited, you can spread these out in whatever way works best for you.

There isn't much you're going to need in the way of special equipment for these tests. You ought to wear something loose and comfortable, maybe shorts and T-shirt or a sweat suit. And you'll need to have a clock or watch with a sweep second hand, a mirror, a tape measure, a ruler, and a scale. A pad, pencil, and some chalk or rope to mark out lines are about the only other items. A number of people have told us that it's enjoyable to have a friend around who is taking her own Self-Portrait while you take yours or is jotting down some of the minutes or seconds or other information you call out as you take these tests. A friend though, while probably an agreeable addition, is not at all a necessity. All you need to do is read this chapter through once and then proceed step by step. You're going to be assessing not only what you are right now but what you can realistically hope to become.

ANTHROPOMETRIC INFORMATION

These are data relating to your body measurements, especially to the amount of body fat you have. Too much fat, of course, means that you haven't been active enough to burn it off and that your level of fitness could most likely use some improvement.

We are including here both a chart where you can find out approximately how much you should weigh according to your height and frame, as well as a graph where you can easily see whether or not your weight falls into the category generally considered average.

As you can see, there is a wide discrepancy in the desirable weight for women of the same height. Someone who is five foot seven, for example, can weigh anywhere from 118 pounds all the way up to 150 pounds and still find her weight on the desirable weight chart. But is her weight really desirable? The variable is the classification of her frame, whether she figures it as small, medium, or large. Some people, as you've probably observed, can look fine and yet weigh more because they have heavier bones. If you are lean around the ankles and wrists and you can see your bony prominences, you are not likely to be a fat person even if your weight is at the higher perimeters of the chart or graph. Your body fat, if you had an excess of it, would cover over your bones at these joints. So this could be your first clue that you are a big person, not a fat one.

Some other clues will be evident when you confront yourself in the mirror. Do you look reasonably proportioned? Your chest girth larger than your abdomen and your thighs not disproportionately larger than your calves? Heavy thighs, a loose and overly large abdomen, striae (colored wavy thin lines) on the belly, wrinkles and flabbiness on upper arms and thighs, all point to the inescapable fact that you are overweight. So if you're the woman of five feet seven who looks like this and weighs 150 pounds, you do not have the large frame you need to carry this amount of weight.

DESIRABLE WEIGHTS

HEIGHT (with shoes on, 2-inch heels)			SMALL FRAME	MEDIUM FRAME	LARGE FRAME
WOMEN	feet	inches			
of ages	4	10	92–98	96–107	104–119
25 and	4	11	94–101	98–110	106–122
over	5	0	96–104	101–113	109–125
	5	1	99–107	104–116	112–128
	5	2	102–110	107–119	115–131
	5	3	105–113	110–122	118–134
	5	4	108–116	113–126	121–138
	5	5	111–119	116–130	125–142
	5	6	114–123	120–135	129–146
	5	7	118–127	124–139	133–150
	5	8	122–131	128–143	137–154
	5	9	126–135	132–147	141–158
	5	10	130–140	136–151	145–163
	5	11	134–144	140–155	149–168
	6	0	138–148	144–159	153–173

(For girls between 18 and 25, subtract 1 pound for each year under 25.)

Still another clue is to determine the amount of fat in your body. There are different ways of accomplishing this, including the elaborate process of weighing you in a tank full of water (comparing your weight above water and under water can give us your body density, which in turn can be used for calculating body fat). We suggest, instead, something a lot easier to do.

PINCH TEST. Lift your arm away from your body and with the thumb and forefinger of your other hand, pinch the back of the raised arm over your triceps muscle, right in the middle of your upper arm. The pinch must be made longitudinally. To make sure you are not including any of the muscle itself in your pinch, bend your elbow so that the muscle under the tissue will contract. Then

76

HEIGHT—WEIGHT RELATIONSHIPS

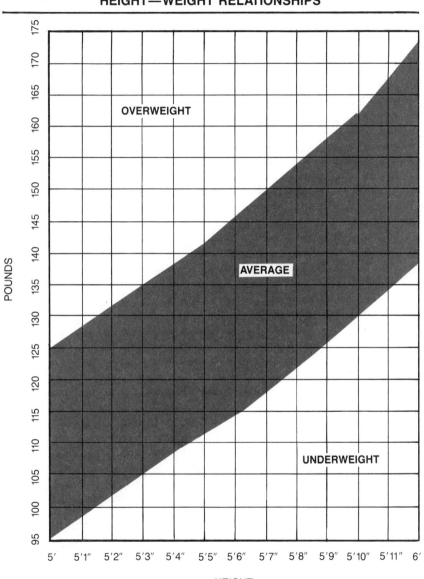

OVERWEIGHT

AVERAGE

UNDERWEIGHT

POUNDS

HEIGHT

look at the amount of skin and fat you've been able to pinch and estimate the thickness (if you've got a friend around, she can actually measure this with a ruler).

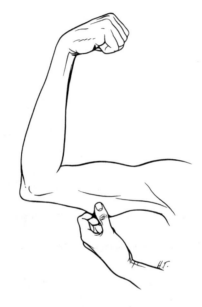

Points for the Pinch Test

More than average	less than ¼″	3 points
Average	¼″–¾″	2 points
Less than average	more than ¾″	1 point

You might get a more exact answer by calculating with multiple measurements on different parts of your body or by using special calipers, but the difference would only be at most a few percentage points. We've found the triceps to be the most reliable part of the body for a single test, and we think your estimation or your measurement with a ruler will come close enough.

MUSCULOSKELETAL EVALUATION

Your inherited body type. This is where you find out just what characteristics you were born with, those qualities that exercise and life-style cannot change. Since these basic body traits have both advantages and disadvantages, no points will be given here for the results of these next three evaluations.

THUMB-FOREARM. Using your nondominant arm, keep your arm bent and flex your wrist with your thumb straight down. Now, with your other hand push the tip of your thumb back toward your forearm.

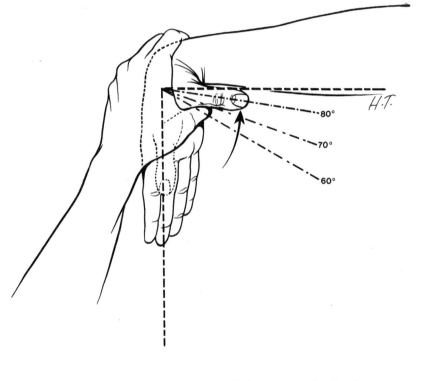

Looser than average	over 70 degrees to entire thumb touching forearm
Average	60–70 degrees
Tighter than average	less than 60 degrees

79

M-P EXTENSION. M-P stands for metacarpal-phalangeal joint, which is the joint where your finger meets your hand.

With your elbow bent, bend your wrist downward so that the tendons in the bottom of your arm are relaxed. Take your other hand and use it to push back your index finger. Then, starting at your wrist, draw an imaginary line extending downward. Estimate the angle between your index finger and this line. We've included an illustration with a silhouette showing possible positions of the index finger and the imaginary line. Just place your own hand against this and see where you fit in.

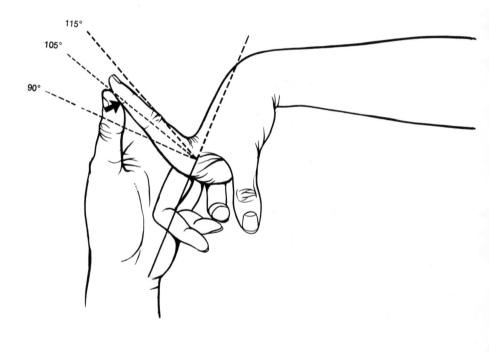

Looser than average	more than 115 degrees
Average	105–115 degrees
Tighter than average	less than 105 degrees

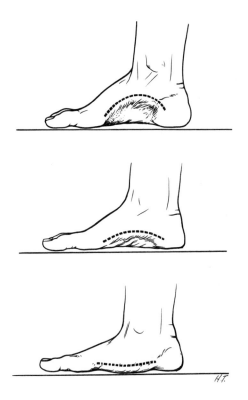

FOOT TYPE. Stand with your feet bare and look at your arch. You'll find this easiest to do if you stand sideways in front of a full-length mirror or a mirror placed on the floor and leaning against a wall. If you have high arches (*pes cavus*), you are also likely to have a tight heel cord and be tight-jointed.

If your feet are flat (*pes planus*), probably your heel will curve outward, and you will be loose-jointed. Most women tend to have this foot type, sometimes having the large toes and bunions that go along with flat feet.

An average arch indicates average flexibility.

If you are not sure of your foot type, just compare your arches to those in this illustration of the three types of feet.

There is a suggested correlation between flexibility and muscle-fiber type, with those who score as looser than average on these evaluations probably having more slow-twitch muscle fiber and those who are tighter likely to have more fast-twitch muscle fibers. Fiber typing has gained considerable interest recently. We know that your predominant muscle-fiber type is an inherited characteristic and that the physical feature of joint flexibility is also inherited. And while your age, sex, and, most important, the amount and type of physical activity you do can influence how flexible you are, the trait characteristics—how you do on the thumb-forearm test and the M-P extension—cannot be changed. Testing these two joints gives us important clues about your particular structure of muscle and ligaments, which in turn tell us about your performance capabilities as well as injury susceptibility.

Those of you who are loose-jointed are likely to be good at dance, gymnastics, cycling, swimming, or running. Your predominance of slow-twitch muscle fibers is best for these endurance activities and patterned movement. The tight-jointed person, on the other hand, is better suited to explosive sports like basketball or hockey. Billie Jean King is a good example of someone having this body trait. Her muscles are more powerful and fast-firing, and she's what we call a "natural" athlete, at least in explosive sports. Still, a loose-jointed woman like Chris Evert Lloyd can become a "developed" athlete in these sports, taking advantage of her stamina by being able to train for hours without tiring. Loose-jointed people tend to have more stamina.

As for injury susceptibility, the loose-jointed woman (and most women tend to fall into this general category) may find she has a popping or a clicking when she moves her shoulders. She's more apt to have ligament problems and partial dislocations. Most of all, she's likely to have knee trouble, with pain and a sliding or slipping of her kneecaps. Strengthening exercises, especially for the thighs, can be the answer for most of these problems. In fact, it's how we treat 90 percent of the patients we see who have loose kneecaps.

The tight-jointed woman has her own set of problems. She's often plagued by muscle pulls and tears, torn ligaments and cartilage, and can suffer from lower back pain. She is also more susceptible to tendinitis of the shoulder or elbow, as well as to pinched nerves. The best way she can avoid these injuries is to realize that she is basically stiff and then compensate for this by stretching her body out with flexibility exercises.

As we've said, your inherited body type by its very definition is something you simply cannot change no matter what you do. But if you're armed with the correct information about your muscle-fiber type and you know whether or not your joints are loose or tight, you can figure out how best to compensate for what you lack, how to avoid the injuries you're susceptible to through the right kind of training, and how to take advantage of your natural gifts by choosing the activities that make the most of them.

Your adaptive joint flexibility. It is possible that because of some sports participation or the physical demands of an occupation, you are flexible in one or more joints while tight in others. So you can see that just knowing your general basic body type will not be enough. These next five tests are what we call adaptive flexibility tests, and they are designed to measure joint flexibility, which improves or declines with age and use. Unlike the results of the thumb-forearm and M-P extension, you can do something about your results on these tests, even if you're inherently tight-jointed and need to train somewhat harder. It is optimum for you to be as flexible as possible, and our point system reflects this, awarding a maximum amount of points for above-average suppleness.

ADAPTIVE JOINT FLEXIBILITY TESTS

Shoulder stretch
Adductor I
Adductor II
Heel cord
Palms to the floor

SHOULDER STRETCH. Standing up with your arms stretched straight out in front of you, hold the two ends of a tape measure or

a belt, rope, or towel that can later be measured with a ruler. Keeping your arms and wrists straight at all times, bring the tape measure or towel over your head and back out behind you as far down as you can. Then look at the distance measured between your arms.

If your shoulders are stiff, you're likely to be susceptible to tendinitis or a hitch in the throwing motion, and you should be working on stretching out this joint. Keep in mind though that if you are extremely loose-jointed in the shoulders, that is if you can do this stretch in under twenty inches, it may indicate an increased possibility for shoulder dislocation and subsequently a greater need for upper body strength exercises (see chapter 7).

Age:	under 25	25–45	over 45	SCORE
Looser than average	under 30″	under 35″	under 45″	3
Average	30″–40″	35″–45″	45″–55″	2
Tighter than average	more than 40″	more than 45″	more than 55″	1

ADDUCTOR I. The adductors are the muscles in the thighs that give the knees their stability. These muscles can easily get pulled in explosive sports and so should be kept as supple as possible.

One test to measure adductor flexibility is to sit on the corner of a rug with your legs stretched straight out in front of you as wide apart as they can go. See if the angle your legs form is as wide as the edges of the rug, less wide, or wider.

Age:	under 25	25–45	over 45	SCORE
Looser than average	over 125 degrees	over 110 degrees	over 105 degrees	3
Average	115–125 degrees	100–110 degrees	90–105 degrees	2
Tighter than average	under 115 degrees	under 100 degrees	under 90 degrees	1

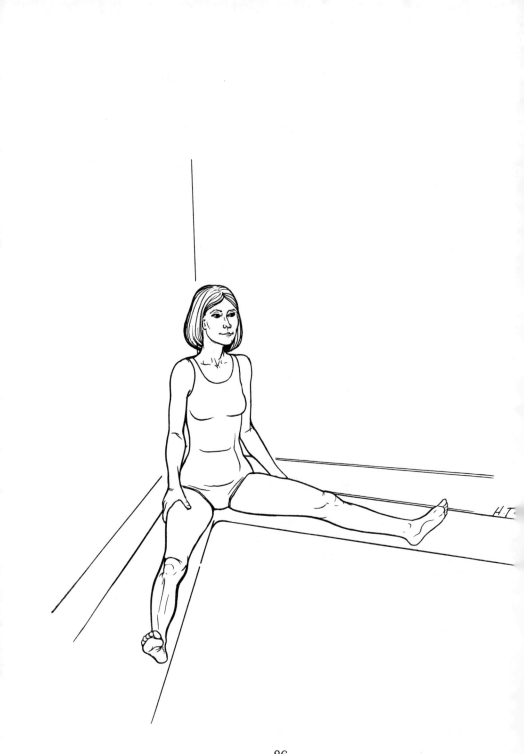

ADDUCTOR II. Sit on the floor with your back straight against a wall. Bend your knees so that they are wide apart in front of you with the bottoms of your feet together. Then pull your feet in toward the groin. Then measure the distance between your knees and the floor.

Age:	under 25	25–45	over 45	SCORE
Looser than average	less than 4"	less than 6"	less than 8"	3
Average	4"–7"	6"–9"	8"–11"	2
Tighter than average	more than 7"	more than 9"	more than 11"	1

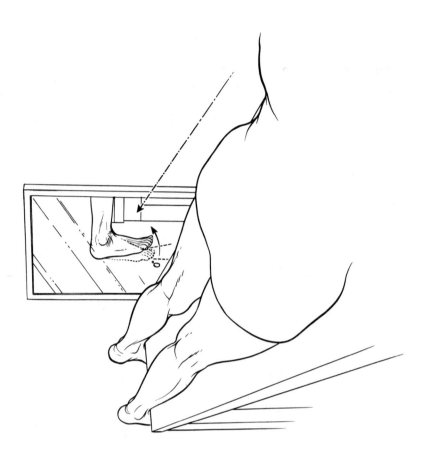

HEEL CORD. In this test you will measure your ankle flexion and tightness of your heel cord. Lying face down on a table or sofa or desk with your knees straight and your feet held off the edge, flex your ankles to pull your feet toward your legs. You will have to estimate the angle your foot makes with your leg so make sure there is a mirror placed next to you if there's no friend available to measure.

(In this test the standards are the same for all ages.)		SCORE
Looser than average	over 105 degrees	3
Average	95–105 degrees	2
Tighter than average	under 95 degrees	1

PALMS TO THE FLOOR. Stand with your knees straight and your feet flat on the floor. Bending over at the waist, reach down with your hands toward the floor. Measure the distance from the tip of the middle finger to the floor. The most flexible of you will be able to rest your palms on the floor while the least flexible will not come lower than 12 inches from the floor.

	under 25	25–45	over 45	SCORE
Looser than average	less than 3″ to touching complete palms to floor	less than 4″ to touching complete palms to floor	less than 5″ to touching complete palms to floor	3
Average	3″–5″ above floor	4″–7″ above floor	5″–9″ above floor	2
Tighter than average	more than 5″ above floor	more than 7″ above floor	more than 9″ above floor	1

PERFORMANCE ASSESSMENT

Strength

While women in general seem to be inherently weaker than men, we know that some weakness is simply adaptive, that is, improvable through exercising. It's not unusual for a man to do regular push-ups, but think of how few women you know who do this or any other upper body exercise. And so it isn't surprising that your upper body is the part of you that requires the most strength training. Test yourself and see how you come out.

Strength Tests
>Modified Push-ups
>Flexed Arm Hangs
>Dips
>Bent Knee Sit-ups
>Wall-Sits

Upper Body Strength Tests

MODIFIED PUSH-UPS. Lie on the floor facing downward. Bend your knees at right angles and place your hands firmly on the floor right under your shoulders. Straighten your elbows as you push yourself up in a straight line from shoulders to knees. Be careful not to sag in the middle. This test (which is also an excellent exercise) should be repeated as many times as you can.

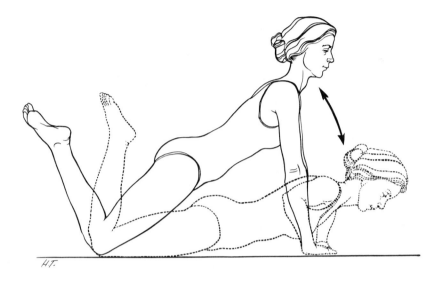

Age:	under 25	25–45	over 45	SCORE
Better than average	more than 30	more than 27	more than 18	3
Average	16–30	12–27	9–18	2
Lower than average	fewer than 16	fewer than 12	fewer than 9	1

FLEXED ARM HANGS. This exercise calls for a chinning bar or a substitute, and, because you may not have access to one, we haven't included this score in the total fitness score. Still, this is a good test that we recommend your trying when you can.

With an overhand grasp so that your palms are facing away from you, hold onto a chinning bar. Your arms should be flexed as you lift yourself off the floor to a height where your chin is above the bar. Hold this position as long as you can.

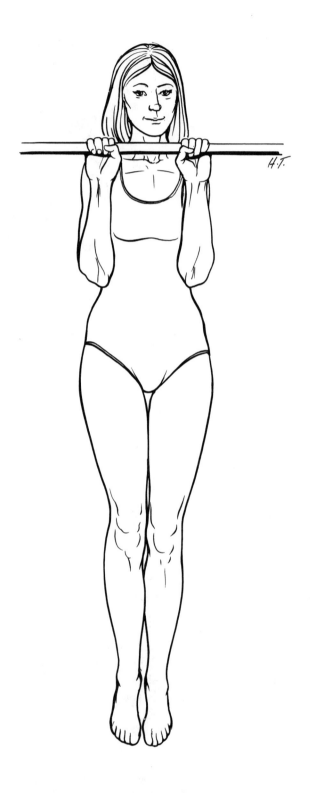

Age:	under 25	25–45	over 45
Better than average	more than 10 seconds	more than 9 seconds	more than 8 seconds
Average	6–10 seconds	5–9 seconds	4–8 seconds
Lower than average	less than 6 seconds	less than 5 seconds	less than 4 seconds

DIPS. Stand between parallel bars or two very steady chairs or a chair back and a table or counter top. With your straight arms supporting you, suspend your body weight, taking your feet off the floor. Then lower your body by bending your elbows and then return to the straight arm position. Try not to jerk your body or kick; keeping a continuous rhythm, see how many dips you can do.

Age:	under 25	25–45	over 45	SCORE
Better than average	more than 8 dips	more than 7 dips	more than 6 dips	3
Average	4–8 dips	3–7 dips	2–6 dips	2
Lower than average	fewer than 4 dips	fewer than 3 dips	fewer than 2 dips	1

NOTE: Dips are far from easy but with training they certainly are possible. Lynn Epstein, a National Championship tennis player, could not support her body on bent elbows. Another young athlete, a University of Pennsylvania junior, could lower her body weight and do one repetition, but this was after five months of training. We are certain that both she and Lynn Epstein will improve, as will you, if you work on building upper body strength.

Abdominal Strength Tests

The abdomen is another area of the body where most women lack strength. If your abdomen is weak, your entire trunk will lack the support it needs to move well. You can see how your tennis game or even your golf swing could improve with stronger abdominal muscles.

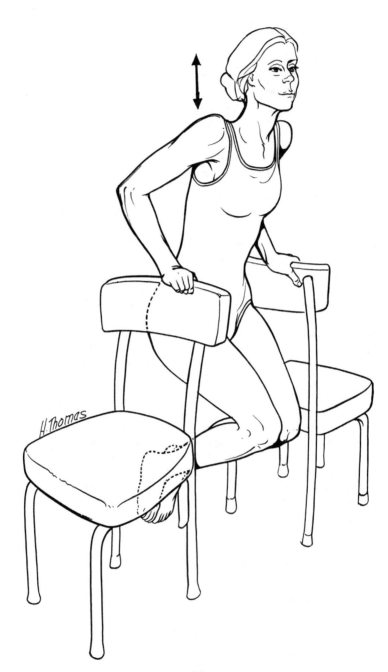

BENT KNEE SIT-UPS. Lie down on the floor facing upward with your knees bent and your feet flat down and as close to your hips as they'll go. If you have a friend around have her or him hold your ankles to keep them from moving. If no one is there, just hook your toes under a heavy piece of furniture to keep them in place. Clasp your hands behind your head and raise yourself into a sitting position. Slowly lower yourself down to the starting position and repeat. Time yourself so that you know how many repetitions you can do per minute.

Age:	under 25	25–45	over 45	SCORE
Better than average	more than 32	more than 30	more than 20	3
Average	28–32	20–30	10–20	2
Lower than average	fewer than 28	fewer than 20	fewer than 10	1

NOTE: You may find that you score best on this test if you leave it for last in this series of strength tests. You will be using abdominal muscles for your push-ups and wall-sits, so if you do your sit-ups before the other two, those muscles may well be sore, affecting your performance.

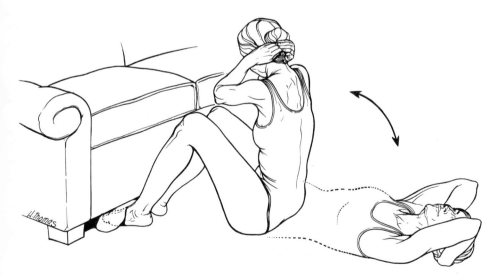

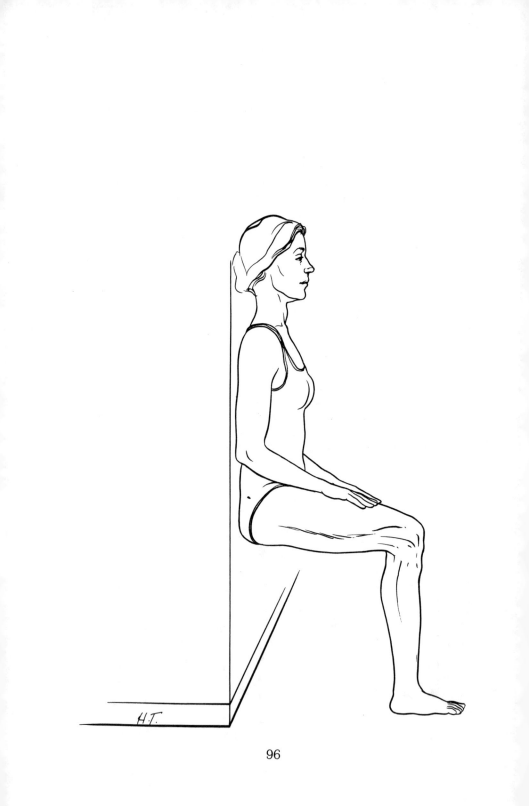

Lower Body Strength Tests

The following test to measure the strength of your quadriceps is also one of our favorite exercises. The quadricep muscles run down the front of your thighs, stabilizing your knees when you move and holding your kneecaps in place. These muscles are critical to the support function of your legs, and we think they're an excellent indicator of your overall lower body strength.

WALL-SITS. With your upper back flat against the wall, lower yourself by bending your hips and knees until they are at a ninety-degree angle. It will be as though you were seated on an invisible straight-back chair. Hold this position for as long as you can.

Age:	under 25	25–45	over 45	SCORE
Better than average	more than 100 seconds	more than 90 seconds	more than 70 seconds	3
Average	90–100 seconds	75–90 seconds	60–70 seconds	2
Lower than average	less than 90 seconds	less than 75 seconds	less than 60 seconds	1

Speed (Power) Tests
    Vertical Jump
    Standing Broad Jump

How you do on the following tests is probably related to your muscle-fiber type. If you have fast-twitch muscles, you are likely to have an explosive type of ability. Slow-twitch muscles, as we've mentioned, give endurance capabilities. None of us is all one or the other, but, instead, a combination of both. These next tests can give you an idea of approximately what percentage of the two kinds of muscle-fiber types you have. Those of you with 60 percent or more fast-twitch muscle fibers will probably jump farther (and also jump higher and react faster). The person who scores in the "average" category most likely has 50 percent fast- and 50 percent slow-twitch muscles, while those of you who perform below average probably have 60 percent or more slow-twitch muscle fibers.

H.Thomas

98

VERTICAL JUMP. Stand with your arms outstretched facing a wall. Mark the spot where your fingertips touch the wall. Then come down to a crouched position and jump as high as you can, with your arms again stretched out to the wall. Mark this second spot where your fingertips touch and then measure the distance between the two marks.

Age:	under 25	25–45	over 45	SCORE
Better than average	over 12″	over 11″	over 9″	3
Average	10″–12″	9″–11″	7″–9″	2
Lower than average	under 10″	under 9″	under 7″	1

In adding up your final score, choose either the vertical jump or the following test, the standing broad jump. Add in your best score of the two.

STANDING BROAD JUMP. Stand behind a line (the edge of your rug or a long ruler or even a stretched-out belt will do). With your feet parallel, bend at the knees and swing out your arms as you jump forward as far as possible. Then mark the spot where the back of your heels land. Try this two or three times until you've gotten the hang of it and then, on your next jump, measure the distance from your starting line to where your heels have landed.

Age:	under 25	25–45	over 45	SCORE
Better than average	more than 5′8″	more than 5′4″	more than 4′9″	3
Average	5′3″–5′8″	4′11″–5′4″	4′1″–4′9″	2
Lower than average	less than 5′3″	less than 4′11″	less than 4′1″	1

17307

STAMINA (ENDURANCE)

Stamina Tests
    Heart Rate Recovery
    1½-Mile Run
    12-Minute Run
    1,600-Meter Run

When you exercise hard enough, your heart rate will elevate. A good way to find out how fit you are is to see how long it takes your heart rate to return to normal after you've stopped all physical exertion. The longer it takes, the worse shape you're in and the more you need a carefully placed, regular program of endurance training.

First, you have to know how to take your pulse. Never use your thumb because it has its own pulse. Instead, use your second and third fingers, placing them along the inside (or thumb side) of your wrist. Press in gently until you can feel the beat of your artery. Looking at the second hand of your clock or watch, count the beats in a ten-second time period and multiply by six to get your rate per minute.

An alternate place for taking your pulse is at the artery in your neck. Again using the second and third fingers, go down from the jawbone and gently push in until you feel your pulse beat. If you find you skip a beat, don't worry—this is quite common and no cause for alarm.

Stamina (Endurance) Tests

HEART RATE RECOVERY. While you are standing, take your *resting* pulse. Then run in place for thirty seconds, keeping your knees as high as possible. Immediately after the thirty seconds is up, take your pulse again to establish your *peak* pulse. Wait one minute and take your pulse to find out your *one minute recovery* pulse. Take it again after another minute to find out your *two minute recovery* pulse.

To find out your heart rate recovery index, figure out the following equations:

$$\frac{Peak \text{ pulse minus } one\text{-}minute \text{ } recovery \text{ pulse}}{Peak \text{ pulse minus } resting \text{ pulse}} \text{ times } 100$$

$$\frac{Peak \text{ pulse minus } two\text{-}minute \text{ } recovery \text{ pulse}}{Peak \text{ pulse minus } resting \text{ pulse}} \text{ times } 100$$

There is no age difference for the results of this test because although resting pulse beat and peak pulse beat are different for different ages, what you are figuring out is the percentage of recovery.

101

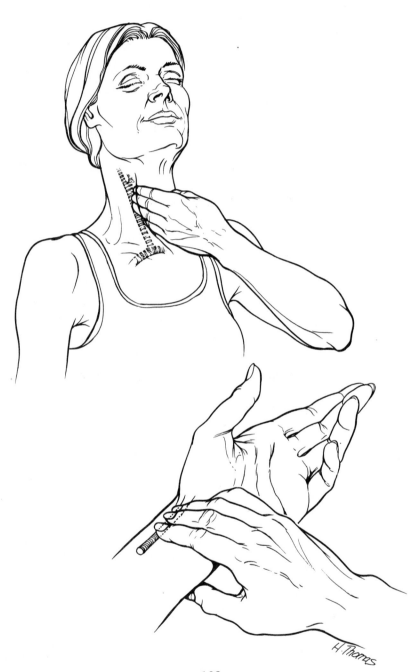

	AFTER ONE MINUTE:	SCORE
Better than average	more than 75% recovery	3
Average	55–75% recovery	2
Lower than average	less than 55% recovery	1
	AFTER TWO MINUTES:	
Better than average	more than 90% recovery	3
Average	70–90% recovery	2
Lower than average	less than 70% recovery	1

This test can be used as a simple screening test. There is no fixed work load since some people will lift their legs up high (which is the desirable position) while others will only be able to shuffle along for the thirty seconds. Even so, despite its being inexact, we've found it a good and highly practical way to learn about your endurance capacity and cardiopulmonary efficiency.

The heart rate recovery is not an endurance test per se but rather a test of your cardiopulmonary efficiency. In order to take an endurance test, you would have to get your heart rate up to a steady state for a fixed period of time and then have the amount of oxygen you've used accurately measured. But because we've found a direct correlation between your overall endurance capabilities —your ability to utilize oxygen during exercise—and your cardiopulmonary efficiency, this simple test can give you a good idea of how you rate as far as stamina goes. Keep in mind that your endurance capabilities improve greatly with exercise.

If the weather is good, you might prefer to run (or walk, depending on your fitness level) outdoors. We are including some tests to be done on a measured outdoor course, which will tell you a little more about your stamina. These scores will not be included in the final fitness score because some of you, because of practical considerations, may not be able to execute these.

1½-MILE RUN. Time yourself as you start and then see how much time to the nearest second it takes you to cover 1½ miles. Take your age into consideration when you figure out how well you did.

Age:	under 25	25–45	over 45	SCORE
Better than average	less than 13 minutes	less than 15½ minutes	less than 17 minutes	3
Average	13–15 minutes	15½–17½ minutes	17–19 minutes	2
Lower than average	more than 15 minutes	more than 17½ minutes	more than 19 minutes	1

TWELVE MINUTE RUN. Starting behind a line, record the time and begin to run (and/or walk) until twelve minutes have passed. Then measure out how much distance you've covered in the time.

Age:	under 25	25–45	over 45	SCORE
Better than average	more than 1.35 miles	more than 1.2 miles	more than 1 mile	3
Average	1.2–1.35 miles	1.1–1.2 miles	.9–1 miles	2
Lower than average	less than 1.2 miles	less than 1.1 miles	less than .9 miles	1

1,600-METER RUN. This test is to be used if you are less than fifteen years old. It's been determined that 1,600 meters is enough to get an accurate picture of the endurance capacity of younger runners (the 1½ mile run that adults use has been found to be too tiring).

Stand behind a line, note the time, and start to run and/or walk for 1,600 meters. The time it takes you to complete this distance should then be figured out to the nearest second.

Better than average	less than 11 minutes	3
Average	11–12 minutes	2
Lower than average	more than 12 minutes	1

Agility Test

——Sidestep

Agility is flexibility and strength in motion, allowing you to change the position or direction of your body easily and rapidly. Being agile is crucial in sports like volleyball, basketball, or tennis. And luckily it is something you can develop through flexibility and strength training, even if you're one of those people who seems to have been born clumsy.

The next (and last) test you will be taking for your Self-Portrait measures the rapidity with which you make lateral movements, changing your direction from one side to the opposite.

SIDESTEP. First you must measure out three parallel lines, each about five feet in length. The middle line should be four feet from each of the outer lines, making the outer ones eight feet apart. If you do this outdoors, you might use chalk lines. If indoors, you can easily improvise with rope or even yarn lines secured in place with pins or tape.

You can sidestep in any way you choose as long as your feet do not cross over one another and they remain pointing parallel to the lines on the floor. Don't turn your shoulders or hips to the side or twist your body in any way.

Start off standing astride the center line with your feet parallel to it. Then sidestep to the left until your left foot crosses the line on the left. Then sidestep to the right, back to the center, and then across the center line. Continue to the right until your right foot is over the right line. Continue back to the left and repeat the whole procedure, moving back and forth from left to right as quickly as you can. This is a test you might like to practice once or twice so that you're comfortable with the movement. When you are actually scoring yourself, you must time yourself for ten seconds. Then count out a point for every line crossed—left, right, and center—in that period of time.

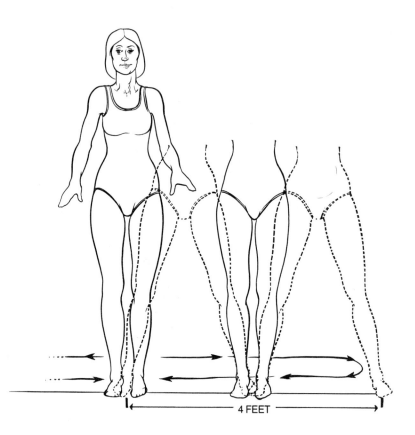

4 FEET

Age:	under 25	25–45	over 45	SCORE
Better than average	more than 17	more than 15	more than 13	3
Average	14–17	13–15	9–13	2
Lower than average	fewer than 14	fewer than 13	fewer than 9	1

Now that you've completed these self-assessment tests, add up the scores to see how your Self-Portrait came out.

NAME OF TEST	WHAT YOU ARE TESTING	SCORE
Pinch Test	Body fat	
Thumb-Forearm	Inherent joint flexibility	no score
M-P Extension	Inherent joint flexibility	no score
Foot Type	Inherent joint flexibility	no score
Shoulder Stretch	Adaptive joint flexibility	
Adductor I	Adaptive joint flexibility	
Adductor II	Adaptive joint flexibility	
Heel Cord	Adaptive joint flexibility	
Palms to the Floor	Adaptive joint flexibility	
Flexed Arm Hangs	Upper body strength	no score
Dips	Upper body strength	
Bent Knee Sit-ups	Abdominal strength	
Wall-Sits	Lower body strength	
Vertical Jump	Speed (power) ⎤ choose the best score between	
Standing Broad Jump	Speed (power) ⎦ these two tests	
Heart Rate Recovery	Stamina	
1½-Mile Run	Stamina	no score
12-Minute Run	Stamina	no score
1,600-Meter Run	Stamina	no score
Sidestep	Agility	

MAXIMUM SCORES POSSIBLE IN SPECIFIC AREAS   YOUR SCORES

Body fat	3
Flexibility	15
Strength	9
Speed	3
Stamina	3
Agility	3

KEY TO OVERALL FITNESS

Maximum Total is 36 points   Your Total Score

Above average	more than 26
Average	22–26
Below average	lower than 22

What have you found out about your physical condition? Are you in as good shape as you thought you were? More important, what are the areas where you need to pay the most attention? You may have noticed that when you climb a flight or two of steps lately you're out of breath, and perhaps you've been concerned about your lack of stamina. Taking the heart rate recovery test and seeing how you line up with other women will give you a good idea of what you can expect of yourself. It will also tell you what kind of exercises you should be doing before you begin your tennis lessons or take the hiking trip your family or friends have planned. How you do on the wall-sit test may offer a clue about what you should be working on before the ski season starts. In this case the test itself contains the answer—what you should be doing is a lot of wall-sits.

We certainly are not recommending your training in just one area, since fitness requires a combination of flexibility, strength, and stamina exercises. But with guidance from your Self-Portrait, you'll know just where you should concentrate the most.

Very possibly this is the first time you've had any objective way of evaluating your physical condition and each of the facets that makes it up. Look at your completed Self-Portrait carefully and see what you can learn from it. If you're not pleased with what you see, keep in mind that you can change most of it. A year from now you might like to take another Self-Portrait, one that looks more like what you want to be.

6

How to
Pick Your Sport

Now that you've learned more about your own capabilities and state of fitness, you'll want to know about the sports available to you and what physical demands they make. Some are activities that almost anyone can take up, while others require a high degree of skill and fitness. Some call for just the very inherent talents you have and the skills you've developed, while others may be just the opposite so that you have to train hard to compensate. Sports, like everything else, have their advantages and disadvantages, and it's a good idea to know beforehand where you may have an edge or where you'll have to make up for a weakness. It's not a question of fitting you into a prescribed slot, but rather of equipping you with enough information so that before you start you'll understand the elements that make up each activity.

The following sports are among the most popular ones. Read about them with your Fitness Self-Portrait in front of you so that you can get a good picture of where you'll more easily fit in or where you'll have to do some remedial training.

JOGGING, RUNNING

The best runners are light and usually tall and lean, able to take long strides. They need basic coordination, knowing something about balance so that they can keep their bodies over their hips, their knees over their feet, can swing their arms rhythmically and step with a heel-toe gait. Good endurance and flexibility help make good runners.

Still, keep in mind, if you don't fit this ideal picture, that running is a sport almost anyone can engage in. People who have the most difficulty—heavy older people with sore knees or tight heel cords—may have to start out on a slow run-walk program since they will lack the strength and agility to support their body weight on one leg at a time while in motion. Short people with explosive-type, tight-jointed bodies aren't really naturally endowed to make good runners and must work hard at training. Still, many of these have finished marathons after they've put enough time into their conditioning.

Running and jogging are basically easy to do and are inexpensive. You don't need any special equipment except for some good running shoes. You can exercise in a short time, just thirty minutes if you're getting your pulse up to an exercise level (¾ of the sum of 220 minus your age). One twenty-year-old tennis player, kept out of competition by an injury, lowered her resting pulse rate almost five beats per minute by running. Another young woman, a bookkeeper who had almost never exercised, lowered her resting pulse by ten beats per minute after running for only three weeks.

Some people believe that running is a complete fitness aid, and this simply is not true. Because it is so repetitive, it uses the same groups of muscles over and over again, so that if you have alignment problems of your hips, knees, or feet, these will be accentuated by the repeated striking of your foot that pushes your weight forward. Your lack of perfect alignment might not have been brought out in sports done in short periods of time and which called for a variety of forces and directions. If your foot strikes the pavement a million times a day running fifteen miles, it certainly will aggravate existing problems.

Also, with jogging and running, some of your muscles, such as the hamstrings, will tend to get developed, while others, such as your thigh muscles, will be underused. Ultramarathoners who run enormous distances actually have extremely small thigh muscles, which have to be compensated for with strength training.

The very repetitive nature of jogging can make it pleasing for some, boring for others. It cannot be used as a good strength trainer since your endurance level will probably stop you before your muscles get trained. If you are tight-jointed and you take up running, be sure to do some concomitant flexibility exercises. If you have knee problems, you should be on a strengthening program. If distance running is your goal, work on strengthening your thigh muscles, which will otherwise weaken as you run.

If you have any excessive shortness of breath when you jog or run, you should stop and check it out. If you have any cardiac or pulmonary condition that can cause you to collect moisture in your lungs, be careful of running in extremely cold weather. Cold air in your lungs can irritate them by collecting fluid that the heart can't pump out.

Some other advice for runners is to wear good waffle-soled shoes that can support your feet and keep you from slipping on pavement. Wear light clothes, in cold weather including a hat, gloves, and good socks to keep your extremities warm. You don't need much covering of your middle because that's where you're generating the heat. Make sure your clothes can breathe so that you don't perspire too much and get a chill as you cool off.

SKIING

Skiing is one of the most physically demanding sports. It requires good leg control, strong abdominal and thigh muscles, and good trunk control. The expert skier has among the highest level of endurance of all athletes and leg strength as great as any top player in any sport. And the strength lies in all the muscles of the leg, not just the quadriceps or knee extensors.

A natural skier would have a low center of gravity, good leg strength, be quick on her feet, and be likely to have had some experience with fast explosive sports like soccer or basketball.

Still, anyone who trains and can bring up her fitness level can begin to ski. Skiing will increase your endurance level and your agility (which is flexibility and strength in motion). Unlike running, though, you can't ski to get fit. You should be fit in the first place before you start a sport as demanding as skiing.

Even when you are in good enough shape to begin, when you first start skiing you'll lack the skill to be able to relax your muscles between contractions. The unskilled skier uses her muscles constantly, holding her abdominal muscles tight in what is almost an isometric contraction, which will quickly fatigue the muscle, getting it to its anaerobic threshold (where it can no longer run on oxygen as a source of energy) much quicker. The skilled skier, knowing how to release a contraction, can avoid the muscle fatigue of the novice.

Cross-country skiing is the most complete form of aerobic conditioning available. It calls for a combination of upper, abdominal, and lower body movement, and to do well you're going to need good arm as well as leg strength. After an initial investment in equipment, the costs for cross-country skiing can be minimal if you live in or near an area where climate and terrain make this sport possible.

Downhill skiing, on the other hand, can be a lot more expensive. Besides the equipment, you have lift fees, which, along with accommodations if you live any distance from the slope, can be awesome, especially when you have a family along with you.

For both downhill and cross-country skiing you should start out with good instruction, and it may take some time for you to comprehend and master the basics. You also have to be prepared to spend a great deal of time on this sport, since you don't ski for just an hour and you are subject to the vagaries of weather and snow conditions. You also can't have a significant concept of the sport (as you can in running) before you go out and do it. Skiing involves elements—altitude, cold, and speed—that most people who are not skiers are not used to in combination. If you weren't brought up in ski country, it can seem extremely foreign to you.

112

The advantages of both kinds of skiing are that they are good for your strength and endurance and get you out of doors, exposing you to nature in an exhilarating way. Skiing is a social event, removing you from what's ordinary in your life. It can be quiet and peaceful and yet exciting. Children who take it up are especially fortunate, since they bring with them a lack of fear and inhibition along with a relaxing familiarity with falling, all of which can help transform them into good skiers. If you have children, their rapid progress through ski classes will amaze you. Even with young children, skiing soon can become a sport a family can enjoy together.

SWIMMING

A good swimmer needs to have cardiopulmonary fitness, flexibility, and abdominal and leg strength. Swimming is also an excellent conditioner, increasing your stamina and forcing you to work your upper body, an area most women do not exercise. It can be an extremely demanding activity and some of the hardiest women athletes—Diana Nyad being a prominent example—have chosen swimming as their sport.

Swimming, like bicycling, is not a weight-bearing exercise, and because it takes the pressure off your antigravity muscles, it can be a perfect activity for someone recovering from injury or surgery. It's also a good sport for someone who is overweight. A fat person often has a hard time running, finding it difficult to support her body with just one leg on the ground. Besides, hard workouts in a pool or lake can help burn calories.

Before starting your laps, try doing stretches in or out of the water. These can help offset any possibility of developing cramps.

If you are a swimmer who is in good shape, you can do some jogging as well or strength exercises to keep your antigravity muscles, such as your hamstrings, in good tone.

113

TENNIS

The demands of tennis include good flexibility, a moderate amount of endurance depending on your level of activity, and some upper body strength, particularly in your wrists and elbows. Women, who tend to get sore kneecaps, may find this condition aggravated by tennis if they don't do some strength training along with the sport.

Tennis can increase your endurance but only if you really play hard or have someone drill you, moving you from corner to corner. If you're made active enough, in thirty seconds you can get your pulse rate up to a good exercising level. The average player, however, plays doubles or stands at the base line in a game of singles, and she's unlikely to get much cardiopulmonary training. A disadvantage of tennis is this fact: it just isn't going to give you a real training effect unless you have a high level of skill or a demanding instructor who keeps you moving.

Tennis is a good movement sport because it involves the whole body—upper body, abdomen, and legs. It can also give you a moderate amount of strength and flexibility improvement; we would suggest you supplement the sport, as do many professional players, with the exercises outlined in the next chapter. Because it offers quick explosive movement, tennis is one of the few sports that many adult women participate in that makes demands on your power. Billie Jean King, after a childhood of playing baseball with her brother and his friends, moved on to tennis when she found that it had all the components to satisfy her demands as an athlete.

HANDBALL, SQUASH, RACQUETBALL

These are excellent endurance sports that also call for flexibility and some amount of strength. The truly great squash players have tremendous amounts of stamina and many of them run sprints, hundred-yard dashes, and do interval training to increase their already high levels of endurance. Of the three, racquetball demands the least learned skill. It's an easy game to pick up so that you can play at a competitive level after only two or three sessions.

A disadvantage with all three of these racquet sports is that they have little strength component and will not do much to increase your flexibility. If you're lacking in these two aspects of fitness, you'll have to get them from some other activity.

The advantages are that these sports give you good endurance training right from the start when you are first beginning to develop your skill. This is in contrast to the slower game of tennis, in which, as we've mentioned, you need a higher level of skill to get training benefits. Squash, handball, and racquetball are all good ways to get into shape, your fitness benefits increasing as your game improves.

GOLF

Golf demands a tremendous skill level and great amounts of concentration since minutiae can make all the difference. You should have reasonable flexibility, good trunk strength, reasonable upper body strength, some amount of endurance, and some amount of power.

Golf does not make great physical demands on you, and few of the top golfers work out, even when they're on tour. This is in marked contrast to a sport like skiing, where the pros do intense training to keep in shape (you as a recreational skier will soon realize you have to do this, too). The discrepancy in golf between the extremely low physical demands and the high skill demands can make it an unsatisfying sport for some people.

Since most of the fitness benefits of golf come from the fact that you walk more than three miles if you're playing eighteen holes, it is essential that you play without a golf cart. If your fitness level is fairly low, just this amount of walking can get your heart rate up to an effective level, making golf a good activity for you. Those women golfers who are in better shape to begin with will have to train as well as play their golf games if they want to get the benefits of exercise.

BICYCLE RIDING

Riding a bicycle requires a certain amount of skill. Balance is essential, along with well-coordinated leg movements so that you can use all the muscles in your legs, not just use a few to the point of fatigue. You also need large amounts of stamina, especially if you go in for competitive bicycling. The recreational cyclist, on the other hand, if she has sufficient balance and skill to ride, can rapidly build up good cardiopulmonary endurance from the sport itself.

Stationary bicycling can be hard work. If you're trying for a training effect with your pulse beat raised and maintained for an effective amount of time, you may find the heavy muscles in your hips and thighs tiring first. If you start out, though, at a low level of physical fitness, just a small amount of working out on a stationary bicycle can be effective. One of the secretaries at the Hospital for Special Surgery who was overweight and underexercised started using the office bicycle for only ten to fifteen minutes daily. In just two weeks she succeeded in lowering her resting pulse rate by ten beats per minute. Since a lowered resting pulse can be an indication of increased cardiovascular efficiency, this significant amount of improvement was an important benefit.

Those of you who are in better shape to begin with won't see such dramatic changes, but for a basically sedentary woman, especially one who prefers to do her endurance training indoors, the stationary bicycle can be a good answer. Like swimming, it doesn't use the weight-bearing muscles and so can be particularly suitable for someone who has recently had surgery or who is extremely overweight. Be sure you stretch both before and after cycling so that your leg muscles will not become sore.

HORSEBACK RIDING

A good rider will probably be someone of average height with reasonably good balance in her trunk and upper body and good leg strength. Most of the muscle work will be in your legs, using your adductor muscles to bring your legs in tight so that you can really grip the sides of the horse. Riding also requires coordination, being able to lift your body when you post and keep yourself from falling if the horse makes a sudden and unexpected movement.

If you're just a weekend rider going along bridle paths, walking in the woods, or trotting down a shore road, you won't require much in the way of stamina unless you ride for very long periods of time. Riding for you will be primarily a skill rather than a demanding activity that requires high levels of fitness.

If, on the other hand, you ride working hunters, jumping fences and riding hard through fields and woods, or if you're involved in polo or if your horse is 16½ hands and weighs 1,500 pounds, riding can be extremely demanding. Some of the toughest athletes we've ever met are rodeo riders, who are strong, quick, and have huge amounts of stamina. Most of these riders have trained bareback so that they can control their legs and posture on a horse without a saddle or stirrups. Controlling your body in relationship to the movements of a horse is good work for your leg and thigh muscles. If you go in for this more strenuous kind of training, riding can be a sport for fitness. Otherwise it's more accurate to consider it basically a pleasurable activity.

FENCING

If you're flexible, have a moderately high level of endurance, but lack a great deal of strength, fencing can be a suitable activity. It is a skill sport that requires excellent coordination, speed, and agility, and it can be a lot of work, constant activity without a break. Because of this, fencing should help you build up good stamina.

GYMNASTICS

To be a good gymnast you need to have flexibility, agility, and strength. For the uneven parallel bars you need a great deal of strength in your upper arms so that you can control your body with your triceps, biceps, and shoulder muscles. The average girl and woman are particularly weak in the upper body so that strengthening exercises may be a necessary adjunct. For gymnastics, as for skiing, the smaller you are, the better, because your lower center of gravity will give you more stability and balance.

Gymnastics helps keep you fit and can be extremely enjoyable. There's no reason why adults can't take it up and learn to master the basics. An instructor is essential, as are spotters, who watch your maneuvers, since without proper training and supervision, the potential for serious injury is significant.

SOCCER

Like basketball and field hockey, soccer demands power, good basic running skills, and endurance. It's an excellent conditioner, developing quickness and lightness on your feet as you rapidly change direction, and building even higher levels of stamina. It can be extremely helpful not only in keeping you fit but in training you for other sports. For this reason soccer has been a favorite sport of many skiers.

BASKETBALL

Large amounts of endurance, reasonable flexibility, good leg strength, and good coordination all go toward making a basketball player. And while you need good upper body strength to throw the ball to the basket, this motion is not as repeated as the throwing motion when you play tennis.

Basketball is an excellent skill developer and the better you become in the game, the more fitness benefits you'll be getting from it. You'll get an excellent workout from running up and down· the court, which will increase your cardiovascular efficiency.

ICE/ROLLER SKATING

You need skill, some leg strength, and flexibility for skating. A certain amount of upper body strength will help your balance, which is especially important in ice skating as compared to roller skating—a single blade, you may have learned, is harder to stabilize than four wheels.

Skating can give you a good workout once you develop the skill to maneuver yourself around. As you improve, so will your endurance level.

SOFTBALL

Softball requires good hand-eye coordination and agility. You really don't need much endurance since you only run short distances. Good upper body strength is helpful, along with flexibility, and a girl or woman with broad shoulders and strong arms who is also supple probably has the makings of a good softball player. If she also has good reaction time, she'll be excellent.

A disadvantage of softball is that it doesn't improve your strength and flexibility or significantly affect your endurance. The advantages are that softball helps develop hand-eye coordination, quickness in running and hitting, and is a good social sport. It's a team sport with a high individual component so that what you do is easily seen.

VOLLEYBALL

Like basketball, volleyball calls for endurance and explosive movements when you spike the ball down over the net. It's an especially good fitness aid for women since it helps develop your arms, which are generally your weaker extremity.

BOWLING

Bowling lies just on the margins of sport and perhaps should be considered more of a skill and activity. You don't have to be particularly fit, nor will you become fit from bowling. A look at people in bowling alleys compared to athletes almost anywhere else will prove this point.

Bowling can certainly be enjoyable and sociable, and it gets your body moving. Still, although your score may improve, it's unlikely that your fitness level will just from bowling.

7

Training
for Total Fitness

No matter how active you are, if your goal is total fitness, you'll
find you need a well-rounded training program. The fact is that
there is no one sport that can possibly give you everything. If, for
example, you run every day, you may be developing your aerobic
capacity (that is, your ability to use oxygen) and the endurance capacity of certain muscles, most specifically those antigravity muscles along the backs of your legs that keep you upright and propel
you forward. But other muscles, such as the quadriceps on the
front of your thighs, are just not going to be developed in the
straight-ahead jogging you're doing, and, in fact, they can even
grow weaker. The runner who wants to be fit has to compensate
with additional strength training along with some work on flexibility.

Other sports, such as the racquet games, can develop one side of
your body more than the other. If you're a right-handed tennis
player, you probably have a left arm that is weaker, with bones and
muscle actually smaller than those in the right arm. In training

you will be working on your entire body, doing strength exercises on your left side, for example, to compensate for all the activity you give to the right side when you're playing tennis. Doing abdominal exercises will enhance body balance and leg control, both major concerns for tennis or squash players.

Training not only compensates for what you're not getting from your ordinary activity, it also helps make up for those natural talents you find you just don't have. If you're slow on the tennis court, a problem many women have, you can make up for this lack of quick reaction by learning how to respond. Since you aren't required to cover a lot of distance on a tennis court—it's usually just two or three steps to get to the ball—if you learn to respond as the ball comes off your opponent's racquet instead of waiting until it goes over the net or bounces on your side, you'll be able to get to it just as fast as someone who is a sprinter. You might never win a hundred-yard dash, but on the court you don't have to. All you have to do is concentrate, watch the ball, and run the short distance you need to get to it. Chris Evert Lloyd, who is basically slow, covers the court as well as anyone because she has learned to respond quickly.

If you need to increase your speed in tennis, having someone hit tennis balls at you again and again will help. Tennis pro Rick Elstein trains women by hitting a series of fast balls right to them. The players act as goalies, protecting themselves with their racquets as the balls come. Once they can hit more and more balls, the speed is increased so that reaction time is continually improving. Eventually players can get their racquets on almost every ball hit at any speed. One young girl who is basically slow increased her reaction time so dramatically that she's been able to win sets from a few of the top nationally ranked women players.

Professional athletes train not only because they want to improve their skills and abilities but because, like you, they often have to compensate for something they don't have. Martina Navratilova has enormous strength but has to work on her flexibility. She does shoulder stretches and has learned to adjust her technique to make up for some innate stiffness. And Abbi Fisher of the United States ski team, a top performer in a sport that demands a tremendous amount of strength, is basically not strong. She has compensated for this by working out with weights in an extremely vigorous program. Perhaps most surprising, marathon swimmer Diana Nyad did not have inherently good endurance. Her training, among the most strenuous schedules we've come across, with a daily Miami–Fort Lauderdale swim followed by a half hour jumping rope and then a twelve-mile run, gives her the necessary stamina for her distance swimming.

Training, besides increasing your performance in a sport and bringing you closer to total fitness, will also help you avoid injury. One of the coaches we've worked with at a New York City high school started his football team on an ankle strength–training program and found that for the first time in twenty years, he didn't have one player with a sprained ankle during the 1979 season.

Women, as a result of their complex history, have traditionally been less physically active than men. And lacking, as most of them do, the experience in sports of their male counterparts, they tend to be more prone to injury. Because of this they benefit greatly from preparation and proper training. Moreover, as we've pointed out, many women are tight-jointed in their lower extremities (legs) and prone to get shin splints. So even before starting to jog or play squash or ski, it's a good idea to do the stretching exercises that can help avoid these injuries. We also suggest strength training, particularly wall-sits, for the thigh muscles. If you're going to run, you'll need to have strong enough muscles to keep your kneecaps in place. Those of you starting on a racquet sport will want to concentrate on increasing the strength in your upper body, the area where women are the weakest. The appropriate exercises, done for the proper amount of time, will help you escape the tennis elbow and slipped shoulder that you might otherwise end up with.

Not only can you avoid injury through training, you can also avoid surgery. In general we can say that there are few orthopedic patients who are not dramatically helped by the proper exercises and activity. Probably close to 50 percent can avoid surgery simply by a proper understanding of the mechanics of what they've been doing and learning to execute the corrective measures with efficient body movements. Take that often troublesome part of the body, the knee. Since we've instituted training programs for girls who have soreness in the kneecaps and pains behind the knees, we've cut down the rate of surgery to about 5 percent or less of these patients. Other patients, with muscle pulls, have been given special flexibility routines that, for many of them, have virtually eliminated this problem. Kristien Kemmer Shaw, whose activity as a professional athlete was halted by a painful back problem, avoided surgery and was back on the tennis court after only two weeks of strength, flexibility, and endurance training. Skier Heidi Preuss, also suffering from backache, saw dozens of doctors, none of whom could help. A great natural athlete and one of the best on the U.S. Olympic team, she was eliminated from the national ski program. Today she's skiing again, purely as a result of training. And one of the most enthusiastic proponents of training, Billie Jean King, has often said that had she started the proper exercises sooner, she would most likely have avoided some of the surgery she's undergone. Younger women on the professional tennis circuit quote Billie Jean King's advice to them to begin training before surgery becomes a factor. And this advice is valid for all women, not only world-class athletes.

With women's interest in physical fitness a relatively recent phenomenon, at least on its current scale, it's not surprising that most women just don't know what it is to exercise really hard. One trainer told us that her biggest problem with women was the fear they had that every ache or pain or strain indicated some sort of permanent damage. It's clear that these women have not exerted themselves enough to feel the muscular fatigue that accompanies a thorough training routine.

We've seen women on exercise programs who complained of making little or no progress. After watching them train it becomes evident that they have no concept of what it is to work their muscles to fatigue. One woman with an elbow problem who was facing possible surgery kept insisting that she had been faithfully exercising with little or no benefit. What she had been doing, in fact, as she showed us, was simply stretching her wrist, pulling it forward and back. She had never considered working with weights and was so apprehensive about strength training that only the prospect of soon being able to go back to racquetball could persuade her to start lifting weights.

It's not only the average woman who doesn't know what total training feels like, it's also the woman world-class athlete. One such woman, who had done some amount of training before, came for a consultation after knee surgery. Even though she was used to playing two to three hours a day, she had never been through a total body workout. Most important, when she worked on the leg involved in the surgery, she had never exhausted the particular muscle she was training. This was something she had to learn before she could begin to build up her weakened muscles.

Often when athletes feel they have done all they can possibly do, we've been able to demonstrate to them that they still have energy in reserve and can go on to do more. Rosie Casals, after training in a gym under the supervision of an expert staff, was shown that she could run twenty minutes more, go on to a series of sprints, and then continue to run even more. Obviously the gym training hadn't brought her up to her level of fatigue. It was only after the last run that she truly experienced what it was to be totally exhausted. It's this feeling of being completely fatigued from physical activity that most women have never known.

For those of you in good health who start gradually and follow the cautions we'll outline, there's no reason for not exercising more often and more intensely than you have in the past. You're going to improve only if you do more—run longer distances, work up your speed, increase the amount of the weight you lift, try for more repetitions of an exercise. If you can overcome the barrier that society seems to have instilled in many women, the mistaken belief that anything beyond the mildest physical activity is somehow basically damaging, there's no reason why you can't go on to train effectively and safely.

WARMING UP AND COOLING DOWN

Purposes of Warming Up
1. Helps prevent sudden abnormal stresses.

125

2. Aids in prevention of injury.

3. Makes muscles more responsive to neural signals (more alert).

4. Increases blood flow to the muscles.

Warming up should accomplish just what it says: get you feeling comfortably warm. You'll find that you have an accompanying increase in circulation along with a relaxation of your muscles. These days there seems to be an emphasis on stretching, and we see runners starting out on a cold gray winter morning working on flexibility routines. It's painful and, in fact, it's useless to try to stretch your muscles when they're tired, tight, and cold. It would be a lot better to start by moving around first, walking or jogging at a slow pace until you feel yourself getting warm. Your muscles will be a good deal looser after a few minutes of movement than from trying to stretch them when your body is not warmed up.

What activity you start off with depends mainly on your current state of fitness. You might walk or jog or stroll, gradually working up your speed. With your body relaxed, you can start moving your arms in small circles to increase your circulation. Swinging arms wildly in throwing motions or making huge circles rapidly can do more damage than good. It's quite possible to pull a muscle or pinch a nerve when you attempt these unusual motions with excessive speed. Just a normal arm motion, a rhythmic swinging, along with the running motion of your legs is all you want to do to start your warm-up. As for the sit-ups, push-ups and other calisthenics some people do before their regular exercise, we would advise reserving these for the strength-training sessions done after a proper warm-up. Calisthenics can get your muscles tight, and when you warm up, what you want to do is just the opposite, loosen and lengthen them.

Once you feel warm, you can start doing some stretches. Begin by moving your arms in a somewhat exaggerated swimming motion, slightly more than you'd use for the Australian crawl. Then, with your arms overhead and together, you can stretch your body from side to side. Standing upright, bend from the waist with your hips forward in order to flex and extend your trunk. Then, pulling

126

your ankle up behind you, you can stretch out the front of your thigh and your hamstrings. Stand on the edge of a step or the curb with your toes up and heels down to stretch your calf muscles. By now you should be ready to start exercising.

How long should all this take? Probably no longer than ten minutes and, depending on how you're feeling that day, maybe only five. In warm weather and on some days, just because you're feeling in particularly good shape, you'll find you need less time than on the days you wake up tired and stiff. Judge for yourself and keep in mind that each person is different. We've found there is no hard-and-fast rule that will be appropriate for everyone.

Cooling down may take a few minutes longer than warming up and should be an extremely gradual process. Run very slowly, only slightly faster than a walk, and make sure your body is relaxed. You should also do some stretching, especially if you've just been running. Running, because it is so repetitive, can tighten and shorten certain muscles. You'll want to stretch these out, specifically the muscles in the fronts of the thighs and hips and the back of the calves. Allow ten to fifteen minutes for the cooling down, which, added to the five- to ten-minute warm-up and the thirty-minute workout (you can alternate strength and stamina workouts, making flexibility exercises part of each session), brings your exercising to under an hour.

Suggested Warm-Ups (gradually work up speed)

1. *Main Street Stroll.* Swing arms briskly and step lively with a fast pace.
2. *Walk with a twist.* Clasp hands behind your head and twist your body to the side, left as left leg swings forward, right as right leg swings forward.
3. *Crawl stroke forward.*
4. *Jog.*

Suppleness

We judge suppleness or flexibility in terms of the range of motion of your joints. There are three factors that affect this range of motion, and the first has to do with the bony structure of the joint.

127

Look at your knee or elbow. The way the bones are put together keeps these joints from extending backward or beyond 180 degrees. The second factor affecting your flexibility has to do with the amount of bulk surrounding your joints. The so-called muscle-bound body builder, the man who has developed huge biceps, may have limited the range of his elbows because his bulky muscles get in the way. And while women don't have this kind of muscle bulk, large fatty deposits may limit motion in much the same way.

The third factor, the one you can do the most about when you work on the following exercises, is the extensibility of the ligaments, tendons, muscles, and skin that cross over the joint. The stretching you will be doing has been designed to help increase this elasticity, giving you as large a range of motion as you can possibly have. Even the connective tissues that shorten with aging, especially those in your back and shoulders, can be actively stretched to their original length and kept that way.

It's best to do your flexibility with a slow control of the movements, stretching your muscles and then relaxing them for several seconds. Your preparatory warm-up exercises should have gotten you to a point where your movements are smoother and better coordinated. Go through the following exercises slowly, stretching the muscles and connective tissue far enough so that you experience the beginnings of some discomfort. Then hold back the stretch to a position just short of that extreme one. In other words, back off a bit from your maximum stretch.

Flexibility exercises should be done frequently, even daily if you can manage it. As you find yourself improving, you can add variations and increase the amount of time you hold each position. But be cautious. Overstretching can actually tighten you and can even cause injury, so don't try to do too much too soon. On some days you'll find yourself a lot stiffer then you are on other days. At these times, when you know you're less flexible, you shouldn't try to surpass a previous goal. It would be wisest even to go back a step or two until your slow stretching corrects the stiffness.

The important thing to remember is that straining is not stretching. You have to learn to distinguish between the feeling of a stretch and the feeling of pain that comes with overstretching.

After a few days of flexibility exercises, you'll be able to judge by how your body feels and responds just what amount of stretching you ought to be doing.

SPECIFIC EXERCISE	AREA OF BODY WORKED	OBJECT AND PRACTICAL PURPOSE
Head circle	Neck	This is to loosen the joints in the cervical spine and stretch the neck muscles. The object is to do a full range of motion.
Over the head	Shoulder	The object of this exercise is to stretch the inner part of your chest underneath the arms, the triceps muscles, and the back of the arm. In addition, it also stretches your shoulder.
Towel exercise	Shoulder	The object is to stretch out the front of the shoulder and increase rotation. The purpose is to prevent shoulder impingement and injuries as well as increase throwing motion.
Shoulder stretch	Shoulder	The object is to stretch your deltoid muscle. This thick muscle surrounds most of your shoulder joint and gives your shoulders their rounded outline.
Extensor exercise	Forearm	This exercise stretches the muscles on the bottom of the forearm.
Pretzel exercise	Back	This exercise stretches out the hard tight band on the side of the leg, which is often involved with soreness in running, and the heavy muscles on the sides of your buttocks, which are the muscles that move your legs out to the sides. These are important for making quick side moves, and they often tighten up from repetitive straight-ahead running. You'll feel a pull in your spine as well as on the outside of your leg and stomach.
Knee to shoulder	Back, hamstrings	You'll feel the stretch in the back of your thighs as well as in your lower back. This exercise should help reduce lumbar lordosis, the forward curve of the lower back, which is aggravated by pregnancy.

129

SPECIFIC EXERCISE	AREA OF BODY WORKED	OBJECT AND PRACTICAL PURPOSE
Toe bend exercise	Back, hamstrings	This exercise should help increase the flexibility of your back.
Chair exercise	Back	The object of this exercise is to loosen up your back muscles and get more extension or curvature of your back.
Standing quad stretch	Quadriceps, front of thigh	The object of this exercise is to stretch out the muscles in the front of the thigh and hip, which often get tight with repetitive running.
Lying quad stretch	Quadriceps, front of thigh	Same object as above. If you have back problems, you should omit this exercise.
Standing object stretch	Hamstrings	The object is to stretch out the hamstrings, which are the muscles in the backs of your legs.
Standing hamstring stretch	Hamstrings, back	This exercise is good for both hamstrings and back. You should feel a pull in the back of your thighs and your back.
Hurdler's stretch	Hamstrings, hip flexors, thigh	When you reach forward you are stretching out the hamstrings and back muscles. When you lean backward, the hip flexors, quadriceps and thigh muscles are stretched.
Seated groin stretch	Hamstrings, groin	When you reach down each leg, you stretch the hamstrings. When you put your hand forward, you stretch out your groin muscles.
Modified Indian stretch	groin, adductors	This exercise primarily stretches the groin muscles.
Side stride stretch	Hamstring, groin	This exercise primarily stretches the thigh and groin. It is not recommended for those of you with kneecap problems.
Stair stretch	Lower leg, Achilles tendon	You should feel the stretch in the lower leg region, specifically in the calf muscle and Achilles tendon.

130

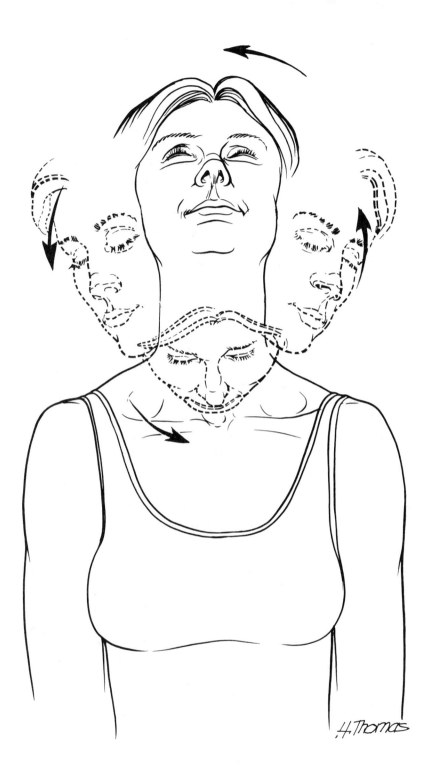

Description of Suppleness Exercises

FOR THE NECK. *Head circles.* Standing straight with your hands on your hips and your feet shoulder-width apart, slowly rotate your head clockwise in a full circle, taking a count of ten to go completely around. An easy way to understand this maneuver is to picture the face of a clock in front of you and think of your nose as moving around that face, from twelve o'clock around to three, down to six, and back up to twelve. After doing a complete circle clockwise, repeat going counterclockwise. This exercise is a warm-up with some amount of stretching and is worthwhile only if done slowly. You may hear some cracking or popping, which indicates that the joints of your spine are loosening up after being held in one position. It is a good idea to do some head circles after driving awhile or sitting at your desk.

FOR THE SHOULDER. *Over the head.* With your arms overhead, hold the elbow of the left arm with the hand of the right. Gently and slowly pull your left elbow back behind your head. You should feel a pull both underneath your left arm and in your triceps, the large muscles in the back of your upper arm. Then reverse arms and repeat. If you have any pain on the top of your shoulder or if you know you have tendinitis in that joint, you should not do this particular stretch because it can aggravate shoulder problems. But if this is not the case and if you play tennis, golf, or any throwing sport, you'll find this maneuver particularly helpful.

Towel exercise. Hold a long object—a towel, tennis racket, jump rope, or even a long stick— over your head with your left hand, letting the object hang straight down your back. Grab the bottom of it with your right hand and move your right hand sideways toward the left as far as possible. Hold for a count of ten.

H.Thomas

H.Thomas

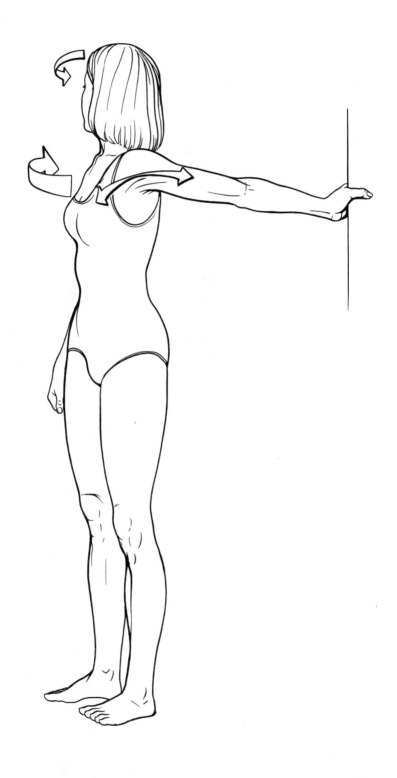

Shoulder stretch. With your left arm holding onto something upright and sturdy, such as a bookshelf or a screen fence around a playground or tennis court, slowly pivot your body in place in a direction away from the wall or fence for as far as you can go. Hold at a maximum point for a count of ten and then repeat the pivot, using the opposite arm.

FOR THE
FOREARM.

Extensor exercise. Hold your arm out in front of you, keeping your elbow straight. Fully extend your fingers and wrist and hold for a count of ten. Then, with the help of your opposite hand, flex your wrist down toward the floor in as close to an angle of 90 degrees as possible and hold. Then extend your wrist up and hold. Repeat, using the other arm.

When your wrist is down, you'll feel the stretch on the top muscles of your arm, and when your wrist is up, you should feel it on the bottom muscles.

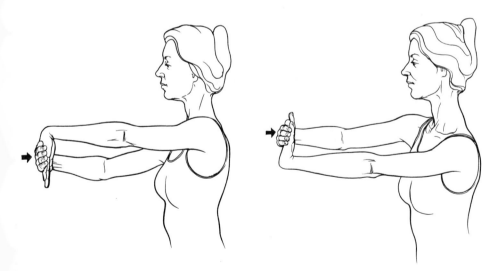

FOR THE BACK. *Pretzel exercise.* This exercise is for those of you who feel ready for more advanced stretching. Sit on the floor with your left leg straight out and then cross your right leg over the left one, placing your right foot flat on the floor. With your left hand reach right in front of you and toward your right hip. Place your right hand on the floor directly behind you. Sitting up very straight, slowly turn your head toward the right so that you can look over your right shoulder. Then stretch your other side by crossing the left leg over the right, your right arm reaching left, and your head turned to the left, looking over your left shoulder.

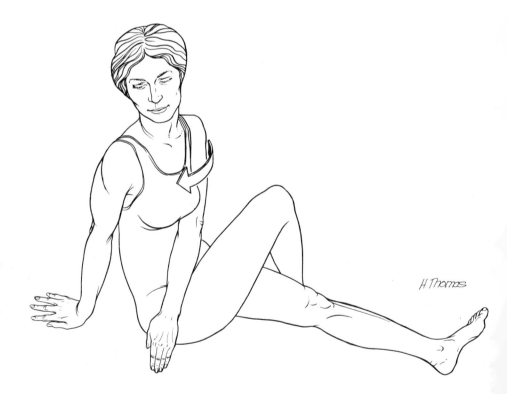

Knees to the shoulder. Lie on your back with a pillow under your head. Your knees should be bent with your feet flat on the floor. First straighten your left leg and bring your right knee up toward your right shoulder. Hold it there for a count of ten and release. Reverse the procedure by straightening your right leg and bringing your left knee up to your left shoulder, holding again for a count of ten. Then bring both knees up toward their corresponding shoulders and hold for ten.

Toe touch bend exercise. Stand with your feet shoulder-width apart and your knees straight. Slowly rotate while bending forward, reaching toward your right foot with your left hand. Hold this for a count of ten and then, after returning to the starting position, reverse the procedure. *Caution:* If you have any back problems to begin with, do this stretch with bent knees.

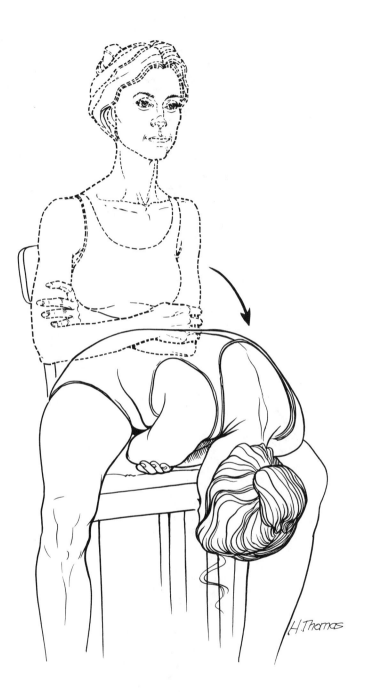

Chair exercise. Sit on the edge of a chair with your legs apart. Lower your head, shoulders, and folded elbows down toward the floor between your legs. Hold for a count of five to ten. This is a particularly good and safe exercise for those of you with back trouble.

FOR THE QUADRICEPS.

Standing quad stretch. Stand on your left foot, keeping your balance by holding onto the wall with your left hand. With your right hand, reach behind you and grab onto your right foot, pulling it back and up toward your buttocks.

Lying quad stretch. Lying on your left side, bend your right knee and grab your right ankle with your right hand. Then gradually move your hips backward until you feel a good stretch in your thigh. Hold this position for a count of ten and then repeat for the left leg, lying on your right side. Your unstretched leg can be slightly bent for comfort. Those of you with back problems should skip this exercise. Arching your back this way can increase lordosis.

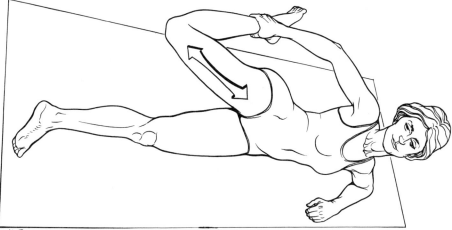

H. Thomas

HAMSTRINGS. *Standing object stretch.* Choose a structure that's at least waist high—any wall, tree, or fence will do. Standing on your straight left leg, lift your right leg until you can place your right heel on the wall at a point below waist high. Then slowly bend forward at the waist, trying to touch your nose to your right knee. When you feel a good stretch in the back of your right leg, hold the position for a count of ten. Then repeat so that you end up doing eight to ten repetitions on each leg.

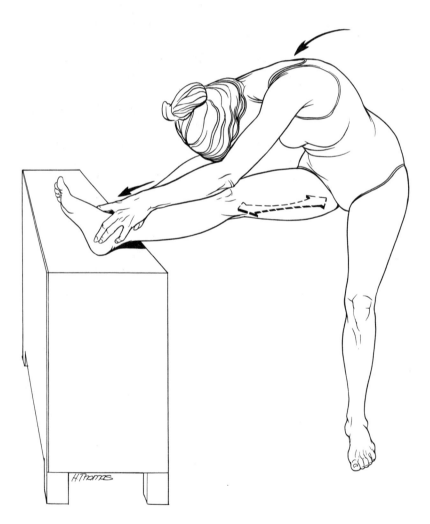

Standing hamstring stretch. Standing with your feet more than shoulder-width apart, bend your right knee and extend your left knee with your toes pointed ninety degrees to the left of your right toes. Try to grasp your left ankle. Repeat this, using the opposite legs. Each stretch should last

143

for a count of ten. With repeated efforts you'll be able to reach farther—if not your ankle, at least a point lower down on your leg.

This exercise is good for the back as well as the hamstrings. You can do it anywhere, holding onto your ankle so that you feel a pull in the back of your thighs and your back.

Hurdler's stretch. In a seated position on the floor, place your right leg in front of you with your knee straight, your left leg behind you in a bent position. Then reach forward and touch your right leg as far down as possible with your left hand and hold for a count of ten to fifteen. Next reach back with your left hand and hold the left leg for the same amount of time. Lean your entire body backward to stretch the hip flexors. Repeat with the left leg forward and straight, the right leg back and right knee bent. You can increase the difficulty of this stretch by positioning your leg farther back each time.

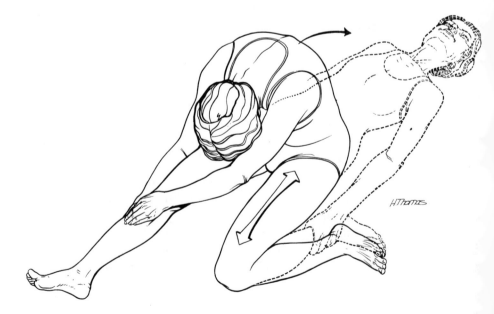

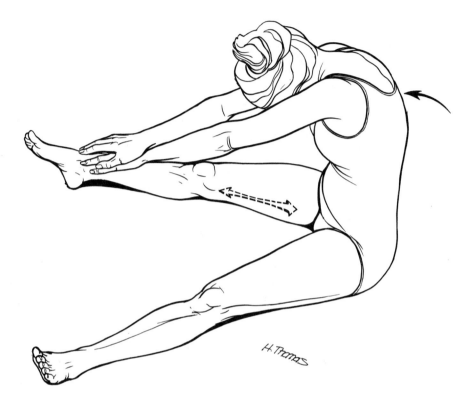

Seated ham/groin stretch. Sit on the floor with your legs apart stretched out in front of you and your feet flexed. Walk your hands down your right leg as far as possible and hold in this maximum position for a count of ten. Then walk your hands down your left leg as far as possible and hold for ten. Then put your hands together and reach out straight ahead and hold for ten. No matter how tight you are, you can usually at least reach your thighs.

GROIN.   *Modified Indian stretch.* Sit on the floor with your back straight and bend your knees so that the bot-

145

toms of your feet come together in front of you. Pull your feet in toward your groin and then push your knees outward toward the floor. Hold for ten.

Side stride stretch. Stand, pointing your right foot forward and left foot sideways, and rotate your trunk to the left. Keeping your back straight, bend your right knee forward as far as possible. Hold this position for a count of ten and then repeat, bending your left leg and rotating left.

CALF.

Stair stretch. You can perform this exercise on a step indoors or use the curb when you're outside running. Stand on the edge of the step or curb with your heels halfway off. Rise up on your toes and hold this position for a count of ten. Next,

H.Thomas

press your heels down below the step and hold again for ten. This second part can be done with one foot at a time.

You should feel a stretch in the lower leg region, specifically in the calf muscle and the Achilles tendon, which attaches the muscle to your heel.

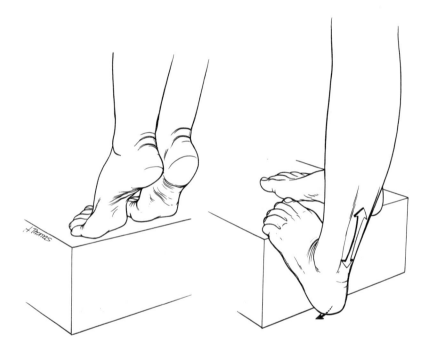

From neck to heel, you've now worked your way down your body, stretching and limbering your joints and muscles. It can help when you do these exercises if you keep a picture in mind of your muscles as elastic, continually capable of stretching and contracting. If your life-style has caused some of your muscles to grow tighter—walking in high heels can shorten your calf muscles, while sitting for hours at a desk can shorten thigh muscles and hip flexors—with training you can lengthen them again. Warm up first and then stretch gradually, letting your muscles relax until they're as supple as they should be. Stretching after an exercise session also helps prevent postworkout stiffness and muscle soreness.

STAMINA

Stamina or endurance refers to cardiopulmonary efficiency, that is, how well your heart pumps blood through your body. Your blood functions as your transportation system, bringing fuel in the form of oxygen to your end organs, which include your muscles, and then removing the carbon dioxide and lactic acid that are the waste products. There's always blood in your muscles, but when your heart works more efficiently, you'll be extracting more oxygen from the blood and into the tissues so that you can run your body longer and harder.

There are three factors in proper stamina training. First, there is the *frequency* of training: three times a week is essential if you want to improve; twice a week is enough to maintain fitness. The second factor is the *duration* of each workout: twenty minutes is minimum. The last factor, the one that will change as your fitness level goes up, is the *intensity* with which you work out.

The simplest and most practical way of figuring out your own particular level of intensity, the amount you have to do to challenge your system with effective exercise, is by taking your pulse. Your exercise pulse rate, the one at which you should be training for endurance, can roughly be figured as 60 to 75 percent of the sum of 220 minus your age. There are more exact ways to measure, of course. The exercise stress test will give you precise maximum heart rate that you can attain. And in a sophisticated laboratory setting there are even more effective ways being developed. How much carbon dioxide you expire compared to the oxygen you take in can be calculated to determine at what intensity you should be working. Or your skin temperature can give us some clues about the efficiency of your system. But unless you have a particular problem or have one of the cardiac risk factors we've discussed in Chapter 4, a rough estimate based on your pulse rate will tell you enough about how much you should be doing. This estimate is the one we use when training professional athletes. Women tennis players training for the Colgate Grand Prix, for example, were recently given drills of extreme intensity. It was clear by their pulse rates, up to about 180 to 200 beats per minute, that they couldn't sustain that high level for the necessary duration of twenty to thirty minutes. We then decreased the intensity of the drills, which in turn lowered the pulse rates of the players to a level which they could sustain for an effective workout. The guideline we use for professional athletes is the same one we'd recommend for you.

Stamina Training

How do you do it? You can run outdoors or on a treadmill, ride an ordinary or a stationary bicycle, swim, jump rope, do aerobic dance, or even get your cardiopulmonary training within a particular sport as long as the proper degrees of duration, frequency, and intensity are accomplished. Some ways, though, are a lot more difficult than others. You can, for example, get stamina training from lifting weights. Probably no other single activity will drive your heart rate up faster. But you need to lift each set of weights one right after the other so that your pulse doesn't drop in between. Sustaining this routine for the necessary twenty to thirty minutes can be too strenuous for most people.

Suggested Activities

Jumping rope
Walking, jogging, running (indoors or on a treadmill)
Bicycle riding (regular or stationary bicycle)
Swimming
or
as part of your regular sport.

JUMPING ROPE. Another activity that can get your heart rate up fast but can be difficult to maintain at the proper level of intensity is jumping rope. This activity may also not work well for you because it requires a certain amount of skill and coordination. Most

150

people land on their toes, causing their calf muscles to contract so that they end up with sore ankles and calves. It might be a good idea, depending on your level of fitness, for you to start off by jumping rope to get your pulse rate up and then continue at some other activity that is less explosive, such as biking or running.

WALKING, JOGGING, RUNNING (OUTDOORS OR ON A TREADMILL). Which of these you'll do depends on what shape you're in. If you can get your pulse rate up high enough by walking quickly, then that's a good activity for you. After a period of time you can combine walking with some jogging.

When you first start on your endurance training, you'll have to stop frequently to monitor your pulse rate. We suggest taking your pulse every five minutes or so until you learn what stride you need to use in order to keep it up at the proper level. You'll get fluctuations, perhaps starting high and then settling down to a good even rate. Get the feel of being at that rate so that soon you'll only have to take your pulse periodically. You should always take your recovery pulse rate one minute after you stop, then two minutes, and then three. You should have a recovery index of approximately 80 percent within three minutes although when you get in better shape, it will take only two minutes. One-minute recovery index of approximately 80 percent of your resting pulse is extremely good, a clear indication of being in excellent cardiopulmonary condition.

BICYCLE RIDING (REGULAR OR STATIONARY BICYCLE). The problem with cycling is that most people don't do it with enough intensity. They may do it long enough or often enough but with the many gears and speeds there's just not enough physical effort involved to get your heart rate up. On a stationary bike you can adjust the amount of resistance and you might consider doing something like that on your ten-speed bike as well, shifting gears to make it harder for you rather than easier.

One other problem that some people have with cycling is that their leg muscles tire before they get the proper cardiovascular workout. It may be a more appropriate stamina exercise for someone whose stamina has been tested first and been found to be low. For this person endurance benefits will come before tired leg muscles.

SWIMMING. While few people swim with the idea of getting endurance training, they can accomplish this if they increase their level of intensity. Swimming is particularly good for anyone overweight, with arthritis, or suffering from certain problems in the knees, ankles, or hips. As with running, biking, and all the endurance activities, when you first begin you have to stop to take your pulse after each five minutes to make sure it's up at exercise level. Those of you who have had very little exercise can begin by sitting at the edge of a pool, kicking your legs in the water, and then proceed to stand in shallow water, working your arms forward in a crawl position. As long as your level of participation gives you effective exercise, you're doing what's right for you.

OTHER SPORTS. As we said in the beginning of this discussion of stamina training, you can get all the benefits in a variety of ways. Almost any sport can do it—field hockey, basketball, tennis, golf— if you play hard enough. If you just stand on a tennis court and hit what comes your way, you are obviously not going to achieve an increased pulse rate. After some time of standing on your half or quarter of a tennis court, you might feel a great deal of fatigue, but since this feeling comes from being static and not from any dynamic activity, it's not the kind of fatigue that indicates you've gotten a proper workout or achieved the right conditioning. But if you can really combine effective stamina training with a favorite sport, it's the best combination. You'll be a lot more likely to look forward to your three-times-a-week endurance training when it's part of an activity you already enjoy.

STRENGTH

Strength training is designed to develop the force of your muscles, and while many people think that activity itself can increase strength, we know that simply isn't true. Activity can certainly train the endurance of your total body and perhaps even the endurance of your muscles, but it can't increase the strength or speed of those muscles.

The only way you can get stronger is by overloading your muscles, that is, working them to the point where it begins to hurt. Start gently and work up to doing more and more until you can actually feel your muscle fatigue. Anyone who is in good health can do this, no matter how old—we'd suggest the same guidelines whether you're eighty or twenty. If, after your Medical Profile, your doctor says you're ready for active sports, you can start the gradual process of working your muscle so that your strength will slowly increase.

There are some facts you should be aware of before you start. First, when you overload a muscle, you are going to feel an ache. This becomes a crisis for some people, who immediately assume something is terribly wrong. Just remember that the soreness from exercise is in the bulk of the muscle itself, usually deep and between the joints. You might not feel it until twenty-four or even forty-eight hours after exercising. This soreness gradually subsides, improving with additional exercise. On the other hand, the pain that should cause you some concern and suggest to you that something is wrong is usually in or near a joint. Tennis elbow begins at the lateral bone of the elbow, for example, and not in the arm muscle. And activity, far from improving it, only seems to make it worse. There are some other clues to distinguish the ache of good hard exercise from the soreness of an activity that is damaging. Ache from exercise comes in the form of a dull pain that is transient, going away when you continue to be active. The pains of a pulled tendon or joint bursitis or a ligament stretch are far more acute. They are aggravated by continued movement, and the afflicted area is extremely tender.

How often should you do strength training? If you want to maintain your condition, you ought to work out twice a week. But if you want to improve, you need to have at least three sessions a week. Many people working out at clubs or gyms have been told to stop for a day in between training sessions. In general, this is a good idea because if you work your muscles to fatigue, it takes twenty-four or even forty-eight hours for the waste product, lactic acid, to get carried away by the bloodstream and for the glucose store of your body to be replenished. But as a practical matter, most people don't fatigue their muscles sufficiently to need this rest period.

153

When you start training, you can work out every day until you find you are really able to work hard. Then the day's rest makes sense for you. Some people like to tone their muscles daily, and they may choose to go through a heavy exercise session one day and a light one the next.

There is variety in the types of strength training available, and each has its advantages and disadvantages. You can join a club and use Nautilus or Universal or Marcy equipment, or you can work out at home with some dumbbells and small sandbags. You can even fill an old purse with cans of soup and use that for weights. We'll describe some of the ways you can effectively strength-train, outlining specific programs for you to follow. Which you choose will depend on what's practical for you.

Isometrics

Isometric exercises involve muscular contractions performed against fixed, immovable resistance. The stressed part does not move. These exercises are not recommended for anyone with high blood pressure or a cardiac condition.

One of the advantages of isometrics is the convenience—it takes little time per session, it costs nothing, and it's not difficult to master. It has another advantage of taking up little room so that you can sit in a crowded jet plane crossing the country and, without anyone knowing it, go through part of an isometric session. These exercises are good for anyone who has to be confined, from astronauts in orbit to students during exam periods. We often recommend this type of strength training for patients whose movements are limited after injury.

On the other hand, isometrics won't increase your strength as quickly and efficiently as other methods, nor is it as good in improving skill and endurance. It's probably wisest to consider these following isometric exercises as suitable for those times when nothing else is possible.

When doing isometric exercises be sure you never hold your breath. If you do, you may experience increased chest pressure as well as elevated blood pressure, which will decrease the flow of blood to your heart. If you hyperventilate (breathe excessively) before you hold your breath, you are likely to faint.

SPECIFIC EXERCISE	AREA OF BODY WORKED	OBJECT AND PRACTICAL PURPOSE
Head isometrics	Neck	This exercise works on building up the strength of your neck muscles in four quadrants.
Chin to opposite shoulder	Neck	The object is to strengthen the muscles around the neck. You should feel the pull on the opposite side of your neck from the direction you're turning.
Face isometrics	Small muscles of the face	This exercise should build up the strength in those small muscles in your face.
Flexed elbow isometrics	Shoulder, chest	The object is to strengthen muscles in your shoulder and chest.
Shoulder shrug	Shoulder	This exercise will build up strength in the trapezius muscle on the top of your shoulder.
Chest isometrics	Chest	The pectoral and other muscles on the front of your chest are the areas strengthened.
External rotation	Chest, shoulder	This will strengthen the muscles that move your arm outward.
Internal rotation	Chest, shoulder	This will strengthen those muscles that move your arm inward.
Forearm extensor	Forearm muscles	The object of this exercise is to strengthen the muscles on the top of your forearm.
Abdominal isometrics	Abdominal (stomach) muscles	This exercise will help strengthen and tighten your stomach muscles.
Wall-sits	Thigh	The object of this exercise is to build strength in the quadriceps, which are the four muscles on the front of your thigh, while your knees are bent.
Quadriceps isometrics	Thigh	The object of this exercise is to strengthen your thigh muscles when they're in the shortened phase, with your knees straight.
Inner and outer thigh	Thigh	Again, the object is to build strength in your thigh muscles.

155

SPECIFIC EXERCISE	AREA OF BODY WORKED	OBJECT AND PRACTICAL PURPOSE
Ankle isometrics	Ankle	This small group of exercises builds up strength in the muscles of your ankle. The outward exercise involves the peroneal muscles, the inward the posterior tibia muscles. The last exercise strengthens the gastronemius muscles, which are the chief extensors of the foot at the ankle joint.

Description of Isometric Exercises

Each exercise should be held for a count of five to ten. Perform two or three sets of ten repetitions of each exercise. Rest two to three minutes between sets.

FOR THE NECK. *Head isometrics.* 1. Sit or stand with interlaced fingers of your hands on your forehead. Forcibly exert a forward push of your head while resisting equally hard with your hands.

2. Sit or stand with your interlaced fingers behind your head. Move your head back while exerting a forward push with your hands.

3. Sit or stand with the palm of your right hand on the right side of your head. Push with your head and neck. Reverse, using your left hand on the left side of your head.

Chin to opposite shoulder. Start by looking straight ahead and then turn your head and neck slowly to the right, trying to touch your right shoulder with your chin. Hold for a count of ten and then slowly return your head to its original, straight forward position. Next, turn your head and neck slowly to the left and try to touch your left shoulder with your chin.

FOR THE FACE. *Face Isometrics.* Smile broadly and hold. Then
pucker up and hold that.

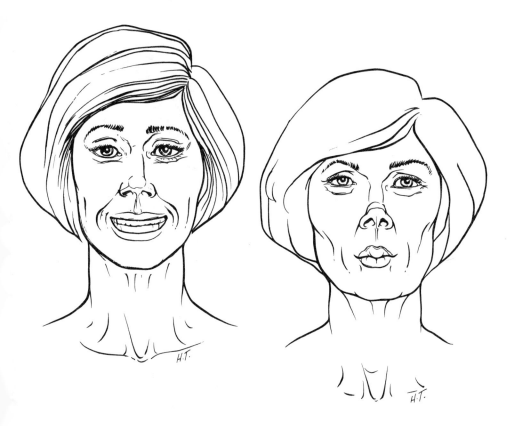

FOR THE
SHOULDER,
UPPER ARM,
CHEST.

Flexed Elbow. 1. Stand with your back next to a
wall. With your elbow flexed at ninety degrees, attempt to press it into the wall.

159

2. Turn so your side faces the wall and try to press your elbow, flexed at 90 degrees, out to the side against the wall.

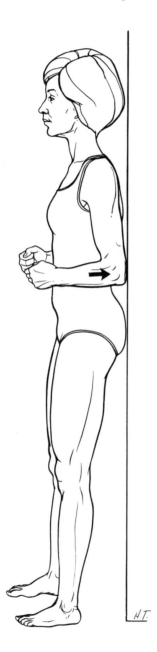
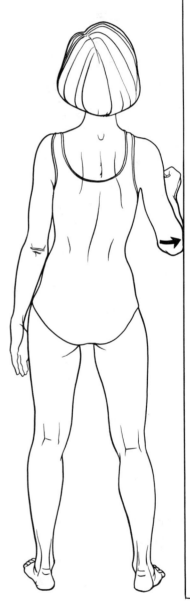

3. Face the wall with your elbow flexed at ninety degrees and attempt to push it forward into the wall.

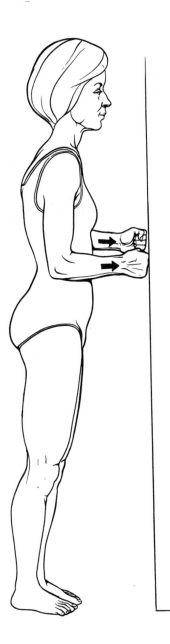

Shoulder shrug. Shrug your shoulders up to your neck and ears and hold. Slowly release.

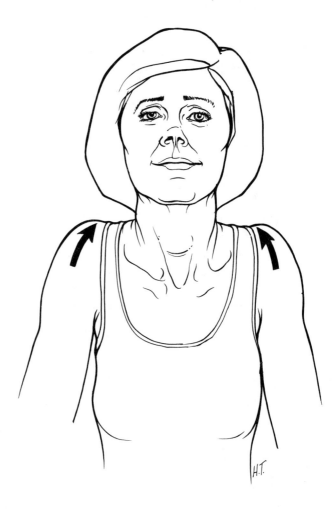

Chest isometrics. 1. Stand with your feet slightly apart and your knees slightly bent. With your arms close to your chest, grip your fingers together and pull hard. Hold.

162

2. Stand with your feet apart and knees bent. Clasp your hands with palms together close to your chest. Press your hands together and hold.

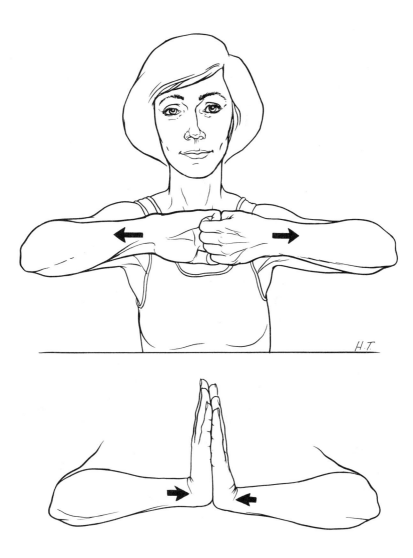

External rotation. 1. Stand in a doorway with your elbows flexed at ninety degrees and held close to your body. Rotate them outward against the door jamb.

2. Lying on your back with your elbows flexed at ninety degrees and held close to your body, grasp the wrist of your right arm with your left hand. Attempt to move your right hand outward, resisting this motion with your left hand. Don't allow your right hand to move. Reverse the process, holding your left hand.

Internal Rotation. 1. Lying on your back with your elbows flexed at ninety degrees and held close to your body, grasp your right wrist with your left hand. Try to move your right hand inward while opposing any motion with your left.

2. Standing in a doorway with your elbow flexed at ninety degrees and held close to your body, try to press inward against the door jamb.

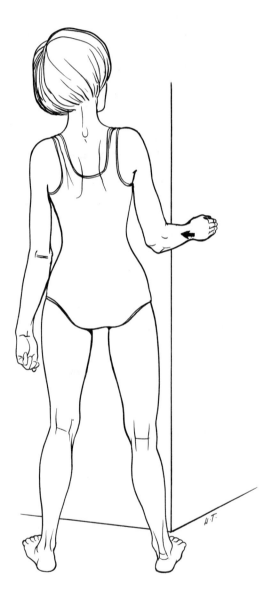

FOR THE
FOREARM.

Forearm extensor. Fully extend your arms, wrists, and fingers out in front of you and hold. Then release.

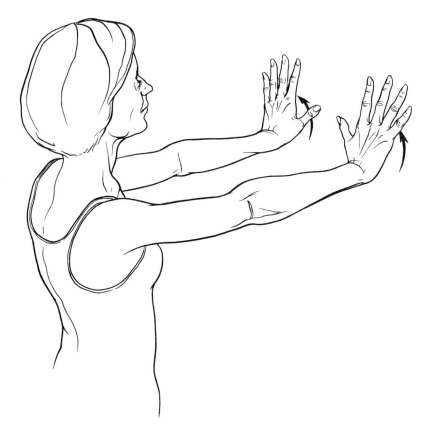

FOR THE
ABDOMEN.

Abdominal isometrics. Stand with your knees slightly bent and your hands resting on them. Contract your abdominal muscles and hold.

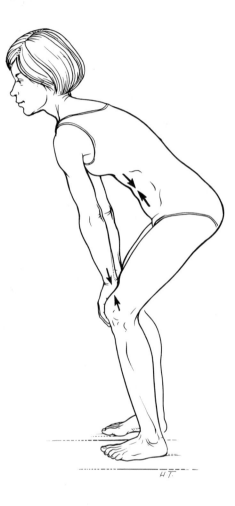

Wall-sits. With your back against the wall, bend your hips and knees to ninety degrees, as if sitting on a chair. Hold for as long as you can, preferably until your muscles are totally fatigued. Those of you with kneecap problems may not be able to start at ninety degrees and can begin higher up, working your way down to ninety degrees in subsequent exercise sessions. If you have pain in your knee-caps, stop. Pain in your thighs, however, shouldn't keep you from doing this exercise, since that means you're getting the strengthening benefits that will help you control your kneecaps.

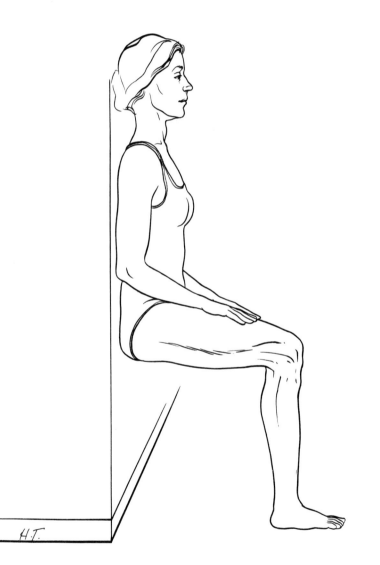

Quadriceps isometrics. Sit on the floor with your legs straight out and then tighten your quadriceps by pushing the back or underside of your knee down into the floor. If there is knee pain, a small rolled pillow can be put under your knees to cushion them as you push. This exercise should be done slowly, tightening gradually and then holding the position. You should release even more slowly.

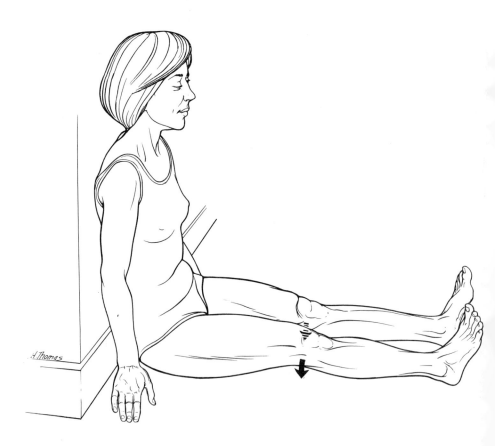

Inner and outer thigh. Sit on a sturdy chair with your legs extended out and press each ankle in against the outside legs of the chair. Hold. Then repeat with your legs under the chair by pressing out against the inside legs of the chair. Hold.

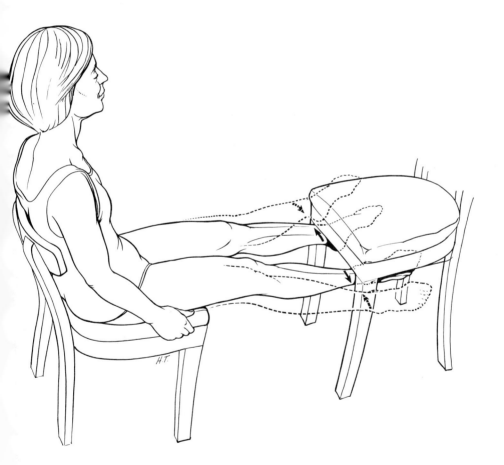

FOR THE
LOWER LEGS
AND ANKLES.

Ankle isometrics. 1. Sitting on the edge of a table or desk, cross one ankle over the other. Try to move one ankle inward while pushing at it with the other. Hold for a count of five to ten and then repeat, reversing ankles.

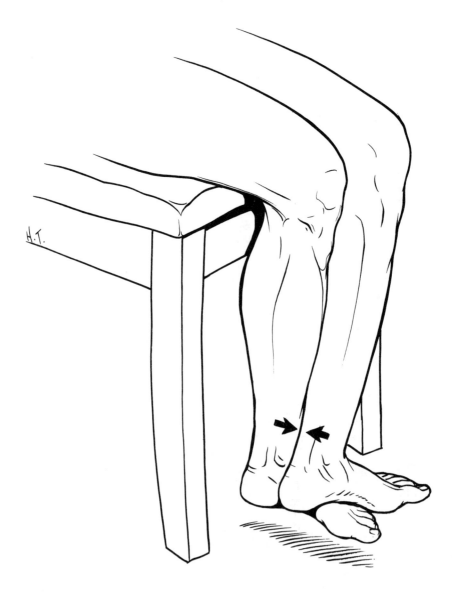

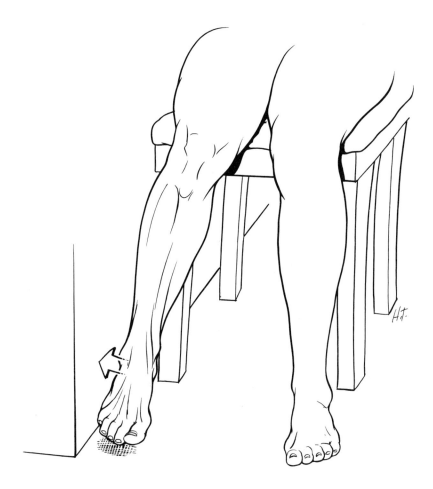

2. Sitting on a chair alongside the wall, try to push your ankle that is closest to the wall outward against the wall. Turn the chair around and now push the other ankle outward against the wall.

173

3. Sit on a chair and try to push your ankles backward against the chair legs.

Isotonics

With isotonic strength training, in which you are actually lifting weights, you'll see improvement a lot faster than you will with isometrics. You'll also develop more endurance and find that recovery from muscular fatigue is faster. The weights you'll use can be anything from barbells to spring grips, cloth bags weighted with sand, coffee cans, a household bucket or an old purse with a good solid handle filled with books, cans, or pebbles.

There are also machines, such as the Marcy or Universal series, which can train the entire range of your muscles because they offer constant resistance. The problem is, though, that while the resistance is always there, it varies during your range of motion. Most people are usually stronger in their midrange than at the ends of their range of motion. This means that the weight you are lifting will feel heavier at those ends of your range than it did at midrange so that sometimes the weight may be too much while at other times, too little.

These machines have the advantage of probably requiring somewhat less supervision than do dead weights because there is less chance for you to be using a wrong and possibly harmful position. With a dead weight such as a bench press, for example, you ought to have someone show you how to sit and position your legs, how to keep your back from arching, and how to select the right amount of weight to lift. But the few disadvantages of dead weights should not make you feel you have to join an expensive club or training facility in order to use these rather elaborate machines. For while the dead weights like your sandbags and weighted buckets train your muscles only in their midrange, this is the functional range that you will be using when you actually perform a sport. If you feel you have to get exercise at the extreme ranges, when your arm is completely straight, for example, or fully bent, you can always change your position to accomplish that. And if you have an instructor or other knowledgeable person start you off by showing you the basic positions you should be using for lifting, you should have no problems with strains or pulls. Just remember to execute all these exercises slowly.

The weight you should be using when you start on the following exercises should be 5 pounds. After you find you can lift this amount easily, increase it by 2½ pounds. You can continue to increase as your strength increases but don't rush your progress. You'll find that significant strength gains take six weeks or longer.

The following exercises should be done in three sets of ten, with two to three minutes of rest in between each set.

SPECIFIC EXERCISE	AREA OF BODY WORKED	OBJECT AND PRACTICAL PURPOSE
Abduction, adduction/ internal rotation	Chest, upper arm	The object of this exercise is to strengthen the muscles of the shoulder girdle and chest.
Horizontal side and front arm lift	Shoulder, upper arm	This exercise builds up the muscles of the shoulder girdle along with those in the upper arm.
Biceps curl	Upper arm	This exercise is to strengthen the biceps, the long muscle occupying the anterior surface of your upper arm.
Dips	Upper and lower arm	The muscles of your entire arm are strengthened with this exercise.
Wrist curl	Forearm	The object of this exercise is to strengthen the extensor flexor muscles in your forearm.
Forearm rotation	Forearm	This exercise builds up the muscles that turn your hand palm up and palm down.
Sit-ups	Back	This exercise strengthens your abdominal or stomach muscles, which are essential for back strength.
Lateral leg raises	Thigh, hip, abdomen	This exercise strengthens the muscles in the outer parts of your hips, thighs, and stomach.
Active bending	Thigh	The object of this exercise is to build strength in the quadriceps, which are the muscles in the fronts of your legs around your knee.
Hamstrings	Back of thigh	This exercise strengthens the hamstrings, which are the muscles in the backs of your legs.
Ankle	Ankle, foot	This exercise is for the muscles around your ankle and foot.

Description of Isotonic Exercises

FOR THE
CHEST AND
UPPER ARM.

Abduction, adduction/internal rotation. 1. Lie on your back and hold the weight up in your arm, which is at a ninety-degree angle from your body. Holding your upper arm down with the opposite hand, bring the weight down to the floor. Reverse arms and repeat.

2. Stand, holding your elbow against the side of your waist. Your elbow should be bent at ninety degrees and your forearm out to the side as far as possible. Hold the weight in your hand and be sure to keep your upper arm against your side (you can use your other hand to hold it in place). Bring your forearm in close to your body and rotate it inward against your chest. Hold. Repeat, using the other arm, and hold.

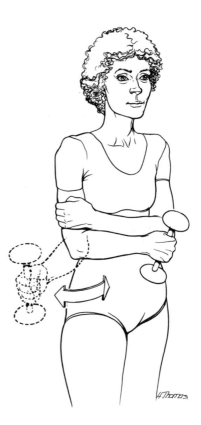

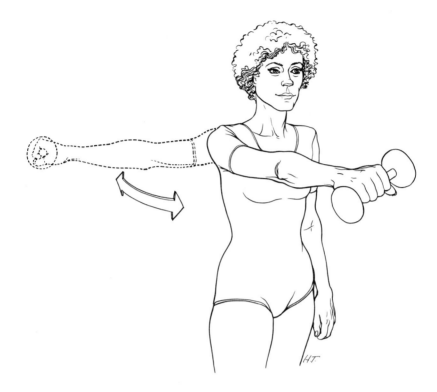

Horizontal side and front arm lift. Standing, lift your arm holding the weight straight out in front of you until it is horizontal to the floor. Hold for a count of five and lower to your side. Then lift your arm straight to the side and hold for five. Repeat, using the other arm.

Biceps curl. Standing, hold a weight in your hand in an underhand grip. The weight will start out in front of your thigh with your arm fully extended down. With your palm facing upward, raise the weight to your chest by flexing your elbow as you lift. Stand erect and keep your elbow in toward your side. Repeat with your other arm.

FOR THE
FOREARM
AND WRIST.

Dips. Stand between parallel bars or two very steady chairs or a chair back and a counter top. With your straight arms supporting you, lower your body until your elbow joints form a right

angle and then return to the straight arm position.
Try not to jerk your body or kick as you perform
this exercise.

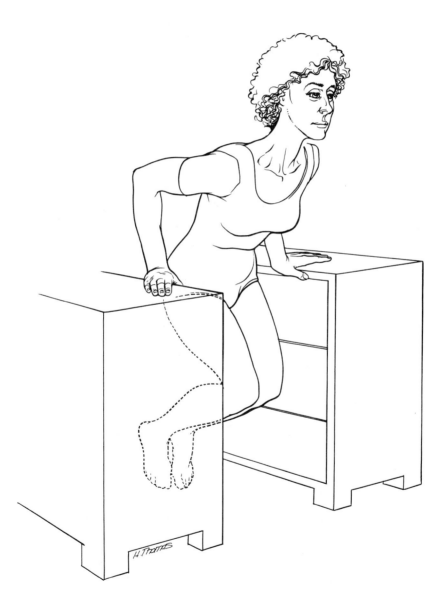

Wrist curl. Sitting, with a weight in your right hand, place your right forearm (elbow to wrist) on your right thigh so that your left hand is past your knee, palm facing down. Keeping your forearm flat against your thigh, bend your wrist up as far as you can and hold for a count of five to ten. Release slowly and repeat with the left hand. You can also repeat this exercise with your palm facing up.

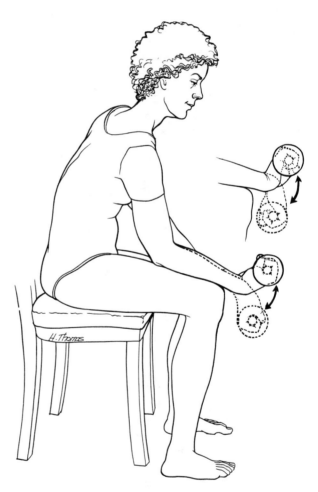

Forearm rotation. Sitting in a chair with the weight in your right hand, place your right forearm on your right thigh with your hand extending past your knee, your palm facing down. Keep your forearm flat against your knee and rotate your right hand clockwise, holding it for a count of five to ten and then counterclockwise and hold. Return your hand to its original position and again hold for a count of five to ten. Repeat, using your left hand. Be sure you keep your wrist as stiff as you can.

FOR THE BACK. *Sit-ups.* This exercise strengthens abdominal muscles, which are essential for back strength. Lie on the floor on your back with your knees bent and the fronts of your feet hooked under some heavy object like a sofa (you might be more comfortable wearing heavy socks or using some padding between the tops of your feet and the underside of the restraining object). With your arms clasped behind your head, come up slowly, putting your right elbow to your left knee. Start by rolling your shoulders off the ground and then your upper chest. Hold for a count of ten and then let yourself back down slowly. Repeat this, putting your left elbow to your right knee and hold for ten. After slowly letting yourself down, reach both elbows out to both knees, hold, and slowly lower yourself down. Perform as many as possible.

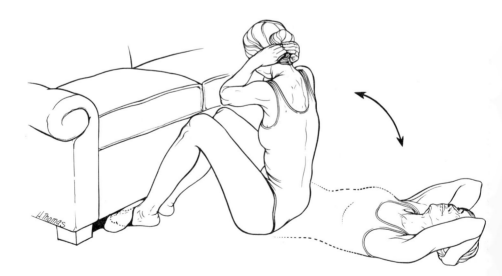

FOR THE
UPPER LEGS
AND SIDE
OF ABDOMEN

Lateral leg raises. Lying on your side with your hip absolutely straight and a weight around your ankle, lift your leg slowly about two to three feet above the other. Hold for a count of ten and slowly lower it. Repeat, using your other leg. As you improve, you can add more weights.

In performing this exercise, be certain you never allow your hips to bend forward, since with the forward bend you would be compensating with another muscle.

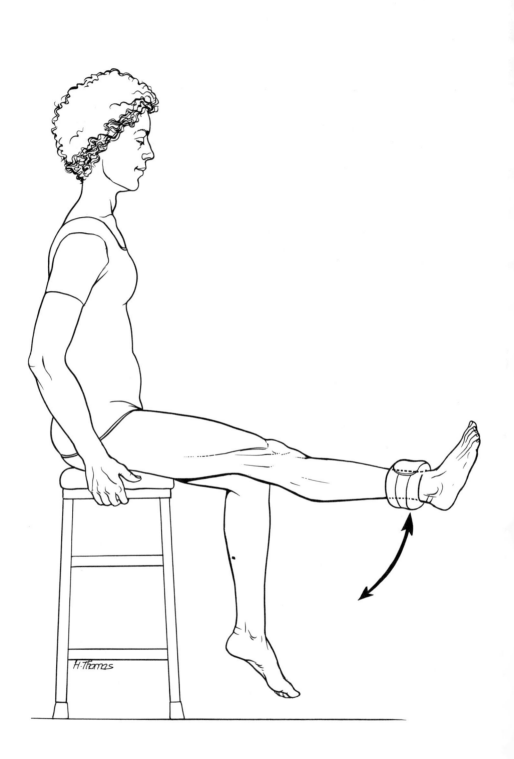

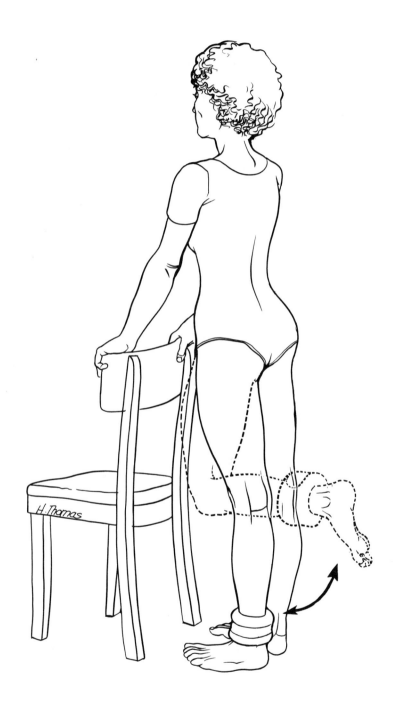

Active bending of knee (quadriceps). Sit on the edge of a desk or table with a weight on your ankle. Lift your lower leg slowly, straight out to full extension. Hold this position for a count of ten and then slowly lower your lower leg.

Hamstrings. Standing and holding on to the back of a chair for balance with a weight attached to your ankle, bend your knee and lift your lower leg back as far as possible from your body. Hold for a count of ten before lowering it to a straight position. You can also do this exercise lying on your stomach.

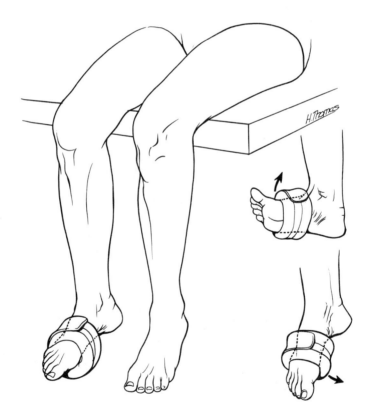

FOR THE
ANKLE.

Ankle strengthening with weights. 1. Sit on the edge of a table or desk with your lower legs hanging down. The suspended weight should be over the instep of your right foot. Make sure it is hanging perpendicular to the floor. Slowly raise and lower your foot with your ankle as the pivot point. Reverse, using the other foot.

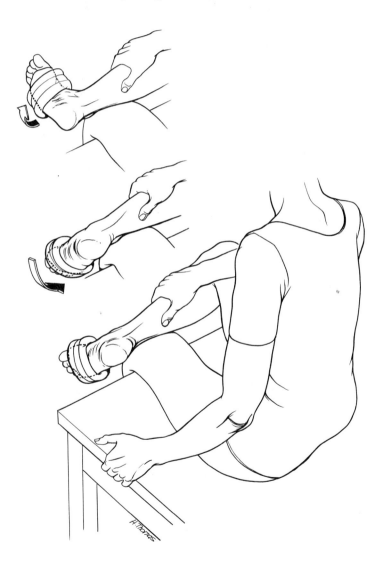

2. Sit and cross your legs with your right ankle over your left knee so that the inside of your right ankle faces upward, toward the ceiling. The weight should be slung over your right instep. Slowly lift your right foot so that your big toe goes up as high as possible and then lower it slowly down to the floor. Repeat, using the left foot.

3. Sit with your right foot over the edge of the table and turn it so that the inside of your ankle points downward to the floor and the outside upward toward the ceiling. Suspend the weight over the outside of the foot and slowly lift your weighted foot up, trying to raise your small toe up as high as possible. Then lower it slowly down to the floor. Repeat, using your left foot.

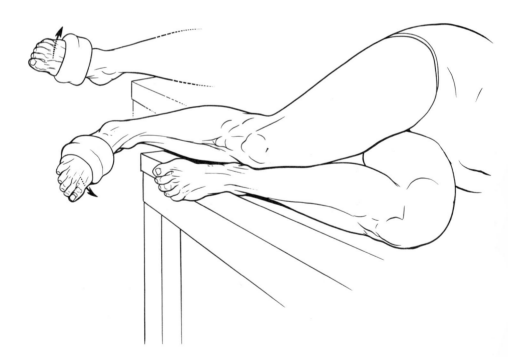

Isokinetics

Isokinetic exercises are done with special speed-controlled devices that give you maximum resistance through an entire range of motion. With the speed preset, you can never move faster, so that if you want to increase your workout, you have to push harder. The manufacturers of these machines believe that they are a more efficient way of training because when they're set at a high speed, what you do with them comes closest to your actions when performing a sport. Whether isokinetic training gives better results than isotonic training has yet to be proven. One problem we've found is that you often get a fast ballistic effect from the machine and if you have a sore joint it can be aggravated. After training with slow resistance weights, isokinetics can give an entirely new feeling and extreme fatigue. While speed is an important component to muscle training, isokinetics has not supplanted other methods of increasing strength.

Skill Training

Skill training for each of the individual sports has different components and emphases. To learn the skills properly, it's easiest to work with an instructor or coach who makes certain you are using the proper motions. Where is your weight? Is it forward, backward, or squarely over your feet? Which way is your trunk leaning? Is your wrist bent or straight? Your knees bent? When you run, is your body relaxed and are your motions fluid? If you're stiff, you can aggravate underlying conditions such as neck pain or spine problems. If you lead with your racquet when you serve a tennis ball, the force can give you painful shoulder problems, and if your wrist isn't stiff enough when you serve, you can end up with a tennis elbow. It would be impossible for us to outline the proper position for every motion in each sport. Magazines for the different sports often have excellent articles about technique along with pictures and diagrams. Working with a coach who understands the dynamics of the game is best, but it can end up being expensive. Since bad habits are hard to break, it would be a good idea to get some good instruction in the beginning if you can and then continue to educate yourself. A perceptive analysis of your game and technique can be crucial to your improvement.

The following is one example of the kind of skill training that can have dramatic effect on your progress in tennis. (This and other drills will be described in a book on tennis training by Rick Elstein and Gary Barrett.)

GOALIE DRILL. Stand behind the net. Your instructor will hit tennis balls right at you at thirty miles per hour. At first the balls will bounce right off your body but after a while, as you keep concentrating on the ball while it's being hit, you'll find you can get your racquet on it—at least enough to protect yourself from the ball. When you can return the balls, your instructor will then hit them to you even faster, constantly challenging you until you can get your racquet on these faster balls as well. No matter how slow you were when you started out, you'll find yourself improving.

Training with a Problem

Not only is it possible for you to train with almost all physical problems, but the right kind of training with the proper modifications can help improve your condition significantly. We've seen patients who had been treated years before for an injury and were told to keep away from strenuous activities or exercise. It's unfortunate for them to have missed out on activities they could have enjoyed as well as benefited by. We've also seen example after example of professional athletes exercising and successfully compensating for injury. There's no reason why everyone can't take advantage of these benefits of training.

Here is a list of some of the problems you may have along with a prescription for the kind of training that will help.

FOR THE NECK. A common complaint is stiffness of the neck with a sore ache felt most often in the morning. The neck-stretching exercises will help, as will the four-way neck isometric exercise, standing upright and then bending laterally from the waist first to the left, then the right, then forward and finally backward. Hold each time until fatigued, that is, as long as you can. A four-way Nautilus machine will also help.

FOR THE
SHOULDER.

Tendinitis is characterized by pain on the top of your shoulder when you try to bring your arm up. You'll feel this when you try to throw a ball or serve at tennis. Hold a light weight—two to three pounds—and extend your arm to the side no higher than horizontal. Lower and raise it again slowly, repeating this until fatigued. Then extend to the front and lower, again repeating until fatigued. Then extend your arm to the front and lower it, repeating until fatigued. Finally, lie down on your back and lift the weight over your chest and then lower it, repeating until fatigued. Do three sets of this.

FOR THE
ELBOW.

Tennis elbow is one of the most common problems afflicting golfers and tennis players. In the average recreational player the pain is on the outside of the elbow while with quality professionals the pain is on the inside. One of the best exercises you can do for the recreational player's tennis elbow is to train your forearm muscles with wrist extensions, going through three sets, each to fatigue, with a two- to three-minute rest between each set. For the professional player, whose pain is often on the inside of the elbow, wrist curls with the palm turned up will help, again three sets, each done to fatigue. This stiffens the wrist. Elbow and shoulder exercises also help, as will technical changes in your game.

FOR THE BACK.

While backaches are somewhat more prevalent in people over thirty, they are common problems in all age groups. You should be cautioned to avoid lifting heavy objects if you can't do this without arching your back. You should also avoid some yoga positions, swimming movements that extend your back, such as the Australian crawl, and doing chest lifts from the floor. You can lift weights if you're in a sitting position, are careful to flatten your spine, and use light enough weights so you don't have to strain. You should also do flexibility exercises to stretch your back along with strengthening exercises to help your abdominal muscles so that pressure can be taken off your spine. See pages 136, 167, and 184. Avoid back extension exercises.

FOR THE KNEES. The most common problem for the knees, especially for women, is sore kneecaps. The most effective training we've found for 85 to 90 percent of those with sore kneecaps is light strengthening exercises with the knees bent from ninety degrees to just short of full extension. See page 168. The exercises that strengthen your thighs will also help. One common injury for tennis players and skiers—and especially for women in these sports—occurs when the anterior cruciate ligament, the ligament that keeps your knee from slipping when your weight is on it, gives way. Athletes with this problem have learned to balance their weight equally on both legs and keep their knees slightly bent. The tennis player must learn to take smaller steps and the skier must try to edge less, going over ice and granular snow with ski bottoms flat. You should carve your skis, that is, set the edge and let the skis do the turning. But the real difference comes with training the quadriceps and hamstring muscles. We've seen some athletes who have trained these muscles build up more strength on the injured side than on the uninjured one.

Other knee conditions can be helped by a knee-strengthening program of active bending and hamstring exercises.

FOR THE CALF. Tight calves, as we've mentioned, are a typical problem among women, who tend to run on their toes. Calf- and heel cord-strengthening exercises (see page 172) will help, as will learning to run with a toe-heel gait.

194

TEMPORARY REDUCTION OF TRAINING

There are going to be times when it isn't the best idea to exercise—at least at a particular hour or on a particular day or until you've recovered from a particular problem. There are also warning signals you should be aware of that point to the need to reduce your activity. The following lists will outline what to look for:

Reasons for Temporarily Reducing or Deferring Physical Activity
    Illness, fever, injury, stomach pains
    Progression of cardiac disease
    Orthopedic problem—fluid on a joint, stiffness after exercise, or acute sharp soreness
    Emotional turmoil
    Severe sunburn
    Alcoholic hangover (although moderate exercise may help mobilize the alcohol and may also have a beneficial psychological effect)
    Cerebral dysfunction—dizziness, vertigo, etc.
    Dehydration—heat stroke on hot and humid days
    Environmental factors—weather (excessive heat or cold, humidity or wind), air pollution (smog, carbon monoxide)
    Overindulgence: large heavy meal within 2 hours, coffee, tea, soda (xanthines and other stimulating beverages)
    Drugs—decongestants, bronchiodilators, estrogen, appetite suppressants (anoretics)

Indications for Discontinuing Exercise Training Program
    Orthopedic problems aggravated by activity
    Progression of cardiac illness unresponsive to medical therapy
    Development of new systemic disease aggravated by exercise
    Major surgery
    Psychiatric complications aggravated by activity
    Acute alcoholism

Symptoms and Signs of Excessive Effort
    (These are indications for reduction of exercise intensity in subsequent sessions.)

During exercise and immediately thereafter:
  Anginal discomfort
  Ataxis (light-headedness, confusion)
  Nausea, vomiting
  Leg claudication (limping), stabbing pain in the calves
  Pallor (paleness) or cyanosis (bluish or purplish discoloration
    of the skin due to deficient oxygenation of the blood)
  Breathing trouble
  Inappropriate slow heart rate
Delayed:
  Prolonged fatigue
  Insomnia
  Weight gain due to fluid retention—salt and water
  Excess ADH (antidiuretic hormone) which can lead to heart
    failure
  Persistent fast heart rate

TRAINING YOU SHOULD *NOT* BE DOING

There are certain exercises that keep getting recommended in books and magazines that can be damaging to your body. Straight-leg sit-ups, for example, can stretch the nerves in your back and spine, and full squats can loosen the ligaments in your knees and tear cartilage. Any exercise that causes you to arch your back forward (a backward "C" shape with your stomach thrust forward) can cause lordosis, an anterior curvature of the spine.

Other exercises you should avoid depend on your present condition. If you have trouble with your shoulders you shouldn't do push-ups. The most common cause of shoulder problems is impingements, in which the tendons get jammed under the bony roof of the shoulder, and push-ups will aggravate the condition. If you have back problems, avoid extending your back with the Australian crawl or butterfly swim stroke, which can pinch your nerves and spinal bones together.

Some of the exercises we *don't* recommend are:

Hip extensions, in which you lie on your stomach and raise your

196

thighs. The exercise value is small while the chance of back injury is great because your back has to arch in order to elevate your legs.

Upper back lifts, in which you lie on your stomach and raise your head and shoulders up, curving your spine back. This can lead to lordosis by putting you in exactly the position you should avoid.

Chair dips (full squats), where you sit on the edge of a chair and, supporting yourself with your arms, lower yourself to the floor. This ends up putting you in a full squat position and so can loosen your knee ligaments.

Hip rotations, where you lie on the floor and move your legs from side to side, are exercises which, while not harmful, are pretty much a waste of time. Instead, you ought to be doing exercises that really work your major muscles.

A few last cautions for you to remember as you train: Don't ever attempt an exercise that's supposed to strengthen your back. You want to stretch your back and keep it as flexible as possible. You should be strengthening your abdominal muscles instead, since they can do the work of supporting your back.

Stay away from exercises that are overly complicated. There's going to be too much room for mistakes and too little chance you'll be tempted to repeat them the necessary number of times. And whatever exercising you do, try to avoid a jerky rhythm, which can cause you pulls and pinches. A slow, relaxed, and fluid motion is what you need for steady improvement.

RETURN TO SPORTS

After any significant illness or injury, you should be checked out by your doctor or some other qualified person before resuming training. A static examination in an office is insufficient, and we advise a qualifying test on a field where you can be observed in motion. The following functional maneuvers should be ones you can comfortably do. If you can accomplish these, then you're ready to begin participating again.

Functional Tests

Running in place

Hopping on one leg

Acceleration—start at zero, run quickly to get your speed up to a half to three quarters of your maximum velocity

Running, making wide figure eights to both the left and right

Running backward

Running straight ahead and then cutting on a ninety-degree angle to the left or right (you should be able to turn comfortably)

Half or full squat (this position is not a good one in repetitive exercises because it strains the cartilage in your knee, but done infrequently, it's an excellent way to test your kneecap)

8

Sports
and Psychology

It's usually easy to see how sports affect us physically. We can watch our endurance improve, our strength increase, and our balance and coordination develop. Participation in sports affects us emotionally, too, and it does so in some ways that are not so immediately evident. It's not only that physical activity can inspire certain feelings—sometimes elation, sometimes frustration and anger after a competitive game, or a sense of well-being if we've played well or of inadequacy if we haven't. Sports can also give us a chance to find out more about ourselves, to develop the strategies we need for our emotional growth.

The emotional significance of sports is one of the areas being considered by the relatively new field of sports psychology. The emphasis in sports psychology ranges from helping the competitive athlete achieve the best possible performance to using exercise itself as a form of therapy. Even among those doctors who do not consider themselves sports psychologists, there is a recognition that important insights can come from studying the behavior patterns of patients as they are manifested in physical activity.

Sports as therapy seems to work, although psychiatrists and psychologists find it difficult to say exactly how. Some patients with unrealistically low senses of their own worth have been able to overcome their feelings of inferiority by perfecting athletic performance. Others, doggedly pursuing some physical activity with compulsive intensity, have come to realize through therapy that they are acting out a fantasy, replaying a rivalry with a brother or sister, or trying to convince a parent of their worth.

If you are in therapy, your involvement in physical activity can be used to give you a more complete picture of yourself. What happens is that sports often highlight different aspects of you, putting you in touch with parts of yourself that you may never have confronted or perhaps you never even knew existed. The resulting self-knowledge can be an important psychological benefit. Dr. Marlin M. Mackenzie, a psychologist at Columbia University, has found another contribution that sports can make to therapy. When his patients come to him directly from strenuous activity, for example, even jogging right into his office, their feelings of well-being frequently make them more willing to communicate during the session that follows than when they attend sessions without some form of prior exercise. Dr. Mackenzie finds that these sessions usually end up being far more valuable than they otherwise would have been.

Dr. Michael Sacks, an athlete and psychiatrist, sees sports as an extremely creative activity, allowing you to get away from the real world and the burdens of everyday living. For a while at least, the strains of reality can be suspended in a fantasy game where you not only come into contact with new sides of yourself but can gratify some long-frustrated desires. For example, you might not feel comfortable in a tank top and scanty shorts in front of three million people—unless, of course, you were in a marathon, at which point your childhood desire for exhibitionism can be gratified. Dr. Sacks believes that such fantasies and gratifications can serve to energize you, letting you return to reality feeling renewed.

For a woman this aspect of sports can have particular value. It is here in the make-believe world of the playing field that a woman can learn about aspects of herself that may have been hidden in her everyday life. How is she as a competitor? How much aggression does she have and how capable is she of dealing with the aggressiveness of others? Up until recently women have seen themselves as having to act very differently from men. Those qualities tradition would have women embrace—passivity and dependency—are the very ones that would stand in a woman's way as a successful athlete (and of course, as a successful businesswoman as well). An ensuing conflict arises between what a woman should be and what it takes for her to win or even to compete at all.

Sportswomen have felt the effects of this conflict to varying degrees, and psychologists have written about it. Psychologist Renee McCormick, herself an enthusiastic athlete, told us she saw sports as a way of diluting the differentiation between the sexes, making it easier for men and women to relate to one another. Other psychologists have talked about sports as an area that allows for androgyny, a state that is neither totally male or female but a combination of the traits of both sexes. Dr. Samuel Perry, a psychoanalyst who has played many sports, believes that women athletes often feel they have entered a man's world when they participate competitively. They associate the aggressive strivings with masculinity as opposed to the more passive and retiring feminine qualities. Dr. Perry emphasizes that women athletes certainly can be quite feminine on and off the field, but in their own minds when they are "killing off" their opponents they feel like "one of the boys." Many women, he points out, may fail to realize their athletic potential because they are uncomfortable with this association with a masculine activity. As more women become successful in sports and publicity makes them accessible as models of identification, the young girl may not have to contend as much with this male-female split.

Sports can end up giving women what it has always given men. For example, it's been pointed out that men learn early on what it means to be against someone on a court or field and then accept the same person as a friend when the game ends. This kind of friendly competition is an essential component of professional life, and so the working woman who has never learned to be comfortable dealing with opponents and who now is at an initial disadvantage can get special benefit from such participation.

The defined rules, the time and space restraints, and the referees to enforce them can make sports an arena in which people can comfortably cope as opposed to the unpredictable real world. And while the sports world can offer a refreshing freedom from anxiety for everyone, for a woman the finite nature of a game offers her something more because it fills an important need. Until fairly recently most women have functioned in a world that presented them little in the way of defined goals. The woman who has found herself in an amorphous world of home and family can gain a more cohesive picture of herself and her accomplishments by participating in sports, measuring herself within the clear demarcations of the physical activity.

Even more basic than showing you what you can do, sports can help you get to know yourself better. Psychologists talk about sports as a way of learning about body boundaries, those perimeters that define you as a complete entity. Women in particular, it has been felt, often lose their own identities as they blend into those around them—their husbands, children, or parents. As they become more physically active, women can become more conscious of themselves as separate, occupying a space in life that is set apart from the space of others.

With its emphasis on the body and on action, sports can be an important factor as well in helping increase a healthy belief in one's own autonomy. Almost all athletes develop an attitude of respect toward their bodies, seeing them as the instruments allowing these athletes to succeed and giving them a sense of control over themselves.

The psychological aids that sports offer are just beginning to be explored as physical activity becomes more and more popular. At the same time, though, some negative effects of sports participation have become apparent. People can use sports as a crutch or security blanket so that it ends up impeding their adaptation to the real world. Their involvement in sports can be so all-consuming that they feel inadequate and withdrawn when for some reason they cannot participate in physical activity.

The sports addict, the compulsive athlete whose whole life revolves around a sport, can be as dependent on a single form of gratification as an alcoholic is. Interestingly, some of the sports addicts have previously been alcoholics. One patient, a woman in her forties who had been an alcoholic for years, gave up drinking and began to run. Unfortunately her running took over her life, just as her alcohol had: all her friends were runners where as formerly she had chosen drinkers; she ate a special runner's diet, went to lectures for runners, and worried about her weight and running time incessantly. What was most striking was that when she didn't run, she felt terrible and had difficulty functioning at all.

There is a tendency to believe that nonchemical addictions such as work or play are better than the chemical addictions such as alcohol. Dr. Sacks, however, thinks it would be difficult to defend such a stand. In any case of addiction, there is a lack of freedom to decide what one can do in life. Accompanying this is often a difficulty in forming healthy relationships. The therapist has to ask: who is more free? who has closer relationships? Another question comes up: is running the physically healthier addiction? Again Dr. Sacks points out that the answer isn't as simple as it might first seem. Runners who are addicts get started in the sport with such intensity that they often develop crippling injuries. Continuing to run despite the discomfort, these people can end up with chronic pain from tendinitis or knee problems, which can cause long-term effects. Clearly, sports for such people can be a very destructive activity.

While a specific type of personality becomes a sports addict, most psychologists and psychiatrists agree that there is no one kind of person who becomes an athlete. Most often your interest in sports is a result of having been encouraged as a child by teachers, parents, coaches, and friends. Many of the women athletes we've talked to say that their first interest in sports was inspired by a parent, often a father, who offered enthusiastic support. On the other hand, there are some children who may be either extremely frail or perhaps obese who have been programmed by others to avoid taking up sports. These children have a sense of not being physically capable, of being clumsy or weak. It is, of course, unfortunate for these children to remain sedentary since physical activity would be particularly good for most of them.

Others might be held back by some personality problem such as a phobia or other neurotic tendency that might make sports frightening or participation with others impossible. These, however, are the extremes. For most people being an athlete of some sort is certainly well within the realm of possibility.

Which type of person is attracted to which sport? It's impossible to generalize about who becomes a swimmer, for example, and who a skier—that is, outside of the economic, geographic, or other unavoidable practical factors. Certainly the nature of particular sports makes them more appealing to some kinds of people. One woman who had been an excellent basketball and field hockey player tried to take up golf and found herself frustrated. She couldn't tolerate having no opponent, and she found the situation of playing against herself instead of against a team hard to take. Some of the long-distance runners we've talked to have stressed the appeal of the individualistic aspects of their sport, the freedom they've felt in having no one to interact with or to have to depend upon. One runner told us that while she had constantly found herself growing furious in playing tennis, in running her anger subsided and her performance improved. But again, within any of these sports, different types of people have been among the most successful.

One important focus of sports psychology has been the international celebrity, the elite athlete. It's been thought that the study of such men and women, those who are the very best in their field, may not only yield information useful to them as competitors but also offer valuable insights to ordinary recreational athletes.

Is there a particular kind of person who ends up becoming an elite athlete? Doctors don't believe there is one special type who becomes an Olympic gold medalist or breaks a world's record. In the tennis world Billie Jean King and Chris Evert Lloyd are clearly very different kinds of women with contrasting temperaments. Some psychological tests have indicated that most elite athletes have one trait in common—that is, stability. It makes sense when you realize that to reach high levels of performance an athlete must practice long and hard. Although there have been some striking if rare exceptions to this, someone who is unstable is unlikely to have trained well enough to reach the highest levels. In competition, too, the elite athlete, if she feels anxiety, must have the stability to be able to deal with it. She will have to be emotionally flexible enough to go along with the variables—the weather, the court or field, her opponent, the people nearby—if she wants to win her match.

If excellent athletes often have the one common trait of being stable, they've also been found in some perceptual tests to have a greater tolerance for pain. Athletes have reported situations where they felt tremendous amounts of discomfort and then, forcing themselves to continue, were able at first to ignore and later simply not to feel the pain. Certainly this has to be true of such athletes as ultramarathoners who run hundred-mile races or swimmers such as Diana Nyad who spend days navigating mountainous waves.

A crucial talent that elite athletes share is intense concentration. Billie Jean King explains that when she plays, she almost forgets the score as she tries to fix her total concentration on the point that has to be played. Sports psychologist Marlin Mackenzie has discovered that the superb athlete has riveted attention, screening out all irrelevant clues and paying attention only to what is important to the game. He describes such athletes as letting their unconscious minds take over, going into an altered state of consciousness where all superfluous outside stimuli cannot intrude. While they themselves may be unaware that this is happening, these athletes develop a tunnel vision, almost like going into deep hypnosis.

Dr. Mackenzie has been studying athletes, observing and recording the internal steps they go through as they reenact their performances. What he is looking for are the internal strategies and patterns that seem to come naturally if unconsciously to superb athletes. These steps, once observed and recorded, can then be taught to other athletes. Assuming that two groups of performers are equally motivated and have similar physiological capacities, Dr. Mackenzie believes that what separates the champions from the less successful is these inner strategies, which are related to motivation, decision making, and task performance.

The elite athlete, as we've all seen, isn't always able to execute the correct strategies and patterns and can go through emotionally painful slumps in performance. If her physical capacities have not declined because of illness or injury, it can become the challenge of the sports psychologist to see just what factors are sabotaging her performance. Fear of success is not an uncommon reason, one which many psychiatrists have noted is especially true of women who are just beginning to enter areas calling for intense competition. The enormous and often unsettling change in life-style that happens to the victor of a major sports event is also a frequent factor. One role of the sports psychologist is to work closely with the athlete, exploring the reasons for her blocks and slumps, which unfortunately exacerbate themselves—anxiety over doing badly leading to more anxiety, fear to more fear, tension to more tension—and helping her to be able to repeat her previous excellent performances.

Another major area of concentration for sports psychologists is the area of sports injury. Clinical psychologist Lawrence Jennings has been working on a study that tries to establish which people are psychologically predisposed to injury. He points out that it is often evident to coaches, trainers, psychologists, and other athletes that certain players at specific times tend to be susceptible to injury. What he is trying to do in his study and what other sports psychologists are also attempting is to pinpoint the many variables that lead to injuries. Problems can arise from becoming anxious in the stress of preparing for competition, and athletes who tense their muscles during repeated practice can end up with painful tendinitis. Sudden fear at executing a dive off a board or a jump from parallel bars can distract an athlete, interfere with her timing, and lead to a fracture.

Dr. Mackenzie believes that many sports accidents are not accidents at all, but situations subconsciously constructed by the athletes. It may be that some anxiety-provoking situation in the athlete's everyday life is intruding. To avoid it, she will suffer an injury, distracting her own attention away from what is producing the anxiety and becoming wrapped up in the sympathetic care and attention from doctors, nurses, family, and friends.

Which athletes will react this way and under what circumstances is something coaches and psychologists together are trying to find out. At the present time, Dr. Mackenzie points out, there isn't enough evidence to make the flat statement that sports injuries can be predicted. Still, he has found enough anecdotal evidence connecting such states of mind as anxiety or depression with injury to convince him that if enough information was available to psychologists, many sports injuries could be avoided.

While anxiety and depression are seen as causing injury in sports, they are often the very states of mind that are relieved by participation in sports. For many of us, vigorous workouts are effective ways of dissipating our tensions while an exciting game can raise our spirits. And our altered psychological state can be seen as clear evidence that sports can play a significant and positive role in our emotional lives.

9

Emergency Sports Medicine

Although being physically fit will certainly lower your chances of being injured in sports, let's face it—there just isn't any way to rule out every risk of having something go wrong. What's important is to recognize what the injury is, know what immediate action you should take, and, often most important, be aware of just which actions you should *not* take. Some injuries are painful but basically minor, while others that give only slight discomfort can be more serious. In all of the instances below, whether they occur to you or to a companion, a sensible response based on valid information can, if not restore you to total fitness, at least alleviate your discomfort or reduce serious risk.

MUSCULOSKELETAL INJURIES

Some conditions, such as severe palpitations of the heart or rapid excessive breathing, which might indicate an accumulation of fluid in your lungs, are true emergencies that require prompt medical attention. On the other hand, most orthopedic problems, except for open fractures or dislocations with artery or nerve involvement, can wait. What is important is to get an early assessment of what the injury actually is. Then, if you follow the RICE treatment—Rest, Ice, Compression, Elevation—you can wait for two to three days before definitive treatment. We suggest to athletes on tour that they make sure they are able to get to experienced medical personnel and to be treated under proper conditions, even if it means traveling some distance. Have an initial evaluation but then don't feel you always have to rush into surgery or a cast. Sort out the facts, make sure you understand the options, and then arrange to be taken to a place that has the facilities and expertise to give you optimal care.

Here are descriptions of the possible injuries to the musculoskeletal system, beginning with the least serious. Learn to recognize them so that you can proceed with the proper emergency treatment.

CONTUSION (BRUISE). A contusion is caused by a blow and is an extremely common minor injury for athletes. You will feel pain and a localized tenderness and may even be unable to use the area of your body involved. You may also have some kind of discoloration, often becoming black and blue.

TREATMENT: 1. Rest, stop exercising.

2. Apply Ice to the area for at least forty-eight hours, each session not lasting more than twenty to thirty minutes with about two hours between sessions. Icing allows for constriction of the blood vessels around the injured area so healing can take place. Be sure the ice is not applied directly to your skin but is wrapped in a towel or bandage.

3. Apply a Compression bandage to the area. This should supply gentle compressive force over the injury to control swelling. However, make sure the bandage isn't so tight as to interfere with your circulation and cause swelling below the injured area.

4. Make sure you have Elevated the affected area above the level of your heart.

This is what we call the RICE treatment. Sometime within the next week your contusion should respond to this treatment, but if it doesn't, that is, if the pain and swelling persist, stop the treatment and see your doctor.

Note: CAUTION, never use heat for a contusion.

MUSCLE INJURIES. These are injuries of the unit of muscles and tendons connecting bone to bone. This unit is elastic and so can contract and expand.

• Strains: A strain, often caused by an unexpected movement, such as slipping, or an abnormal muscle contraction, is an overstretching of a muscle, tendon, or group of muscles.

First-degree strain: You will feel a localized weakness and tenderness as well as spasm (a sudden involuntary contraction of your muscle).

Second-degree strain: Symptoms are more severe, with a loss of motion (you won't be able to use the area involved), swelling, and possible discoloration along with spasm and local tenderness.

Third-degree strain: Symptoms include severe spasm, a loss of motion, point tenderness, swelling, discoloration; and you will be able to feel actual muscle separation.

Note: Degree of pain is not necessarily an indication of severity.

TREATMENT: For all degrees of strain use the RICE treatment prescribed for contusions. Second- and third-degree strains should be seen by your doctor.

RETURN TO PLAY: It is essential that you restore your muscles to their previous level through strength training before you resume your sport. Weaker muscles are susceptible to reinjury. In addition, make sure that you allow for extra warm-ups and more time for stretching.

• Muscle cramps: These are severe and painful uncontrollable contractions of any muscle. The following are the most common causes:

1. Lack of electrolytes (salts) from excessive perspiration or a poor diet.

2. Overfatigue.

3. Sudden changes in temperature.

4. A sudden blow to your muscle.

5. A local impairment of your circulation, sometimes caused by tight clothing.

6. Overstretching your muscle (or a strain, discussed above).

7. Forcing your muscle to do an unaccustomed action (which may also involve a strain).

TREATMENT: Loosen any restrictive clothing or tape in the area of the cramp.

Administer fluid, especially an electrolyte drink, if you suspect the cause to be lack of fluid.

Massage the area to restore circulation.

Note: CAUTION, do *not* massage if the cramp is caused by a direct blow or by overstretching.

RETURN TO PLAY: If no other injury is present, you can resume playing as soon as the cramping stops.

• Hernia: This is an outward protrusion of normal tissue from its natural position. You will be able to see your muscle bulge and then the bulge disappearing when your muscle is contracted. There is likely to be local discomfort and possibly some swelling.

A hernia can be caused by strain, uncontrolled torsion (twisting), or weakness in the tissue that covers a muscle. Inadequate conditioning can also be responsible.

TREATMENT: Hernia requires your doctor's attention

LIGAMENT INJURIES. Ligaments attach bone to bone. When your joint is sprained, that is, forced beyond its normal range of motion, the ligament is injured. In general, you may feel a crunching or tearing sensation, although there are different characteristics for the three degrees of severity. Keep in mind that the amount of swelling does not necessarily indicate the severity of your injury.

• First-degree sprain: You will feel a sudden pain in your joint and then suffer some mild disability with some amount of weakness, point tenderness, and possible swelling.

• Second-degree sprain: You will feel a sudden and prolonged

211

pain in your joint with point tenderness, swelling, weakness, and some bleeding (hemorrhage) within the joint, which shows up in black and blue discoloration.

• Third-degree sprain: This involves sudden, severe, and constant pain, loss of motion, tenderness, swelling, and hemorrhage.

TREATMENT: Use the RICE treatment, utilizing crutches if necessary. In cases of second- or third-degree sprain, see your physician.

Here are some additional observations about two of the most common injuries for athletes, ankle and knee sprains.

• Ankle: Before you return to play after a sprained ankle, make certain you can walk normally, have normal range of motion, and have equal strength in both ankles. Take the following three tests to be sure you are sufficiently recovered so you won't reinjure yourself. Make sure you can run

1. first accelerating to a maximum speed and then stopping as quickly as possible and, if so,

2. then side to side, using sidesteps, and if so,

3. finally, in a course forming figure eights, making wide figures and then tighter ones in both directions.

• Knee: What you remember about your knee injury can be of considerable help to your doctor. If you hear a pop, click, snap, or some other noise, you should see an orthopedist as soon as possible. If there is swelling or your knee seems locked in position, you also need medical attention. Besides any sounds you may have heard, try to recall if your knee just seemed to give way, whether it was bent or straight at the time of injury, and what it looked like right after the injury. All this information can furnish important clues for your doctor to use when he makes his diagnosis.

Here are five functional tests you should pass after a sprained knee to make sure you're ready to go back to sports:

1. Run in place for thirty seconds, lifting your knees as high as possible. Ask someone to check you for symmetry of running pattern.

2. Jump as high as you can on your uninjured leg and then on your injured one. If you are recovered, there should be virtually no difference in sensation.

3. Do a full squat and then a duck walk.

4. Run figure eights first wide and then tighter in both directions.

5. Run backward.

FRACTURE. These are breaks in the continuity of the bones. Although there are a great many degrees and types of fractures, they can roughly be placed into two categories:

• Simple or closed fractures: involve a break in a bone without external exposure.

• Compound or open fractures: involve a break in the bone that extends through the outer skin layers, exposing the bone.

Fractures occur when there are stresses that force a bone through an abnormal range of motion, when a direct blow is inflicted on an unprotected bony protuberance, or when prolonged and constant stress is placed on a bone and its surrounding structures.

How can you tell if you have a fracture? You'll feel point tenderness and significant pain, and you may hear a grating sound at the fracture site. You may see swelling, possible discoloration, and when you compare one side to the other, you may see a certain amount of deformity. Of course, with any significant injury, it is essential to have X rays.

Emergency first aid for suspected fractures includes covering all wounds, splinting the fracture where it lies, and then carefully transporting the patient to a hospital for X rays and further treatment.

NOTES ON SPLINTING FRACTURES:

1. Cut away or remove clothing from any suspected fracture.

2. *Before* moving or transporting the patient, *splint first,* improvising if necessary, using smooth pieces of wood or heavy cardboard from cartons.

3. The splint should immobilize the joint or bone both above and below the site of the injury, so make sure it is long enough and sufficiently rigid.

Note: CAUTION, make sure there is always good circulation below the fracture. Loss of circulation for any significant length of time can cause severe damage.

213

DISLOCATIONS/SUBLUXATIONS. In a dislocation, damage to the joint and ligaments allows one or more bones of the joint to be displaced. A subluxation is a partial dislocation. Both of these can be caused by a twisting force applied to a bone that is near a joint, some force that moves the joint past its normal range of motion, or a direct blow to an exposed joint, such as a finger. With both dislocation and subluxation, there is a loss of function so that you are unable to use the limb, point tenderness, and in many cases extreme pain as well.

TREATMENT: Treat as you would a fracture, that is, immobilize the area with a sling or splint and get to a doctor.

Note: CAUTION, do *not* attempt to move the joint into place.

BLEEDING AND WOUNDS

Bleeding (hemorrhaging) is the escape of blood from arteries and veins. It can be external or internal, and enough bleeding will cause shock or even death.

EXTERNAL BLEEDING. This category includes abrasions, lacerations, incisions, punctures, and avulsions (forcible tears).
• Abrasion: This is a loss of the first layer of skin due to scraping of the skin or some other kind of localized friction. You will feel local pain, stiffness, and tenderness, and you'll notice some redness and loss of skin. An abrasion or mild abscess, properly protected, needn't keep you from sports participation.

TREATMENT: Wipe the wound with a sterile bandage, hold it under warm running water, then wash with a sterile gauze pad using hot, soapy water. Apply an antiseptic and sterile bandage, and make sure you change the dressing daily.
• Laceration: This is a cut or gash that leaves a jagged edge and will give you considerable amounts of pain, bleeding, and tenderness.

TREATMENT: *Immediately* get to a doctor. Don't attempt to wash the wound, although you may apply an antiseptic and sterile bandage.
• Incision: This is a clean slice where the bleeding can be rapid and heavy.

TREATMENT: Wipe the wound with a sterile bandage, apply pressure to stop the bleeding if necessary, and then apply an antiseptic and sterile bandage.
• Puncture: This is a narrow, deep entry of the skin that can result in infection. Local pain, bleeding (which may be internal), tenderness, and even shock can be among the symptoms.

TREATMENT: Get to a doctor as soon as possible. Allow the wound to bleed freely and do *not* wash it. You can apply an antiseptic and a sterile bandage.
• Avulsion: This is a forcible tear that may result in a separated body part.

TREATMENT: Get the victim to the hospital immediately (make sure to take any severed part along as well, putting it in a towel and packing it with ice).

Try to control the bleeding, either by applying pressure to the wound or by tying a tourniquet, made from a bandage or strip of fabric, near the wound to stop the flow of blood.

INTERNAL BLEEDING. This can be caused by stomach ulcers, bleeding from closed fractures, a lacerated internal organ such as a liver or spleen, or a rupture of blood vessels. Internal bleeding, although often not visible, can be extremely serious. Bleeding that you can see, that which comes from the mouth, ears, rectum, or is in the urine, can indicate serious internal injuries.

Symptoms of internal bleeding can include:

Abdominal pain and/or extreme swelling
Nausea and/or vomiting
Possible extreme thirst
Dizziness or light-headedness
Possible coughing up of bright red blood
Shock (see symptoms of shock below)

TREATMENT: If the injury is in an extremity, apply a pressure bandage and splint. If not, make sure the victim lies down on her side with her clothing loosened. If it is available, she should be given oxygen while an ambulance is called.

Note: CAUTION, give the victim nothing by mouth.

215

SHOCK

Shock is the collapse of the vital functions that often accompanies or follows many injuries. It is a complex entity, caused by some of the following factors:

Heavy bleeding from internal or external injuries (e.g., rupture of liver, fractures, or lacerations)
Puncture of the lung (often by a broken rib)
Injury to a sensitive area
Fractures
Spinal cord damage
Fluid loss

A person in shock has one or more of the following symptoms:

A weak and rapid pulse
Cold and clammy skin
Profuse sweating
A pale or blue (cyanotic) face
Shallow, labored, rapid, or possibly irregular respiration
Dilated pupils
Extreme thirst
Nausea and/or vomiting
Faintness (or total collapse)
Extreme drowsiness

TREATMENT: The first thing to do for an athlete in shock is to try to order an ambulance and get medical attention. Then attempt to secure and maintain a clear airway for her, giving her oxygen if you have it available. Keep the athlete on her back and transport her on a stretcher, controlling any bleeding with gentle but firm compressions. Splint any fractures, trying not to move the athlete unnecessarily. Try to elevate the lower extremities unless the injury is there. If the injury is to the head, or if the athlete has difficulty breathing, elevate the shoulders instead of the legs.

Prevent the loss of body heat by putting blankets around the

216

athlete and record her initial pulse, blood pressure if you can, other vital signs, and keep a record of this for each five-minute interval until she's admitted to a hospital.

Note: CAUTION, do not give the victim any liquids.

HEAT PROBLEMS

Everyone should be aware of the dangers of heat illness since it can be a life-threatening situation that in almost all cases is avoidable. When you exercise in warm weather, your body is going to need more water and salt to function normally. Be sure there is an adequate supply of water nearby so that you can replace your body's water supply. Your clothing should be loose to allow heat to escape and permeable to moisture to allow heat loss through sweat evaporation. White clothing is especially good because it reflects the heat. Gradually increase your workouts as you become more and more accustomed to the heat.

• Heat cramps: These can occur after strenuous exercise if there is a low concentration of salt in your body or if you have lost too much fluid. Even while exercising or shortly after your exercise has been concluded, you may find you have muscle spasms, muscle twitch, fatigue, reduced alertness, perhaps some heavy sweating, and cold, clammy skin.

TREATMENT: Rest in a shaded area, drinking plenty of cold water. Taking salt is necessary only if you've lost more than four quarts of sweat (represented by eight pounds of body weight), and even then, drink lightly salted liquids so that you are also taking in large amounts of water.

Note: CAUTION, do not take salt tablets when you are suffering from these symptoms since concentrated amounts of salt can draw water out of your cells in order to dilute the salt, leaving muscle cells even more dehydrated.

To relieve the cramps, have someone apply pressure to the area affected while your muscle is being stretched in a slow static pull. After the pressure has been applied, make sure it is released gradually in order to prevent recurrent tightening.

217

RETURN TO PLAY: As soon as your symptoms have been relieved, you can resume activity.

• Heat fatigue: Heat fatigue, because it can decrease your alertness and so make you more vulnerable to injury, should never be ignored. It's likely you have heat fatigue if, when you are exercising in hot weather, you find yourself easily tired, suffering from a headache, sweating profusely, having a high pulse rate (which can be so fast that it is unpalpable), and if your breathing is shallow, appetite poor, and you later have trouble sleeping.

TREATMENT: Rest is essential as is increasing your intake of fluids and spending more time in a cooler and drier atmosphere.

• Heat exhaustion: Far less dangerous than heat stroke, heat exhaustion is an excessive loss of salt and water from the body with symptoms that develop very gradually and can include:

> Pale appearance of skin
> Heavy sweating
> Weak, rapid pulse
> Normal or below normal temperature
> Dilated pupils
> Cramps and tight muscles
> Cold and clammy skin
> Shallow breathing
> Generalized feeling of weakness
> Headaches
> Possible vomiting
> Possible shock

TREATMENT: Stop your activity immediately and retreat to a cool place where your feet and legs can be elevated and your head be kept lower than the rest of your body. Have someone cool you down with an ice bath or sponging, drink cold water, and make sure your clothing is loosened or removed.

A physician should be called since this condition can progress into heat stroke, a medical emergency.

• Heat stroke: This is a condition that results in a breakdown of your body's sweating mechanism. It can occur suddenly or may be preceded by heat exhaustion. Learn these signs of heat stroke carefully since it's quite possible that knowing them can save your or someone else's life:

Flushed, red appearance
Dry, hot skin, becoming ashen or purplish. No sweating although you may have previously sweated heavily
High temperature that rises sharply. The degrees can register from 105 to 110 Fahrenheit
Weakness
Headaches
Heat cramps and loss of muscle tone
Constricted (pinpoint) eye pupils
Strong and pounding pulse
Deep and rapid breathing
Note: A coma is common.

TREATMENT: Get a doctor immediately or get the victim of heat stroke to a hospital. This is a medical emergency, and any delay can be fatal. Cool the patient immediately, even on the way to the hospital. Apply cool water or even an ice whirlpool if possible, to reduce her body temperature. Massaging her trunk and extremities with alcohol can help return muscle reflex.

COLD PROBLEMS

Like all sports, winter sports bring with them not only pleasure and physical benefit but also a certain degree of hazard, and chief among these is exposure to cold. When planning your activity, you should take into consideration not only the temperature but also the wind-chill factor, which relates the velocity of the wind to the outdoor temperature in order to figure out how your body will react. A temperature of ten degrees Fahrenheit with a thirty-mile-per-hour wind, for example, will feel as cold to you as a temperature of minus thirty-three degrees with no wind at all. Always get an up-to-date weather report and make sure your clothing is adequate for the environmental conditions.
• Frostbite: What happens when you are exposed to extreme cold

or heavy winds is that the blood vessels closest to the surface of your skin constrict so that you become pale, even grayish, in the affected spots on your body. Particularly vulnerable are your extremities, which include your fingers, toes, ears, and nose. These are the areas to watch for any change in color when you're skiing or ice skating, since such changes may well signal frostbite.

TREATMENT: Cover the frostbitten part and try to get indoors as soon as possible.

Note: You may walk on a leg or foot that is frostbitten provided it has not been thawed. Once your leg or foot is no longer frozen, you will have to be carried, with the affected area supported and protected.

Take in warm fluids and put on dry clothing.

Remove rings or anything constricting, since frostbitten extremities tend to swell when they thaw.

You can try to restore circulation in the frostbitten areas by immersing them in comfortably warm—never hot—water. Do *not* follow the folklore remedy that calls for applications of snow or cold water.

You can pat the areas dry if you are extremely gentle, careful *never to rub*. Frozen cells contain ice crystals, which can cut or kill the surrounding tissue. If you wish to bandage to protect from contamination, make sure the bandage is loose.

If blisters appear, this is a good sign, which indicates only partial damage. Don't open the blisters but instead protect them with a loosely wrapped dressing.

As frostbite thaws you may notice some of the following:

> the area may get temporarily blue or purple
> it will probably begin to swell
> there may be stinging or burning because of injury to the nerves
> it is possible to end up with increased sensitivity in the frostbitten area, possibly even permanent tenderness and sensitivity to cold

• Hypothermia: This condition is severe body cooling, caused by exposure to low or rapidly dropping temperatures, cold moisture, snow, or ice. Some of the contributing factors, in addition to the extreme weather, are the victim's own hunger, fatigue, or extreme exertion, exactly the circumstances that can often occur at the end of a long day's hard skiing.

The symptoms of hypothermia start with shivering, which is the body's mechanism for warming itself. Next, the victim will grow apathetic, sleepy, listless, and indifferent as her body temperature rapidly lowers. She will then become clumsy, stumbling when she walks and slurring her speech, and will show some amount of mental confusion. Quickly, after these symptoms appear, if she remains cold, she will lose consciousness and have a slow pulse rate, slow respiration, and a glassy stare.

TREATMENT: This is a medical emergency that requires a doctor's help as soon as possible. In the meantime, to prevent further heat loss, get the victim into a sheltered area and replace wet clothes with dry ones.

You must try to do more than just supply a blanket or sleeping bag. Provide external heat in the form of a hot-water bottle, a campfire, or even your own body heat and that of other rescuers.

If the victim is conscious, give warm liquids.

If she is unconscious and is not breathing, give mouth-to-mouth resuscitation. If there is also no pulse, you should give chest compression along with the resuscitation. Both these emergency techniques are described in detail later in this chapter in the section on cardiac problems.

ALTITUDE

Another atmospheric condition that can affect the athlete is altitude. While most people will experience no serious adverse reactions exercising at high altitudes, some may feel some minor discomforts following a rapid ascent to areas over 8,000 feet. You may find yourself feeling lethargic and drowsy, suffering from headaches, and unable to sleep soundly. With Acute Mountain Sickness, you may also have such other symptoms as loss of appetite, an intolerance for fatty food, and possibly occasional nausea and vomiting.

221

TREATMENT: For most people, adaptation to high altitudes will occur rapidly and without difficulty. If, however, you find you have AMS, your symptoms can be diminished by a diet high in carbohydrates and low in fat, as well as by taking aspirin for your headache. Try to avoid strenuous exercise for the first day at a high altitude.

Note: CAUTION, avoid taking sleeping pills because they depress breathing and can aggravate your symptoms.

WATER ACCIDENTS

Since water-related fatalities are the third leading cause of accidental death in the United States, it is important for you to understand the mechanics of drowning and crucial for you to learn how to treat a drowning victim.

Drowning, usually defined as any water death or near-death, is suffocation in or under water. What happens is that water enters the victim's mouth and nose, causing coughing. She may swallow water while trying to take in a deep breath or, if her head is under water, she may involuntarily inhale large amounts. If the water enters the trachea (windpipe), spasms can occur that may end up sealing the airway of the trachea from the victim's mouth and nose and from her lungs. The resulting lack of oxygen can cause her to lose consciousness, and if she does so while under water, her spasms will then relax, unfortunately allowing water to enter her lungs. If it is salt water, pulmonary edema (abnormal amounts of fluid in the lungs) can result because the salt in the fluid inhaled can cause the surrounding cells to release their own water content. If it is fresh water that the victim has breathed, it will be absorbed into her bloodstream, where it can end up damaging blood cells and lungs.

Rescuing a drowning person doesn't necessarily involve swimming. Hold out a pole or rope (be certain your hold is secure but if you feel yourself being pulled into the water, let go) or throw out anything that will float.

If you are going to enter the water yourself to help someone, be

222

sure you are trained in lifesaving and have sufficient command of the pool or lake or ocean so that you are not putting yourself into jeopardy. The safety of the rescuer must always be considered.

The drowning victim must first, of course, be brought to the surface as promptly as possible. Before you remove her from the water, however, try to find out if she has sustained any spinal injuries, certainly a possibility if she has fallen from a boat. Ask if she has any loss of feeling or diminished sensation in her arms or legs. If she does, she should be put on a board or stiff surface of some kind before she is lifted out of the water so that her spine is not damaged even further.

TREATMENT: First, the victim's airway must be cleared—open her mouth wide and clear the back of her throat with your fingers, making sure nothing has lodged there.

The airway must also be open. Place the victim on her back and by hyperextending or stretching up her neck and pulling her lower jaw forward, you will cause her tongue to go forward, opening up her airway.

Now, begin mouth-to-mouth resuscitation. Pinch closed her nostrils so no air can escape and place your own mouth tightly over hers, making certain your mouth is sealed so that no air can escape. Next, inhale and exhale gently but firmly, twelve to fifteen times per minute if you are treating an adult and seventeen to twenty times a minute for a child. Continue until the victim's own breathing begins or until a physician can take charge.

If the victim is unconscious and her heartbeat has stopped, use the chest-compression technique described in the following discussion of the emergency treatment for cardiac problems.

MEDICAL PROBLEMS

The following are some of the conditions or diseases that you may find yourself having to deal with within the context of sports. If you know that you have these or any other special conditions, it is a wise caution to tell your partners or teammates as well as in-

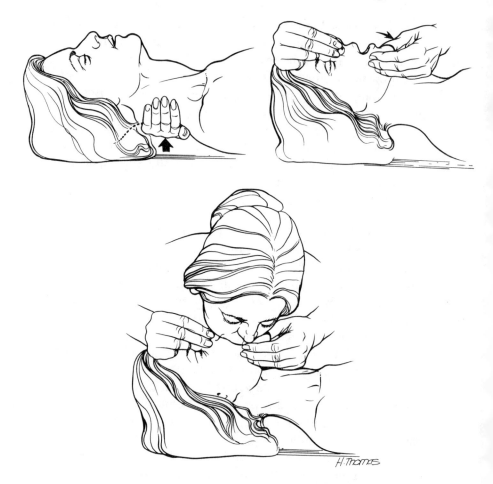

structors or administrators at sports facilities so that they can deal intelligently and efficiently with those symptoms that might arise.

CARDIAC PROBLEMS. These generally require as prompt medical attention as is possible.

• Angina pectoris: This is a chest pain caused when the heart has too little oxygen for its needs for more than several seconds. These symptoms can include:

Chest pain; the pain can radiate down the left arm

The pain comes during exertion and should diminish when the exertion stops

The sensation is a feeling of pressure or squeezing, lasting between three and ten minutes

Additional symptoms can be shortness of breath, nausea, and sweating

If this is the first time that you or your companion has had these symptoms, see a doctor as soon as possible. When with someone who has these symptoms, ask if she has ever had them before. If she has, she is probably under a doctor's care and likely to have with her nitroglycerin or some other medication, which she should immediately be given to relieve her chest pains.

Next, call for medical help; while you wait, loosen the victim's clothing. If breathing seems difficult for her, prop her up so that she gets as much air as possible. Try to keep her as calm as you can.

Severe angina may progress to a heart attack and should be treated as such. See below:

• Myocardial infarction (heart attack): This is caused by a narrowing of the coronary artery so that there is a diminished oxygen supply for the heart muscle. Unlike angina pectoris, which can be brought on by increased activity or stress, myocardial infarction can occur at any time and is not necessarily relieved by rest or medication. Symptoms may include:

Chest pain under the sternum (chest bone), which is a squeezing sensation that radiates down the left arm or possibly both arms

Dilated pupils, indicating a lack of circulating blood

Cyanosis, a bluish color of the skin, caused by a lack of circulating blood

Possible fainting

Lack of pulse, which indicates the heart has stopped beating

TREATMENT: This is a medical emergency that requires a doctor as soon as possible, and until then, if there is no sign of pulse (check the carotid pulse at either side of the neck near the throat), the victim will have to be given resuscitation. In an ideal situation, the person giving cardiopulmonary resuscitation would have received proper instruction, and we encourage you to take advantage of one of the CPR courses that are currently offered by, among other organizations, the Heart Association, Red Cross, and many local Ys. The techniques taught are not difficult to master and the results in saving lives certainly make the effort worthwhile. For those of you, however, who have not yet taken a CPR course and find yourselves in an emergency situation with an unconscious person whose heart has stopped beating, we recommend the following:

What you must attempt to do is to breathe for the victim by mouth-to-mouth resuscitation while circulating her blood through chest compression. The first part, using the same techniques you would for a drowning victim, is to clear her airways by hyperextending her neck and lowering her jaw. Next, pinch closed her nostrils, place your mouth over hers, and breathe in and out, filling her lungs with air.

The chest compression part of the treatment is a good deal more strenuous and carries with it some risk to the victim. An inexperienced person, one who has not been properly trained in CPR, may cause one or more of the victim's ribs to be broken. Still, because the victim has no heartbeat, it is sensible to risk injuring her in a treatment that gives her a chance for survival.

Chest compression involves putting pressure on the victim's chest, which in turn compresses her heart, forcing blood through the chambers of the heart and into the lungs and tissues. First, stand or kneel beside the victim, who should be resting on a firm surface. Then place the heel of your hand about two thirds of the way down the chest bone with your fingers pointing toward the victim's head. Put your other hand on top of the first and, in order to utilize the force of gravity, place yourself in a position in which you are pressing straight down. Keep your arms straight and move forward, pressing down firmly, and then move back. Do this fifteen

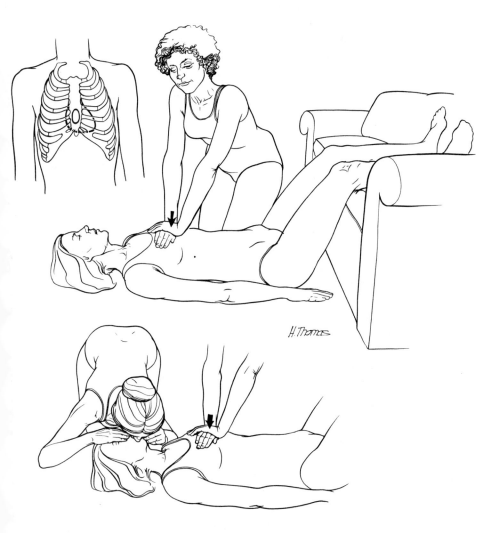

H. Thomas

times at the rate of one time per second and then stop the chest pressure and administer two breaths of mouth-to-mouth resuscitation in order to inflate the lungs. Repeat the sequence of fifteen compressions and two breaths until the victim is revived or a doctor tells you to stop.

If someone else can help you, one of you can inflate the lungs between every fifth and sixth compression. Position yourselves on opposite sides of the victim's body so that both of you can easily switch positions from airway to chest if you choose.

Again, we want to emphasize that your confidence, skill, and consequently your effectiveness in administering these emergency techniques would be vastly increased with a course in CPR under qualified instructors.

DIABETES. A diabetic is unable to use sugar normally and needs additional insulin to enable the sugar to go from the bloodstream into the cells of the body. There are two possible medical emergencies that a diabetic can develop, insulin shock and diabetic coma. Both require quick attention.
• Insulin shock: This is caused by an insufficient amount of sugar in the blood, probably because too much insulin has been given or because not enough food has been eaten or possibly because the diabetic has engaged in excessive amounts of exercise. Symptoms include:

Pale, moist skin
Dizziness and headache
Rapid pulse of normal strength
Possible fainting or even seizures

TREATMENT: Give the patient a sugar solution, which may be any sweet drink, including fruit juices.

Note: CAUTION, an exception to this treatment occurs when someone with insulin shock is unconscious. It is extremely dangerous, under any circumstances, to give liquids to an unconscious person. Instead, quickly transport her to the nearest hospital.

• Diabetic coma: This is a more serious condition, caused by an imbalance between the sugar in the bloodstream and in the body cells. Acidic waste products build up in the blood with an accompanying loss of fluids. The symptoms include:

Air hunger, which shows up as rapid and deep sighing respiration (In contrast, someone in insulin shock breathes normally)
Dehydration, with warm, dry skin
Sweet or fruity odor of breath caused by acid in the blood
A weak, rapid pulse
Various degrees of unresponsiveness

TREATMENT: Someone in a diabetic coma needs insulin and other medication. Transport her to the hospital for immediate treatment.

EPILEPSY. This is a common disease that can be controlled by proper medication. While there are two types, petit mal and grand mal, only grand mal causes what is usually thought of as an epileptic seizure. With grand mal there are uncontrollable contractions of body muscles, contraction of the jaw muscles that can lead to biting the tongue or lips, a possible loss of bladder or bowel control, and unconsciousness. (The other type, petit mal, causes so slight an episode that it may be undetectable.)
TREATMENT: Using a hard, flat object, try to keep the patient from biting her tongue or interfering with her own breathing.
Note: CAUTION, don't place your fingers between the patient's teeth since it's quite likely you'll get bitten.
Once the seizure is over, transport the patient to a hospital emergency room.

ASTHMA. This respiratory disease is an abnormal spasm of the airway passages and can be an allergic response to insect stings or substances inhaled, ingested, or injected. Someone with an asthma attack has a characteristic wheeze when breathing out. Chest pain is rarely present.

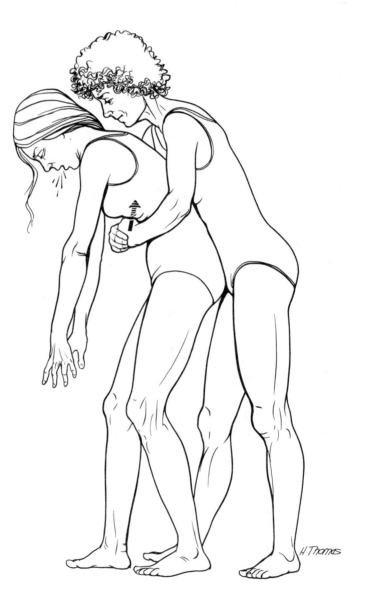

TREATMENT: Stop activity and get the victim to relax. If she has medication with her, make sure that she takes the proper dosage to relieve symptoms. A doctor should be consulted.

CHOKING

Although choking on food or some foreign object is not especially common in sports, it can happen in the excitement of vigorous activity, and participants should be cautioned against eating food, chewing gum, or sucking on candy while engaged in any sport.

While a choking victim can resemble someone suffering from a heart attack, one way to distinguish between the two is that someone with a heart attack can speak while someone choking is unable to do so. If you see someone choking—unable to speak or

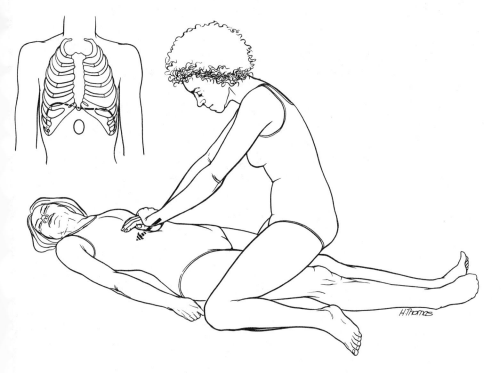

breathe, turning blue, or collapsing—you should immediately attempt the following maneuver since each minute counts in a choking accident.

TREATMENT: The Heimlich Maneuver has proven itself the most effective way of dislodging an object that is blocking the airway of the victim.

Position One: Victim is standing or sitting with rescuer standing. First, stand behind the victim and wrap your arms around her waist. Next, grasp your fist with your other hand, placing your fist against her abdomen slightly below her rib cage. Press your wrist inward and upward in a hard thrust. If this movement doesn't dislodge the object, repeat again until it does.

Position Two: Victim lying face up with rescuer kneeling. With the victim on her back, kneel astride her hips, facing her.

Place one hand on top of the other with the heel of the bottom hand on her abdomen slightly below her rib cage. Press into her abdomen with a quick, upward thrust. Repeat if necessary.

In most of the emergencies that arise, the wisest recourse is getting to a hospital emergency room or a doctor's office, and the most that you can do is simply keep yourself or someone else as comfortable as possible in the meantime. Sometimes, however, as you've seen in this chapter, your actions can not only avoid further injury or aggravation to a condition but, in a few instances, actually save a life. For these reasons we think it's essential for you and those around you to know how to distinguish an emergency and be able to take those appropriate first steps that can be so crucial.

10

Fitness Facilities and How to Rate Them

Less than ten years ago there were few people exercising with any frequency at fitness facilities. Even many professional athletes, particularly women, weren't yet aware of what regular training sessions could do for their performance in a sport, while the rest of the population for the most part considered exercising basically an activity for producing muscles. Today, though, most people are aware that if their heart and lungs and joints are well exercised, they can function more efficiently. The concept that a gym is not just a place for prize fighters to jump rope or punch leather bags has certainly taken hold as physical activity—exercise and sports—has become increasingly popular. Health clubs and training centers have sprung up all over the country, mushrooming so rapidly, in fact, that the situation may seem chaotic and confusing. If you've decided to look into joining a health club, you'll probably be faced with many choices that raise a lot of questions. First of all, what should a facility have to offer? Then, what qualifications should instructors and supervisors have? Are there clues that can reveal a facility as unsatisfactory? Since a well-run, well-equipped health spa can be an important aid to fitness, it's worthwhile to explore your options.

One of the first confusions deals with something rather basic: the definition of a health spa. When the Federal Trade Commission held lengthy hearings in 1979 about the physical fitness industry, there were relatively few comments about what would constitute a broad definition. Jimmy Johnson, Executive Director of the Association of Physical Fitness Centers, offered a description of the various types of establishments. The first type he called the "urban country club," which offers a full range of facilities and services. The clubs not only have gymnasiums and pools but also have whirlpools, saunas, food services, tennis courts, and other facilities. Obviously a huge investment is required to build such a place, and fees reflect this. A second type of spa provides full facilities, including a gym, pool, sauna, and steam room, but on a smaller scale with less space. The third group of spas cater to either men or women, the women's facilities usually categorized as "figure salons." If there aren't wet areas, these spas constitute a fourth type of business, which often operates in a storefront with carpet, mirrors, exercise equipment, and one or two employees.

All the above, from the lavish to the spartan, are actual fitness facilities. There are other establishments, however, that are sometimes mistakenly put in that category. One is the "passive exercise salon," which sells treatments on a vibrating table or other passive device. These treatments offer no physical benefits and are basically a waste of time and money. Still another kind of facility that has deceptively called itself a "health spa" is the massage parlor, which actually offers sexual services, usually for men.

The federal government has proposed defining "health spa" as "An establishment which provides as one of its primary purposes services or facilities which are purported to assist patrons to improve their physical condition or appearance through change in weight, weight control, treatment, dieting or exercise." Within this broad category we would recommend your choosing a facility capable of getting you to improve through a concept of complete training, that is, working on all three elements of strength, stamina, and flexibility.

If you live in a large city, your options may seem almost too abundant, with everything from advertising in newspapers to handouts on street corners offering you a fitness program. And these days even in smaller cities and suburbs you generally have a selection. In most areas, whether urban or suburban, there are public community centers that can offer excellent programs, as can the Ys. Many of the Y's services are free, below cost, or at cost, making it an attractive bargain. Sally Stewart, Physical Education Director of the McBurney Y in New York City, runs a program that includes a cardiovascular class. This group meets three times a week for forty-five minutes and includes a diverse group of men and women ranging from twenty-two years old up to one woman in her seventies. After a ten-minute warm-up, which consists of low-level aerobic activity and stretching, each member goes on to work at his or her own level, walking, cycling, or jogging. Sally Stewart's staff at the Y is not only well trained but selected for their ability to get along well with people. Part of her program is educating the public about health—speaking to older people about the benefits of brisk walking or educating children about how their hearts function. Her Y, while well equipped, is a plain and some-what somber place compared to the mirrored, carpeted spas, but the difference in price can compensate for decor.

Another kind of facility that's growing more and more common is the company fitness program open to employees of some of the large companies and corporations. It can be an attractive extra for personnel directors to point to and can benefit the company by helping increase fitness among workers. Dennis Colacino, who is in charge of a fitness facility for Pepsico, and Gretchen Regan, who recently started one for Remington, have found that more and more employees have been attracted to the programs. Good medical screening is followed by carefully supervised programs that include weight lifting, flexibility exercises, and aerobic activity. There are also leisure activities, such as swimming and softball, which fall under the supervision of the exercise director. The object of these programs is not only to get everyone well exercised but also to teach each something about his or her own level of fitness. Employees are encouraged to include some aspect of the program in their working day at least three times a week, and some employees manage to make use of the facility daily. At Pepsico, company policy allows staff members to exercise at any time as long as it fits in with the working schedule of the department involved. At both Remington and Pepsico the classes never segregate the sexes. A growing trend at Ys and health spas as well—men and women working out and training together in an unself-conscious and relaxed atmosphere—has been an aspect of exercise programs that many instructors proudly point to. One woman told us that she felt the exercise classes she took with male staff members increased a feeling of camaraderie and mutual regard that carried over into other aspects of corporate life.

Most people, however, don't have company fitness programs to join and so they have to turn instead, if not to a community center or other facility with special funding, to a commercial health spa if they want organized training and instruction. An initial consideration has to be whether or not you can afford a program that can be quite costly. When you consider price, try to estimate accurately how often you'll use the facility. A club costing $400 a year to join can end up being cheaper than going to the movies if you're going to use it two or three times a week all year round. Unfortunately a lot of people start out enthusiastically and then, when the novelty wears off, go rarely if at all. This phenomenon, according to a lawyer who testified at the FTC hearings, is one that some health spas are counting on as they sell more memberships than they can possibly handle on the expectation that you won't stick it out. You have to size yourself up realistically so that you can anticipate how faithful you'll actually be to a new regime.

Another practical consideration is the location of the facility. It should be near either your home or your office or on your way between the two. It should be in an area that is safe and easy to get to, with good parking facilities or near public transportation. Try to figure out beforehand what your routine is likely to be and if there is anything inconvenient or off-putting about where the spa is. You'll be far more likely to make use of the facility if you can occasionally go over during a lunch hour or, if you're an early riser, before your workday starts.

What should the facility look like? First of all, it ought to look clean. Not only is a lack of cleanliness unhygienic and unpleasant, it also points to carelessness and an uncaring management whose inattentive attitudes will no doubt surface in other areas. Some spas have mirrors everywhere, and while these may possibly contribute to the aesthetics, they can also interfere with the concentration necessary for executing exercise maneuvers properly. A bright, agreeable look can be important in encouraging your attendance, as can the availability of the facilities you need in order easily to incorporate strenuous exercise into your everyday life. This will include lockers, showers, hair driers, and whatever else you need so that you can return home or to your office after a workout looking the way you want to look.

The most important objects for you to examine when you're considering a spa are the exercise equipment. One women's facility in New York, in the midst of the Madison Avenue advertising agencies, has Nautilus and other worthwhile equipment but everything is in disorder, with two of one machine, none of another, and no logic to what is being offered. Strength equipment should be well organized into stations, each of which exercises a particular muscle or group of muscles. A full complement of machines is important for total body strength. Nautilus and Universal are among the most practical because they require the least supervision, but it's certainly possible to have a good strength program with just weights or sandbags along with dumbbells and a slant board. For this kind of program you should be carefully programmed and instructed, at least in the early stages of exercising.

Your facility should include an open area for warm-ups and cooling down as well as for classroom demonstration. You should also have an aerobic or cardiopulmonary training area where you can use a treadmill, jump rope, stationary bicycle, or any of the other devices for elevating your heartbeat to a training level. Swimming is a good aerobic exercise and if it's one you'll be doing, it will be particularly important to you that the pool be long enough for you to swim laps without worrying about bumping your head.

There should be easy accessibility to all the exercise areas and the equipment they contain. Make certain there is plenty of room around each machine or station and that the lighting is sufficient.

Notice the state of repair, again a reflection of the concern or lack of it on the part of the management.

Several people testifying at the FTC hearings about health spas expressed their opinion that instructors at the fitness facilities should be certified. These statements will be particularly surprising to much of the public which is under the impression that instructors have had to be certified all along. Unfortunately, at too many places it doesn't take much to be put in charge of an exercise class. One woman from a club in Ann Arbor, Michigan, said that she was hired with no specific qualifications and was encouraged to deceive customers with false body measurements. Another young woman who worked at a well-known New York health spa told us that few of the instructors she worked with had any certificate or degree in physical education. Making matters worse, they were given little on-the-job training and often ended up creating their own exercises, some of which would do little good and a few of which were actually harmful. These instructors rarely knew enough to teach clients about the proper use of the exercise machines. Many of the ill-informed instructors were overly timid, nervous when they saw any sign of exertion, and so stopped their clients from exercising long and hard enough to accomplish anything at all.

John Dietrich, president of the American International Health Industries, believes that instructors should be certified. "Lifeguards, masseurs and masseuses all need licenses," he said, "so why not instructors who are teaching people how to push around hundreds of pounds of weight?" His instructors all have to have at least a bachelor's degree in physical education and must take sixty hours of training at the Sports Training Institute in New York. We suggest you talk to exercise leaders and supervisors, asking them what their sports background is and what their experience has been in giving people guidance in the use of exercise equipment. Find out just how qualified the person is who will be telling you what you should be doing. You ought to be supervised to make sure you are executing an exercise correctly, even if you are experienced in using exercise equipment. You can also benefit by an instructor's objective assessment of exactly where you are and how much you can do. Just how close the attention is that's paid to you can't help but be a function of what *you've* paid—one-to-one weight training in a gym is going to be far more expensive than a yoga class at a Y. Still, even when training several people at once, an attentive and informed instructor can give you sufficient supervision.

Besides a physical education background and an interest in sports, it would be helpful if someone training you had some background in sports medicine, understanding concepts of injury prevention and rehabilitation. The person supervising or actively consulted about exercise programs should be an exercise physiologist, preferably with a master's degree and experience in training both athletes and ordinary people who want to exercise. The supervisor should be able to discuss with you aspects of training, special conditions that require modifications, and should communicate to you an enthusiasm and ability to motivate instructors and trainers.

The staff of a fitness facility should also be prepared to deal with emergencies. Recently in New York City, a member of a major health club had a heart attack while working out. None of the instructors or other personnel were trained to give emergency first aid so that the victim ended up unattended for forty-five minutes. Ask the representative of the spa who is soliciting your membership what is done in such emergencies. Are there staff members certified by either the American Red Cross or the American Heart Association to give cardiopulmonary resuscitation (CPR)? If so, is one of them always on duty? Has an arrangement been made with an ambulance service? Nearby emergency room? Attending physician? A health spa should have considered the possibility of medical emergencies and taken steps to insure immediate first aid along with reasonably prompt attention from a doctor.

Another important aspect of safety is medical screening. Some health clubs ask everyone over thirty-five to have a clearance from a doctor. We would suggest that anyone starting out on a new fitness regime have her doctor do a medical profile as described in Chapter 4. Be sure to call attention to recent operations, infections, conditions such as hypertension and respiratory problems, as

239

well as recent muscle pulls or problems in your bones or joints so that they can be checked by your doctor. Find out if any limitations are recommended before you start your program, and make certain your doctor's advice is passed on to your instructors.

One club in New York, the Paris Health Club, besides asking for a doctor's clearance for prospective members over thirty-five, also conducts its own tests for heart and blood pressure. Your resting pulse rate must be no higher than 100 to 105 beats per minute and your blood pressure should be no higher than 150/90. As for other problems a member might have, the club has had good experiences with overweight members, some others who are blind, and one man with cerebral palsy who swims daily. Rather than putting off the other members, those who are handicapped seem to inspire others with their diligence and enthusiasm.

We think there are very few conditions that should screen you out of a facility. People with missing limbs, diabetes, rheumatoid arthritis, and other disorders or handicaps should, of course, be cleared first and given specific recommendations, but they can usually benefit from exercise. Anyone under recent care of a physician for an acute respiratory or heart problem or anyone having undergone a recent operation should in most cases stay out of an exercise program at a health spa, at least temporarily until there has been a marked improvement in physical condition.

Once in a program, your safety and general well-being will be helped by doing warm-ups before and cooling down after exercising. Many people end up rushing into a class at the last minute and then rushing back off to work or back home without allowing the five to ten minutes before and after to acclimatize themselves to beginning and stopping vigorous activity. It's probably wisest for instructors to realize this fact and incorporate the proper warm-up and cooling down into the actual exercise session. For individual workouts with weights, members should be reminded by instructors or trainers to warm up beforehand so that they can get the most out of a session without injury.

Take your resting pulse before you start. Then try to exercise at approximately three fourths of your predicted maximum (220 beats per minute minus your age). It's good to find out what your heart rate is when you're working the hardest during an exercise so you can do sprint work or other high-intensity activity to drive your heart rate up. Then let it come down to your exercise rate and keep it there for twenty to thirty minutes in order to get a cardiopulmonary training effect. Some exercise classes have everyone stop periodically to check their individual rates, a practice we approve of because too many people exercise for long periods of time without actually improving their cardiopulmonary efficiency. Without your pulse up high enough, you simply can't accomplish this desirable goal.

Make sure you're comfortable when you work out. You should wear light, airy clothing. Cotton, because it breathes better, is a good choice. As for shoes, they should be carefully fitted, have high counters and slight arch support, and be wide enough. Neither basketball shoes nor tennis sneakers are right for running, and we've seen many women with shin splints that started because they ran in tennis sneakers. You simply can't land comfortably on the heel of a tennis sneaker and so you tend to develop stiffness and tightness in your feet.

There is quite a lot that a good fitness facility can do for you. Classes can add inspiration and sociability to what otherwise might be impersonal training. An instructor can give you the guidance and confidence for you to work intensively enough to really gain the benefits of exercise. The pleasant atmosphere can tempt you away from less positive ways of spending your time, and the emphasis on health can give you an awareness you'd lacked before. If you're a serious competitor, your activity at a fitness facility can make a difference not only in your performance but in your injury rate.

On the other hand, it's impossible to ignore the many abuses that some fitness facilities have perpetrated. First, there are the contracts you sign, which can be rigidly binding and one-sided in that most of the terms favor the health spa, much as a standard form apartment lease favors the landlord. One spa member spent a night in a hospital after almost drowning in an unguarded pool at a spa. She tried to cancel her three-year contract but couldn't. Another woman, who told the facility that she had arthritis and migraine headaches, joined anyway and found her migraines intensified by exercise. She tried to invoke the disability cancellation clause in her contract but couldn't because her disability was a preexisting one. Still another member became aware of a heart condition after using the spa for a few months. Even with a letter from her doctor, the facility refused to cancel her membership.

One young woman who worked for a large chain of health clubs told us that she was taught the most overwhelming program of promotional tactics she'd ever seen. She was given lessons in selling, pamphlets, and cue cards, and she discovered to her amazement that it all worked—saying just what she was supposed to say got people joining up one after the other. Sometimes she appealed to the vanity of the prospective member, asking them questions ("Just how long have you been overweight?" "Who else in your family has weight problems?" "Do you think it runs in your family?") that were supposed to show an interest.

"If you answered enough of my questions, I could be pretty sure you'd join no matter what your answers were," she said. "You'd get involved because it seemed as though we all cared about you."

After joining up, the turnover rate at these same clubs was astronomical. The equipment was poor, the classes far too short—fifteen minutes—to do any good. But if people dropped out, this presented no problem for the spa. The dropouts were paid up already, and there were others to take their places. "As much as I needed the job, I just had to leave," the young instructor told us. "My conscience still bothers me for ever having been a part of that rip-off."

An instructor at still another chain of spas told us that the sales pitch she had been taught included totally fabricated statistics to scare people into joining so that they could fend off the encroaching coronaries and strokes. Other tactics we've heard about include "specials" that are really the same fees just stated in a different way, or unsettling you, making you feel guilty or inadequate if you express any reluctance about joining ("Can't you make up your own mind?" or "Wouldn't your family prefer to see you in better shape?" are some of the remarks designed to get you to sign there and then).

Some state laws call for a cooling-off period so that a customer can think about what she's gotten herself into. It's been suggested that all health spas follow the practice of refunding membership fees within the first three days after signing, a practice we think makes a great deal of sense.

Abuses and dishonest tactics continue in some spas after the high-pressure selling has landed the customer. The facility may refuse to limit membership, so that it becomes uncomfortably over-crowded. It may promise services such as a special medical examination or special diet and then simply give out some mimeographed papers full of general recommendations. Although it can be hard to foresee exactly what will happen to a club after you join, there are telltale signs you can search out so that you'll be less likely to make a costly mistake. Some facilities allow you to be a guest for a day, and even if a fairly large fee is involved, it can be worth it to have a firsthand look. If you can't spend some time using the equipment, be sure you make the most of your introductory tour.

WHAT TO LOOK OUT FOR IN A FITNESS FACILITY

1. If salespeople in a facility try to sell you a membership before taking you on a tour and explaining the program and equipment to you, you should walk out. The sales policy is clearly irresponsible, indicating an attitude you should want to stay clear of.

2. If a salesperson seems to be in a great hurry and pressures you into making up your mind quickly, we suggest that you have no time for that particular health spa. Salespeople should be sensitive to the fact that your decision has to be a thoughtful one.

3. Be sure to see the spa during the actual hours you'd be most likely to use it. If you're going to be dropping in after work, generally the most crowded hours in most health spas, looking around at three in the afternoon won't give you a good picture of what it's going to be like for you.

4. Is there enough equipment or are people standing in line waiting?

5. Is the equipment hardly being used at all? This may indicate it was a poor purchase, inappropriate for a spa.

6. Is the equipment in a good state of repair? Broken equipment of long standing indicates a careless attitude.

7. If there are weight machines such as Nautilus, Mini Gym, Marcy, or Universal, make sure there is a full complement so that you can get total body exercise.

8. Is the facility too empty? If during the busy periods—lunch hour in a business area and six to eight P.M. generally—there aren't many people, you should try to find out why. It may indicate that the club isn't doing well and is in danger of going bankrupt, at which time you'd end up losing your money.

9. Are people just standing around and talking? If they are exercising, are they exerting themselves enough to work up a sweat and otherwise show signs of making a significant effort? If not, the members may not be motivated or receiving the proper supervision or instruction. In any case, we'd advise against joining such a club.

10. Look around. Are the showers and lavatories clean? Does the steam room smell dank? Are there wet towels lying around in corners, wet bathing suits draped around the sauna? Are there burned-out light bulbs? Hair driers that don't work? Lockers that don't lock? All these are clear indications of how the club is being run, and any of them is sure to wear on you after you join.

11. While you tour the club, be sure to stop and talk to some of the members. Tell them that you're thinking of joining and ask them what they think of the facility. If the salespeople or management object to your questioning members, that in itself can be a clue that there's something to hide.

12. Ask whether there are many extras and what they cost. It may be that something you thought you'd get automatically will end up costing so much in addition to your membership fee that the club becomes impractical for you.

13. Ask to take a sales contract home with you so that you can read it over carefully. If the salesperson says you can't because the contract is part of a numbered sequence, offer to have it Xeroxed.

14. Write down expenses as they're being quoted to you. Some-

times salespeople will quote so many figures that you get confused and can't remember what sounded reasonable or what you'd agreed to.

15. Even if a salesperson claims you will save money by signing up immediately instead of thinking it over, don't make up your mind that moment. It's worth risking an extra amount of money to avoid being pressured into what might end up an even costlier mistake.

16. While on your tour, talk to some of the staff. Their general appearance, ideas about training, their education and experience and ability to express themselves can be crucial factors in whether or not you'll get much from the club.

If you decide to join a health spa, you can use it to best advantage if you relate what you'll be doing there to your Fitness Self-Portrait. Once you've determined your own particular deficiencies, discuss them with your instructors so that they can help you to figure out a program that's best for you. If you are tight-jointed, for example, it would be a good idea to spend extra time on activities promoting flexibility, such as yoga classes.

When you start exercising, follow the general guidelines for training in Chapter 7, making sure your intensity and the time you spend are enough for real improvement. Take advantage of everything offered that's appropriate to your own training program, because, despite the abuses in this relatively young industry, there are significant benefits to be had. Chief among these—especially for those who are less likely to be self-starters—are the convenience and regularity their exercise programs offer.

11

Girls
and Sports—What
Schools and Communities
Have to Offer

One look at the ages of the two winners of the United States Open in 1979, the twenty-year-old John McEnroe and the sixteen-year-old Tracy Austin, and you can see how dramatically the level of performance and skill have risen for the young. Just a few years ago athletes this age would still be working at mastering the rudiments of the sport, leaving the top ranks for players in their twenties. Today, skill levels seem to be sorted out earlier, with those juniors showing the most talent not only encouraged to participate at a younger age but placed into programs that make greater demands and, in turn, get better results.

On the other side of the coin, however, are the many youngsters whose physical fitness level has steadily declined. Hours watching television and a diet of junk food have produced children who are too often overweight and unhealthy. One study of 400 Michigan schoolchildren found that almost 50 percent of them showed one or more risk factors for heart disease, including high blood pressure and high cholesterol levels. What makes this poor state of physical fitness particularly unfortunate is that the young have an excellent capacity for a high level of fitness and athletic skill. If you've ever been part of a sports instruction class that included children or teen-agers, you may have discovered for yourself how much faster than adults they can be in mastering the elements of a parallel turn or a backhand. They haven't as yet developed some of the inhibitions that could keep them from moving their bodies in the way the instructors demonstrate, no matter how unfamiliar the action may be. As for the physiological advantages, younger people starting in a sport have not yet developed the tightness of the heel cords, groins, or hamstrings that are adaptive characteristics of many adults.

As long as it is geared to their attention span and level of desire, a sports program for the young is not only appropriate but desirable. Physical exertion has never been shown to have deleterious effects on children. In fact, daily physical activity is important for the proper development of the functional capacity of a child's heart and lungs and the strength of her muscles and bones. There is no exercise we can think of that is beneficial for adults while at the same time not good for children or teen-agers. In fact, because daily activity of the young involves more of the types of motions that are part of exercising and sports—quick starts, for example, or jumps—it is likely that some of the difficulties adults encounter in training and some of the cautions they might need to take would not hold true for younger participants.

This is true for the young in general, but what is the picture for girls in particular? We strongly believe that there is no physical activity that is all right for boys to do but is potentially injurious for girls. When we asked Margaret Wigiser, who is the supervisor of the girls athletic program for New York City public schools, what she thought of the concept that it was bad for girls to throw overhand, her immediate response was, "Nonsense." She went on to point out that too many girls hadn't been taught to throw and while some might pick it up naturally, others end up pushing from the shoulder with no idea of the proper motion. Boys, on the other hand, if they hadn't automatically grasped the concept of throwing, would have had the chance to learn it during those early years when they still had the natural ease of motion. As she points out, "Now, at forty or forty-five, if the woman who never learned to throw correctly decides she wants to take up tennis, she may find that she's just too tight in her arm and shoulder to play well."

Most differences between boys and girls, such as throwing motion, are adaptive. Still, there are the inherent physical differences between the sexes that should be understood so that they don't cause discomfort or injury. Most important to take into consideration is that girls are generally more loose-jointed than boys and often have sliding and slipping kneecaps. Many of the problems that can stem from this can fortunately be avoided by exercises of the thigh muscles with wall-sits, knee extensions, or other quadriceps routines (see Chapter 7). One caution we would add here is that operating on the kneecaps of young girls should be done with extreme caution. Sometimes surgery can result in severe weakness, limitation of motion, and pain that may far outweigh the original underlying condition, the loose kneecaps. Strengthening exercises may well be the answer to this problem, which is the most common one among physically active girls.

One other difference, this an adaptive one, was pointed out by Cathy Heck, head trainer of women's sports at Michigan State. She had observed that, on a university level, many girls started becoming active in sports after long periods of inactivity in high school. Because they had not been encouraged, as boys had, to participate in sports, they had remained relatively sedentary. Not in active training, if they don't have a proper coach who recognizes the need for careful conditioning and skill training, they can be subject to overuse syndromes such as stress fractures and tendinitis.

Cathy Heck also noted that strength exercises were often not part of a girl's training routine. We advise girls in sports programs to include training with weights, concentrating especially on the arms and shoulders when involved in sports that stress the upper extremity. Even in sports that are thought of as lower body exercise, such as running, the control you can get through training your upper body will help your abdominal muscles stabilize your legs.

There is no evidence that weight lifting hurts the growth centers. In fact, the opposite may be true. When there are stresses across the joint through lines of force, the response may be increased growth through increased strength. Repetitive, controlled weight lifting does not have any significant detrimental effects that we have seen or have been told about, either for girls or for boys.

As for the female biological function, as we've pointed out in Chapter 2, menstruation should not be a problem for most women or girls in athletics. Some runners or swimmers have reported temporary cessation of their menstrual periods, but this amenorrhea stops when endurance training is over. Many girls in athletic programs have reported fewer and less severe menstrual cramps then they had before participation. It may be that vigorous activity helps by delivering more blood to the glands that control hormones, by mobilizing fluid from the tissues, or simply by distracting you from your discomfort. Dr. Elizabeth Coryllus, a pediatric surgeon, points out that after the onset of menstruation, most girls, and especially those in athletics, may find they need iron supplements to maintain the oxygen-carrying capacity of their blood at optimal levels. Unexplained fatigue and failure to improve performance even with increased training are often due to borderline anemia caused by an unreplaced loss of iron in normal menstrual flow.

Injury rates for girls have not been significantly higher than for boys. Dr. Sandra Scott of the New York State school sports program found that most injuries for both sexes were minimal. As for girls, once the coaches realized the social truth, that girls often start out in high school programs with less conditioning than boys, they compensated with more practice periods and the injuries began to decline. How new the sport is for girls seems to be another factor. Dr. Coryllus has found a high proportional accident rate among girls playing soccer, an activity only recently becoming popular for girls, and far lower accident rates for swimming and figure skating, sports girls have been doing for generations. Informed coaches who insist on the proper conditioning of girls in these sports have undoubtedly contributed to the lower rates.

At West Point and the other service academies, the young

249

women who are most physically fit are the ones who have the fewest injuries, a fact that should substantiate the need for careful conditioning for girls who, more often than boys, have been less active. Many of the injuries reported, by the way, are minor aches and pains that female cadets, less involved in physical activity in the past, are simply not used to. After several months there is generally a great decline in infirmary visits for these kinds of complaints. The reason probably lies in a combination of a better state of fitness for the women cadets along with an understanding of which transient physical sensations of discomfort they can safely ignore.

The real difference between the sexes in school and community sports programs is a matter of attitude rather than any physical fact. The long-standing lack of emphasis on sports and fitness for girls, along with what had been for the most part a second-rate school sports program, ended up producing girls who, despite their inherent potential, came nowhere close to the athletic performance of boys. Today that's beginning to change. Cathy Heck, head trainer at Michigan State, says that the female athletes she trains are now so highly motivated that her biggest problem is getting them to stop. The level of skill that these athletes achieve, in turn, reflects this enthusiasm.

When university athletes are this enthusiastic, it reveals a growing interest in sports that's starting on the high school level. Women we've talked to who have been competitive swimmers or runners as children frequently reported that their parents urged them to transfer their interest away from sports when they reached adolescence. One thirty-two-year-old woman, who completely dropped sports from age twelve until recently, sums up a situation and attitudes that have been all too prevalent. "When I was nine, my father made me a special cabinet where I could display my swimming medals and trophies, but by the time I was twelve, he and my mother stopped bragging to their friends about what races I was winning. I got the message quickly enough, and besides, as my big sister pointed out, when you swim every day, you have to go around school with your hair looking limp. For some reason, this seemed an immensely important reason to stop swimming."

250

This same woman, an art director at a major New York department store, now runs almost every day. Sometimes it's hard to fit the running into her busy schedule, but she always manages to get in some exercise. "I know it's frantic," she told us, "but I guess I feel I have to make up for lost time."

Today the picture in high school in most communities has changed. Ingrid Boyum, the number-one nationally ranked fourteen-year-old squash player, says that among her friends and classmates it's good for a girl to be athletic. "Nobody puts you down anymore. In fact, you know how kids think it's great for a boy to be a good athlete? Well, that's how they think about girls too in my school." The coach at a New Jersey high school said she used to have trouble getting enough girls to try out for the softball team. These days she's swamped. The girls who make the team are pleased at having people know who they are when they walk down the hall. Just as pleased, the coach points out, as the boys on the teams have always been.

On the junior high school level, girls' sports have still not progressed far enough to be able to feed well-trained athletes into the high schools. Margaret Wigiser finds in many of the girls she supervises in the New York City public school programs a lack of poise when competing, and sometimes a lack of reliability and commitment. The experience that boys get at age ten with Little League, church leagues, and the like, girls traditionally haven't gotten on any large scale until college competition at seventeen or eighteen. Once the junior high schools' girls' programs improve along with community programs, the next groups of high school girls will not be as far behind boys in training and sophistication.

Randee Burke, a former competitive swimmer and now the assistant trainer for the University of Wisconsin football team, believes that the growing involvement with sports among girls not only reflects their attitudes toward physical activity but also affects their attitudes toward life. In sports as in life, girls are beginning to learn how to accept winning as well as defeat, how to deal with rigorous training, and how to function with the different temperaments of teammates as well as coaches and trainers. The high school girls in Madison, Wisconsin, where she lives, are offered ex-

251

cellent coaching in a large variety of sports, and their growing skill reflects this. Their involvement is enthusiastic, and she finds it in marked contrast to the attitudes of many of the older women who have stayed away from exercising because they consider it unfeminine. The older women voice a fear of getting muscles, of sweating, of being short of breath or appearing awkward, and it's been a difficult job trying to dissuade them. These women, of course, have not had the chance to develop the habit of being physically active and the attitude that sports can be tremendously enjoyable. Many of the Madison high school girls, on the other hand, will be able to look forward to a life of being active, along with gaining an understanding of what it's like to be physically fit.

The biggest change in school sports for girls and women has to do with Title IX. In 1972 Congress passed the Education Amendment to the Civil Rights Act of 1964, and part of it, Title IX, specifically prohibits discrimination on the basis of sex in educational programs and institutions that receive federal funding. The Department of Health, Education and Welfare, after attempting to investigate complaints of alleged discrimination, decided to provide further guidelines as to what constitutes compliance with this law. The feeling was that there were many serious misunderstandings the department wanted to correct, and so a policy interpretation was set forth to clarify the regulation and offer clearer guidelines.

Title IX, as it was redefined in December of 1979, is a lot more flexible than it had been thought to be. There is now no per capita concept that would determine, for example, that because ten uniforms were purchased for men, there have to be ten for women. The only area today with rigid requirements for compliance is in scholarship money, and here there has to be per capita breakdown of funds. If there are sixty male athletes and forty female athletes, then 60 percent of scholarship money will go to men and 40 percent to women.

There are no other dollar-for-dollar requirements as far as the other areas that are dealt with. These areas are: equipment and supplies; locker rooms, practice and competitive facilities; scheduling of games and practice times; assignment and compensation of coaches and tutors; travel and per diem allowances; provision of

252

housing and dining facilities; opportunity to receive coaching and academic tutoring; provision of medical and training facilities and services; and publicity. Individual universities will be able to assess their own special needs and the needs of the individual students. The government will base its compliance determination on whether the policies of the university are discriminatory and whether there are substantial and unjustified disparities that deny equality of athletic opportunity.

Another important aspect of Title IX is that the university itself is responsible for finding out from its student body what the level of interest is of its male and female athletes. If, for example, there are women interested in basketball, the university should accommodate that interest and establish a team. If no interest is evidenced, then there is no need to create an artificial situation, that is, an unwanted women's team simply because a men's basketball team is in existence on the same campus.

Colleges and universities have been waiting for this last redefinition. Joan Bernstein, HEW and, more recently, HSS general counsel, expects that now most will comply. Representatives of universities have been invited to come in and talk to the department in order to work out a plan, and this plan need not be implemented immediately. The federal government considers itself adaptable to the differing natures of athletic programs and, because of this, feels hopeful about the cooperation of the universities. "It can't be to the interest of any institution of higher learning to defy the government, at least without trying first to work out a way of complying," Joan Bernstein points out. Since the federal government has taken the position that its prescriptions for eligibility for federal funding are very broad, it can cover all areas, not just the specific programs that might be involved. As Joan Bernstein notes, "If the government takes the position that any institution that wishes to be eligible for student loans must comply with Title IX, Title I, or any other title, a student who has a federal loan is likely to ask something like, 'Listen, are you in compliance with government titles? If not, I can't go to your school because I won't be able to pay my tuition.' That's a very effective and far-reaching sanction that few institutions can afford to ignore."

Laws like Title IX are basically reflections of the attitudes of the people they would govern. The growing understanding of the importance of physical fitness and an awareness that physical activity benefits women as well as men, along with an increasingly widespread conviction that women should have equality of opportunity, all have a lot to do with the creation of this amendment in the first place. The real motivation behind the growth in women's sports, according to many of the coaches we've talked to, has been the women themselves—their wanting to participate. Title IX, in a way, is a means of underscoring this and accelerating progress. An important result of this law, even though it hasn't really been enforced until this last redefinition by HEW and now HSS Secretary Patricia Harris, is that there's been a dramatic rise in the number of women participating in intercollegiate athletics as well as a growth in the number of sports that more and more institutions are sponsoring for women. These, of course, are bound to continue to increase as the effects of the amendment become more far-reaching.

The dynamics of the changing scene have been exciting to watch as the changes in attitudes toward women's sports accelerate. "It's really unbelievable," tennis professional Janet Newberry notes. "Only eight years ago there just weren't tennis scholarships for women. I was the number two eighteen-year-old in the United States, second only to Chris Evert, and I was a good student besides. I ended up having to pay my entire tuition while today I'd have my pick of universities."

Margaret Wigiser remembers what New York City public school athletics for girls were like in the sixties. Competitive interscholastic events were not allowed because "girls cry when they lose." Gradually, with the help of a new director and some sympathetic colleagues, she was able to get permission for girls to represent their schools in interscholastic activities. "Of course, we had to do it without any money, but that didn't stop us," she recalls. "We went into areas like volleyball and basketball where I knew we'd do well and finally, in 1972, we got a budget. At last we could pay our coaches, who had mostly been volunteers, and we could offer more sports. Now, with Title IX, we've made real advances. We've gotten equal salaries for our basketball coaches as well as for our officials at sporting events. High school girls are pushing for more, and I'm hoping junior high school girls and their parents will start pushing, too."

Sports programs are changing, girls are changing, and so, of course, are coaches. Cathy Heck of Michigan State sees a new breed of coaches, young women who have actively participated in sports in high school and college and know intimately both the skills of a game and what it's like to play it. These are some of the qualities that can make for a good coach. Parents of girls high school age and younger often ask us how they can evaluate their daughters' coaches, and so we've come up with some guidelines.

HOW TO EVALUATE YOUR COACH

First, you should start by asking your daughter's coach some questions: Does your job depend on whether you win or lose? What is your training and background? Were you a physical education major?

Requirements vary from one school system to another, and a shortage of coaches has sometimes led to hiring unqualified instructors who, despite good intentions, can lack the knowledge to teach athletics. You might ask your coach if she's played the sport in question. Has she coached this or other sports? Participated in them herself? She can't be a good coach without a genuine interest in and enthusiasm for both athletics and children, and she's likely to manifest these in past work with children on some level and in her own participation in physical activity.

Does your coach understand the components of athletic performance? An athlete can win just by sheer determination and yet lack good hand-eye coordination or the skills to make lateral moves. These need to be developed if your coach is aiming for an optimum total performance.

In community sports the coaches can frequently be inexperienced although enthusiastic athletes. Or they can be simply men and women who are especially fond of children. Even more than with school programs, there is a tremendous range of ability among these volunteers. We can sketch for you three types of community coaches so that you can see the characteristics of good and bad coaches and just how they can manifest themselves.

Coach I. This woman believes that all children are innately competitive, a contention with which we disagree. During the match she stalks the sidelines, shouting and screaming at her team. She rarely gives credit for a skillful maneuver, and she is overly concerned about the place her team is currently in. She never works at building confidence among the young athletes, never bothers to teach skills or movement dynamics, and seems determined to instill aggression in every member of her team.

From our experience and observations, children are not nearly as competitive in sports as adults are. One of the most successful and popular ski programs is the Nancy Greene Ski League in Canada, where young skiers are taught racing maneuvers, turning around gates, for the purpose of improving their skills rather than winning any competition. These skiers get pleasure and excitement from activity and improvement, not from victory and defeat. We've found that especially when they are preadolescent and not yet programmed into competition, children enjoy playing for the fun of the game.

Coach II. This coach knows her sport well and, largely because she is a good teacher, has ended up with a winning team. But as her team improves, she herself has fallen into the trap of loving to win. She's now more critical and more competitive, identifying with the team so that every victory seems a personal gain for her, every defeat a bitter blow she suffers. She's working on developing the sense of competition among the children and, as this increases, parents have noticed the atmosphere becoming more and more tense.

Coach III. This last coach never chastises anyone. From the first day she knew every child by name and her final words after each game are "Good job," even after those games that the team has lost by a large margin. She has a warm personality and a soft but clear voice, and she looks every young athlete straight in the eye as she

256

gives advice about playing the sport. The children who started on this team have remained on it, showing up faithfully for practice sessions even in the worst weather. Whatever kinds of athletes this last group of girls eventually becomes, their initial experience with team sports has made the concept of physical activity a good one.

Next, what about safety? That's often the first question parents of participants ask, and it's an area that certainly merits exploration. Everyone seems to have heard stories about inadequate medical supervision or lack of emergency equipment. A girl falls in a gymnastic event in a New York private school, and she's probably broken her arm. The school nurse will allow no one near her until a doctor, coming from some distance away, arrives to alleviate the girl's pain and take her to his office for X rays. Or another girl, obviously suffering from a dislocated shoulder after a forceful encounter in a basketball game, is driven by her coach to the emergency room—only she isn't quite sure where the local hospital is and the twenty-minute trip ends up taking an hour.

What can you, as parents of a school athlete, ask in order to determine if your program is safe? First, find out what kind of equipment is being used and what safety measures go along with it. If a trampoline is used, there must be spotters sufficient in number to watch each child who is exercising at one time. If there are ropes, are they frayed? Are mats worn so that they've lost resiliency? Are there enough mats for the number of children participating?

Ask to watch a typical class so that you can see for yourself what's going on. Are children being carefully watched and properly supervised? During competitions is there a system for dealing with injuries? If there is no doctor at an athletic event, your coach or some school official should have an arrangement for transportation, with a car ready to take an injured athlete to a doctor. Someone coaching the team should have a basic knowledge of first aid. She should be able to deal with an asthmatic attack and an epileptic seizure, should be able to splint a bone, and, besides having a car—preferably a station wagon—handy, should know how to get to the nearest hospital. At out-of-town games she should know where the hospital is and what kinds of doctors are available there.

Does the hospital only treat outpatients, or can an injured or seriously ill athlete be hospitalized there? Your coach should also know how to get emergency ambulance service in the event of a life-threatening situation such as heart failure. It's certainly fair for you to ask the coach what she would do in the various situations that might come up. If she can't answer your questions and hasn't even thought about these eventualities, you might question her ability to handle emergency situations.

What emergency equipment is necessary? This can depend on the age of the participants and the nature of the sport. Contact sports, for example, may require more. But most coaches should have something, such as pressure bandages, to stop bleeding and strips to close up a cut. Ice packs should be part of basic equipment along with collapsible air splints, which can be good temporary aids for fractures or sore knees. These take up little space before they're blown up, are inexpensive, and a doctor can X-ray right through them. Tongue blades or curved mouthpieces to keep someone in a seizure from swallowing her tongue are another feature of a basic first aid pack.

Sports safety is greatly improved in those situations where coaches are well versed in sports medicine. In New York State coaches have requirements for recertification that include taking sports medicine courses. In these they're given information about body function and fitness as well as injury detection, all of which is reflected in better safety records.

In those larger sports programs where trainers are involved, they, too, should have requirements in the field of sports medicine so that they can recognize injuries and understand skill development. Since part of a trainer's function is to help select equipment, tape an athlete when necessary, and do initial screening of injuries, trainers need qualifications similar to coaches'. We would recommend that certification as either student trainers or as full members of the National Athletic Trainer Association be a requirement. A knowledgeable trainer, by taking over many of the paramedical responsibilities, can leave the coach free to concentrate on developing skills.

A crucial part of safety in school programs is the thorough

screening of athletes. While most school programs require a doctor's certificate and some states require an examination by a specific physician employed by the school system, too many examinations are inadequate. Young athletes who continue to participate with undetected fractures, particularly carpal-navicular fractures of the wrist, can eventually end up suffering from arthritis. A girl with sore kneecaps will have increasing pain if she plays basketball or field hockey without first undergoing the proper strengthening therapy.

At Michigan State two family physicians examine athletes. Cathy Heck reports that a large number of freshmen women are put on rehabilitation programs right from the start so they don't have a chance to get hurt. Those who make the freshman varsity teams are in good shape, fit enough to handle the vigorous routine.

Good screening not only keeps some players from joining a program but allows the participation of others who might have been kept out. Some physical conditions have been misunderstood or misinterpreted, resulting in excluding the students who would most benefit from sports. We know, for example, that many cardiovascular and pulmonary problems can be helped by activity if the proper modifications are followed.

Static examinations of school athletes—taking blood pressure and pulse rate and listening for clear lungs—are simply not enough. Observing students while they are active and testing them after exertion will provide a far more complete picture of the condition they're in. Students should be asked to run in place so that their pulse recovery rates can be measured. A physical examination should include a musculoskeletal profile to determine specific joint function, range of motion, stability, general body looseness or tightness, presence of pain, and the ability to execute certain functional tests such as hopping on one foot or walking in a full squat (duck walk).

Here is a questionnaire and suggested examination we have developed for the Sports Medicine Service at the Hospital for Special Surgery in New York. We recommend it as a guideline for preseason evaluation.

259

HISTORY

1. NAME: _____ 2. SOCIAL SECURITY NO. _____

3. HOME ADDRESS: _____
   No & St.   City   State   ZIP

4. PHONE: _____ 5. SEX: _____ 6: AGE: _____ 7: BIRTH DATE: _____

8. MARITAL STATUS: _____

9. PRESENT TEAM: _____

10. LEVEL OF COMPETITION: a) professional b) college c) high school d) varsity e) JV

11. Whom shall we notify in case of an emergency? NAME: _____
    Relation: _____ Address: _____
    Phone: _____ Business Phone: _____

12. HEALTH INSURANCE: Name: _____
    Name of persons insured: _____
    Policy Number: _____

13. During participation, do you wear: (a) contact lenses (b) glasses (c) dental appliances (d) mouth protector

DISEASES AND ILLNESSES (PAST AND PRESENT):
Circle number of all appropriate conditions.

Details of circled conditions.

14.
1 ___ Congenital generalized abnormalities/absent organs
2 ___ Blood disease
3 ___ Infectious mononucleosis, pneumonia, or others
4 ___ Epilepsy
5 ___ Hepatitis, jaundice
6 ___ Diabetes
7 ___ Sugar, albumin, pus, blood in urine
8 ___ Cough up blood
9 ___ Allergies (to drugs, etc.)
10 ___ High blood pressure
11 ___ Concussion/knocked out (give #)
12 ___ Recurring headaches/blackouts
13 ___ Blurred vision, sties, pink eye
14 ___ Chronic nose bleeds
15 ___ Skin infections, boils, impetigo, etc.
16 ___ Congenital heart disease, rheumatic fever, murmurs
17 ___ Appendicitis, hernia
18 ___ Chest pain during exercise
19 ___ Tuberculosis
20 ___ Chronic cough
21 ___ Frequent indigestion, heartburn
22 ___ Ulcer (location)

23 ___ Kidney or bladder diseases
24 ___ Heat exhaustion/heat stroke
25 ___ Hearing problems
26 ___ Mental illness
27 ___ Any other illness not listed

15. Are you presently taking medication? What kind? _____

What dosage? _____

16. OPERATIONS OR HOSPITALIZATIONS:

TYPE	DATE	HOSPITAL	DOCTOR'S NAME & ADDRESS

17. Any diagnostic tests performed? EKG, electroencephalogram, electromyogram, arthrogram, etc? _____

18. BONES AND JOINTS (ORTHOPEDIC HISTORY): circle where applicable.

1. Head
2. Neck
3. Shoulder-Clavicle
4. Arm, Elbow, Wrist
5. Hand
6. Spine
7. Ribs
8. Hips and Pelvis
9. Thigh
10. Knee, Kneecap
11. Leg
12. Ankle
13. Foot

Details of circled regions (explain type of injury or condition, i.e., arthritis, calcium deposits, nerve injury, fracture, etc.).

19. Do you have any bone grafts, spinal fusions, plates, screws, etc.?

20. Do you wear any type of brace, splint, or orthopedic appliance?

FEMALE SUPPLEMENT

21. Menstrual History: Age of onset: _____   Interval: _____   Duration: _____

    Last menstrual period: _____

22. Conditions: a) dysmenorrhea b) varicose veins c) pregnancy d) other _____

23. Contraception: a) rhythm b) birth control pills c) IUD d) other _____

I hereby state that, to the best of my knowledge and belief, my answers to the foregoing questions are correct.

_____   _____
Signature   Date

(TO BE FILLED OUT BY PHYSICIAN)

1. NAME: _____ 2. HT: _____ 3. WT: _____ 4. BP: ____/____

5. PULSE: _____ Normal reading after 1 minute of running: _____

6. VISION: Without glasses: R: _____ L: _____; With glasses/lenses: R: _____ L: _____

7. HEARING: R: _____ /15 L: _____ /15

8. SKIN: (a) dry (b) moist (c) coarse (d) smooth (e) rash (f) scars (g) nail changes (h) telangiectasia (i) discoloration
   (j) needle tracks (k) other: _____

9. SCALP: (a) normal (b) tenderness (c) scar (d) other: _____

10. LYMPH NODES: (a) present (b) absent (c) location: _____

11. EARS: (pinna, external canal, tympanic membrane) (a) normal (b) discharge (c) other: _____

12. NOSE: (septum, sinus) (a) normal (b) tenderness (c) obstruction (d) discharge (e) other: _____

13. THROAT & MOUTH: (lips, tonsils, buccal mucosa, tongue, pharynx, teeth, gums) (a) normal (b) abnormal

14. NECK: (thyroid, trachea) (a) normal (b) mass (c) other: _____

15. BREAST: Right (a) normal (b) mass (c) scar _____ location
            Left (a) normal (b) mass (c) scar _____ location

16. CHEST & LUNGS: Inspection: (a) normal (b) abnormal
                   Auscultation: (a) normal (b) abnormal

17. HEART: Auscultation: (a) normal (b) abnormal

18. SPINE: (a) normal (b) lordosis (c) kyphosis (d) scoliosis

19. ABDOMEN: (liver, spleen, kidneys, stomach, appendix, intestines)
    Inspection: (a) flat (b) distended (c) scaphoid (d) scars (e) other: _____
    Palpation: (a) normal (b) rigid (c) tender (d) mass (e) rebound (f) fluid wave (g) hernia

20. GENITALIA: External (a) clitoris (b) labia _____
    Pelvic (a) cervix (b) uterus (c) adnexa

21. NERVOUS SYSTEM & REFLEXES: Pupils: (a) equal (b) unequal
    Knee Jerk: (a) normal (b) abnormal
    Ankle Jerk: (a) normal (b) abnormal
    Romberg Test: (a) normal (b) abnormal

22. IMMUNIZATION: FLU: ___/___ TETANUS: _____ POLIO: _____
    RUBELLA: _____

23. LAB STUDIES: Albumin: _____ Specific Gravity: _____
    Urine Glucose: _____ Other: _____
    Blood CBC: _____ Blood sugar: _____ Sickle Cell: _____ Other: _____

24. SPECIAL STUDIES: (A) CHEST & OTHER X RAY FINDINGS: _____
    (B) EKG/ECG STRESS TEST: _____
    (C) ELECTROMYOGRAM: _____
    (D) MUSCLE TESTS: _____
    (E) FITNESS EVALUATION: _____

1. NECK: (a) normal   (b) pain in range of motion   (c) limited rotation   (d) limited flexion   (e) limited extension

2. SPINE: (a) normal   (b) excess lordosis   (c) kyphosis   (d) scoliosis   (e) limited motion   (f) pain with motion   (g) decreased reflexes   (h) sensory change   (i) increased weakness   (j) + Leseque's

3. SHOULDER: (a) normal   (b) limited range of motion   (c) pain throughout range of motion   (d) pain and limited range of motion   (e) atrophy

4. ELBOW: (a) normal (absence of hyperextension, i.e., extension = 180°)   (b) hyperextension (greater than 180°)   (c) flexion contracture (less than 180°)

5. WRIST: (a) normal   (b) limited range of motion   (c) pain with motion

6. M-P EXTENSION: (a) <70°   (b) 70–89°   (c) =90°   (d) >90°

7. THUMB-FOREARM: (a) >45°
   (b) 1–45°, not touching
   (c) +
   (d) ++
   (e) does not apply

8. HAND: (a) normal   (b) limited in flexion   (c) limited in extension   (d) limited in rotation   (e) pain in flexion   (f) pain in extension   (g) pain in rotation

9. FUNCTIONAL TESTS: (Scores: 0 = can't perform, 1 = can perform with discomfort,
2 = can perform well)

    (a) Up and down stairs: _____   (b) Running in place: _____

    (c) Hop on one leg: _____   (d) Half squat: _____   (e) Full squat: _____

10. PALMS TO FLOOR: (a) >10 inches from floor

                        (b) <10 inches from floor

                        (c) Tips to floor

                        (d) Fingers to floor

                        (e) Palms to floor

11. HIP: (a) normal (b) limited in flexion (c) limited in extension (d) limited in rotation (e) pain in flexion (f) pain in extension (g) pain in rotation

12. KNEE:

Alignment: (a) varus

                 (b) valgus, 0–14° normal

                 (c) valgus, greater than 15°

                 (d) flexion contracture

                 (e) normal

                 (f) hyperextension

Range of motion: (a) normal (b) limited in flexion or extension (c) limited in flexion and extension
(d) less than 90°

Thigh sizes: (a) equal (b) 1–2 cm. difference (c) greater than 2 cm. difference

Stability: (for all stability scores, answer must include both # and letter)

(A) LCL: (5) Normal = opposite leg
(4) Mild instability in flexion
(3) Moderate instability in flexion
(2) Instability in flexion and extension
(0) Gross instability
(a) Hard end point
(b) Soft end point

(B) MCL: (5) Normal = opposite leg
(4) Mild instability in flexion
(3) Moderate instability in flexion
(2) Instability in flexion and extension
(0) Gross instability
(a) Hard end point
(b) Soft end point

(C) ACL: (Anterior Drawer Sign)*
(5) Normal = opposite leg
(4) Slight jog
(3) Moderate jog
(2) Severe in neutral
(0) Severe in neutral and rotation
(a) Hard end point
(b) Soft end point

(D) PCL: (Posterior Drawer Sign)*
(5) Normal = opposite leg
(4) Slight jog
(3) Moderate jog
(2) Severe in neutral
(0) Severe in neutral and rotation
(a) Hard end point
(b) Soft end point

*Test to derive score

Palpation:
Scar: (a) yes (b) no
Pain: (a) yes (b) no
Effusion: (a) yes (b) no
Soft tissue swelling: (a) yes (b) no

Excursion: (a) ½ inch (b) 1 inch (c) 1–1½ inches (d) 2 inches (e) >2 inches

Displacement: (a) medial (b) lateral (c) straight

Apprehension Test: (a) yes (b) no

Crepitation: (a) yes (b) no

14. ANKLE: Range of motion: (a) normal (b) limited (c) painful

Stability: (a) normal (b) + anterior drawer sign (c) + medial//lateral talar shift

Heel cord tightness: (a) >90° (b) 90° (c) <90°

15. FEET: (a) *pes cavus* (high arches)
(b) normal
(c) splay
(d) flat (*pes planus*)
(e) pronated

16. EXAMINER'S IMPRESSION (DIAGNOSIS):

17. RECOMMENDATIONS:

18. EXAMINER: _____

Once an athlete passes the careful scrutiny of a medical examination and wants to join a team, some further assessment ought to be made. J. Kenneth "Dutch" Hafner, who has recently retired as director of field services for the New York State Public High School Athletic Association, believes that 99 percent of the prevention of injuries lies in starting the athlete off right. This means placing her in the correct situation where she's competing with and against her equals. Among children and adolescents, there are tremendous differences in rates of maturation, and this should be taken into consideration. Participation on a particular team shouldn't depend simply on age or grade but rather on the level of maturation, skill, and fitness. Such judgments, of course, will need frequent reassessment because of differing growth and maturation patterns.

How can a coach determine if athletes are fit? With the following tests she should be able to screen out those who would be more likely to suffer injuries and so require more conditioning. Students who can reach or surpass these norms, and who, of course, have already been evaluated in the initial screening procedure, are fit enough to make the team.

SUGGESTED FITNESS LEVEL FOR TEAM PARTICIPATION

STRENGTH	Modified Push-ups	13 or more
	Flexed arm hangs	10 seconds or longer
	Sit-ups	30 in one minute
	Wall-sits	for over one minute or longer

upper body weights—arms: lift half body weight, pressing it away from her. (A 100-pound girl should be able to lift 50 pounds.)
lower body weights—legs: should be able to press twice her body weight. (A 100-pound girl should be able to press 200 pounds.)

POWER	40-yard dash in 5.9 seconds or less
	standing broad jump (long jump) 5'3"
	vertical jump 12"

AGILITY *Sidestep:* starting at a center line and sidestepping alternately left and then right across two outside lines 8 feet apart. Should be able to do 14 or more side steps in 10 seconds.

ENDURANCE   mile-and-a-half run in 17 minutes
FLEXIBILITY Bend and stretch   6.0 inches
             Adductors   110 degrees
             Shoulder stretch II   40 inches with hands
                                     straight going across
             Palms to the floor   8 inches or closer

Once coaches have a good idea of the level of fitness of their athletes, they can start training programs. Besides overall conditioning, players should practice by using the muscles and tendons they're going to need in the sport. For example, as Dutch Hafner of the New York State High School Athletic Association points out, if your team keeps practicing one motion, such as an overhand throw, indoors in a gym during the winter and another, such as throwing a curve ball, outdoors in the spring, they're likely to have sore elbows and shoulders as the softball season gets under way. Coaches can avoid this by having athletes in January execute the movements they'll be using in March.

Conditioning should be a year-round program, but most schools, certainly most high schools, have neither the facilities nor the funds to support this. Still, coaches can make recommendations for training during the off-season so that fitness levels don't drop. Running, bicycle riding, swimming, or some other aerobic activity should be done about three times a week. The quickness and agility called for in soccer make it an excellent off-season activity for many athletes, including skiers. Running is also popular for skiers during the summer season, and it's been found useful as well for tennis players in winter. Strength exercises, working with free weights or with weight resistance machines, should be done twice a week for maintenance and three times a week for improvement. Flexibility exercises should be done faithfully every day. Power training, with high-intensity starts and quick stops, can easily be incorporated into the running program. If coaches stress the fact that it's infinitely easier to maintain than to improve, it's more likely that their teams will work out during the off-season.

After training starts, what signs should parents and coaches watch out for? Young athletes should not develop excessive fatigue or weakness or dizziness. Rapid respiration and an inability to recover as quickly as others do after a period of exercise is also a warning that something may be wrong with the heart or lungs. Pains in any joint or abdominal cramps are indications that there are difficulties in the musculoskeletal system. Problems in the neurological system can manifest themselves in spasms, contractions, or significant weakness of one limb. Any of these symptoms needs checking out although none of them would necessarily preclude physical activity.

Despite thorough screening and intelligent training, injuries can occur, so it's wise to make sure that you have adequate insurance. Too many policies for schoolchildren have a $200 deductible and then a $1,000 maximum. These days that just about gets you inside the door of a hospital, what with X rays and blood tests. If your daughter has surgery and requires a week's hospitalization, your insurance money will not begin to scratch the surface of the expenses. Check your policy again and make sure you have sufficient coverage.

Of course, serious injuries are extremely rare, and an awareness of their possibility should never become a preoccupation. All the more so since it might deter some parents from allowing their children to participate in athletics. It seems to us crucial for parents actively to encourage their children since early involvement in sports will tend to help form a lifetime habit. Physical fitness is just one element of what these children will gain. Equally important is the great pleasure—physical and emotional— that sports participation can offer both the child and the adult.

12

Fitness
over Forty-Five

Since recorded time we know that women have always lived longer than men. At the turn of the century, the average life span for an American man was forty-nine, while for a woman it was fifty-three. In the years since, these average life spans have increased for both sexes, but for women the gain has been disproportionate—to seventy-seven compared to a man's sixty-nine. There is speculation as to why this is, with various theories that credit estrogen or steroids. Whatever the reason, it's a fact that the concerns of aging have become even more the concerns of women. Your enjoyment of these later years depends enormously on the shape that you're in, and that shape can be continually improved through an appropriate fitness program.

Take your weight, for example. As you get older you need fewer and fewer calories, but because your eating habits are so ingrained by now, you're going to find it increasingly difficult to maintain your weight. This is a particular problem for women, who, compared to men, start out with more body fat in the first place. Exercise can help keep your optimum weight, a factor affecting not only your appearance but, more crucial, your blood pressure. Weight becomes critical if you are one of the large number of people (30 percent of all Americans over sixty) who has hypertension. Increased physical activity will not only help by keeping your weight down but it also actually functions to lower your blood pressure.

Another condition that can be dramatically improved by exercise is diabetes, a disease that affects close to 20 percent of the American population over sixty. Exercise can stimulate your body to produce more of the needed insulin, consequently reducing your external requirements. Diabetic tennis player Hamilton Richardson, because of the stresses of a long match, produces so much insulin that sometimes it's even been in excess of what's necessary. You may not get up to the level of exercise of a top tournament player, but your increasing activity will be a great aid in controlling this disease.

When you exercise, your entire cardiopulmonary system becomes more efficient. This, in turn, offers a whole list of vital benefits. If you have angina, your chest pains may diminish in intensity because of a lessening in the resistance of your heart muscle, which can cause constriction. Besides this desired result, being more active will also increase the flow of blood in the heart and other muscles, moving it into more vessels so that those not working well will have other vessels to take up the slack.

Women who exercise have been found to have less frequent attacks of coronary artery disease, less intense heart attacks if they occur, and better collateral circulation, which helps maintain the health of the heart muscle. For those inactive, the risk of death from cardiovascular disease is two to three times greater than for those who exercise.

When you are physically fit, your red blood cells increase so that there are more of them to carry the oxygen that your system runs on. You have fewer triglycerides, which we think are related to plugged blood vessels. Thrombosis, the stopped-up veins that can cause swelling limbs in older people, is decreased by changes in your blood chemistry brought on by physical activity. Other benefits are decreased blood cholesterol and increased high-density lipoproteins which are associated with less coronary artery disease.

As for your lungs, exercise will help them make the exchange— of fuel oxygen for the waste product carbon dioxide—more efficiently. If you have asthma, emphysema, or some other pulmonary disease, an appropriate exercise program will soon have you breathing more deeply and evenly.

Most of us have simply assumed that when we get older all of our bodily systems will decline. We'll hear less acutely, see less sharply, and our bodies will ultimately grow weaker. Some of the changes that come with age are, we know, measurable fact—many of us do end up needing reading glasses, for example, or having some other actual deficiency. Most of the physical changes in older people, however, are mistakenly attributed to aging when, in fact, the actual cause is a lack of proper conditioning. We believe that most of the so-called frailties of age are social phenomena and, as such, avoidable.

Take the musculoskeletal system. It doesn't change all that radically because of the normal aging process but because we've allowed it to. When we don't exercise, when we sit for long periods of time or allow ourselves every step saver from golf carts to electric can openers, we can find our powers diminishing. If a normal, healthy person of any age spent a week resting on a sofa or in a bed, she could lose as much as two inches in the circumference of the muscles. As for her bones, they would quickly lose density with disuse. The astronauts, as soon as they were weightless, suffered from this bone loss. We don't know the reason for what happens but we do know that in the bodies of the physically inactive, the calcium needed to give bones their hardness washes away into the bloodstream. What's left will be brittle bones, capable of breaking easily.

One bone disease that is more common among older women than older men is osteoporosis. Women with this condition (about 10 to 15 percent of those over sixty) have such thin bones that they can get actual fractures in their spines. There has been a great deal of research trying to show that this disease is related to losses of hormones or calcium. Still, there's been no real proof that we can change the density of bone by any known medication. The one thing we are certain will change the density is exercise. When an older person has curvature of the spine or hunched shoulders, it's assumed that age is responsible. She'll be treated with pills or injections, which is easy—the prescription of an exercise program may be a lot harder for her to take, but that's exactly the path to follow. Exercise is the one factor we know will be helpful to the musculoskeletal system, with beneficial changes that are almost instantaneous.

Arthritis occurs in two basic forms. One, osteoarthritis, which is characterized by excess bone deposits, limits your motion and makes you feel stiff. Stretching and strengthening exercises will help take the pressure off those of your joints that are afflicted. As for the other kind of arthritis, rheumatoid arthritis, the problem is progressive stiffness and disintegration of a joint that can end in crippling. Again, as with osteoarthritis, stretching and strengthening exercises will help alleviate many of the joint symptoms since, as the bones deteriorate, the concomitant muscles tend to weaken. We've found good results with exercising in warm water—showers, tubs, or warm pools.

As for backache, from our experience with patients we've concluded that about 95 percent of it is probably due to muscular imbalance and/or poor posture. Here again exercise can relieve the condition. Heidi Preuss of the United States ski team, one of the top ten women skiers in the country, was washed out of the program because of her back problems. After less than three months on a strength and flexibility program she was back again, skiing as well as she ever had and no longer troubled by back pains.

When you're older and have back problems, too often your aches are assumed to be inevitable, something you can do nothing about. We believe though that rather than the aging process, what's bothering the backs of so many older people is a lack of exercise and just too much sitting.

Other musculoskeletal aches, such as tendinitis of the shoulder or elbow, can also be cured through training. We've seen patients with tendinitis who have been advised to undergo surgery or a series of injections and have been cautioned against any physically demanding activity at all. Yet 98 percent of our patients have gotten over tendinitis of the elbow (that is, tennis elbow, which could also be called golf elbow or even knitter's elbow since there are many activities that can bring it on). When you use muscles to a degree for which they have not been conditioned, your joints can end up suffering. Strengthen the muscle and you can cure the tendinitis. We've found that, in general, any joint or muscle problem benefits from exercise.

What should be particularly encouraging is the rapidity of the improvement you'll see in your musculoskeletal system when you begin to exercise. It's not unusual for women over forty-five and on up into their eighties who have been exercising properly to have levels of fitness close to those of women in their twenties and thirties. As for your cardiovascular system, after starting out on a good fitness program you'll move right out of the high-risk category and into the low-risk one. Being sedentary will have caused little harm that is irreversible. For the most part, you can change your systems so that they'll start working more efficiently for you.

Among the other benefits you can look forward to when you're fit is a decrease in insomnia. Several older women have told us they had the first uninterrupted deep night's sleep in years after a vigorous session of stamina training. We've also gotten reports that headaches have disappeared or gotten less severe, and that stomach complaints have eased. These are subjective observations that, along with our own conclusion that women (and men) who are active have better color and firmness to their skin, can't be considered scientific fact. Still, these are benefits we've noted and think should be passed along to you.

Before starting on your exercise program, we recommend you see your doctor for the Medical Profile we've outlined. Next, you should assess your own inherent physical traits and present condition with a Fitness Self-Portrait. If you're over forty-five and have never exercised before, or if you have any history of cardiac disease, you should have an exercise stress test. We don't feel that you need this, though, if you've been active in the past and are presently in a good state of health. Dr. Marc Weksler, the head of the division of geriatrics and gerontology at Cornell University Medical School in New York, agrees with this. He believes that for many reasons the best stress test of all is simply the slow progression of exercise itself. It can guide you far more wisely than can the exercise electrocardiogram. There are more and more medical tests these days that can uncover many subtle abnormalities, but it's important not to allow these tests to confuse the basic issue, which is whether or not you should exercise. It could be argued that a stress test done prior to exercising might not only suggest you shouldn't exercise but also foreclose the opportunity for exercise to improve your results on a subsequent stress test. You may end up not being active when you're someone most in the need of a program of physical activity. It's possible these days to get involved with so much medical technology that you're on an endless (and expensive) treadmill. If you're feeling well, your family doctor finds you healthy, and you're well motivated toward becoming fit, we would encourage you to start.

OVER FORTY-FIVE FITNESS PROGRAM

When you begin your exercise program, you may be starting out at a level of fitness that's below that of a younger person. But even if your increment is different, you'll still be continually improving. In fact, you may find that your improvement is even more vitally important in its effect on your daily life. A younger woman who has kept in shape generally has considerable reserves. Her exercise is not only making her more fit but is giving her something extra to keep on tap. Only if she's a serious competitor will she need to draw on all of those resources. An older woman, though, who has spent years being sedentary, will find each increase in fitness immediately useful. Without conditioning she may lack the stamina not only to win in a sport but possibly to play at any sport at all, or not only to run around a track but perhaps to get up a flight of stairs without panting. So if you're over forty-five and have not been active, you may start lower, but the changes that your rising fitness level will make will have a tremendous effect on the quality of your life.

Begin by warming up. A brisk walk can do it or a jog-walk if your level of fitness makes that an appropriate activity. Careful stretching should follow since the elasticity of your muscles and tendons hasn't been tested in a long time. Cooling down is essential after you've completed a workout. When you exercise, more of your blood goes to your working muscles so that if you stand still or sit immediately afterward, the blood will pool in your legs. You'll be dizzy and may even lose consciousness. Avoid this unpleasant physical reaction by tapering off from activity. Walk around until your heart rate is within twenty beats of your resting pulse, no matter how long that takes. As you exercise more, you'll find the cooling-off period shortens, with your heart functioning more efficiently.

If you're exercising out-of-doors, be sure you protect yourself from the sun, which is a great foe of aging skin. Ultraviolet waves break apart collagen molecules and can cause changes in the skin that may result in skin cancer. If you're exercising outdoors at a high altitude, the risk of sunburn is even greater since there's less density of air between you and the sun. There's also less oxygen so that you may have to reduce your activity until you acclimate to the atmosphere.

Allow time for exercise. If you're in too much of a hurry, you may be active at a time too soon after a meal. The process of digestion requires the blood you also need for exercise so it's dangerous to combine the two activities.

Your cardiovascular activities can be swimming or jogging. A good alternative, and one that can be used in all weather, is a small exercise bicycle on which your legs do not have to go through large sweeps of motion.

It's been shown that age itself is no deterrent to endurance training. The relative change in maxVO$_2$, an excellent measure of cardiovascular fitness, is similar for both older and younger women. Just remember to stress your body gradually and to stop or slow down if your pulse rate gets too high. You can figure out a rough estimate of your target pulse rate, the rate you'll want to maintain during endurance training, by subtracting your age from 220 and multiplying this by .60 to .75. After your warm-up, start your stamina activity and keep taking your pulse to see that you're keeping up this target rate for approximately twenty minutes. Follow your exercise by a gradual cooling down.

Strength exercises are appropriate for you if the weights are kept

279

between three and five pounds, at least when you first start out. Many repetitions with light weights will work best. Some of the exercise physiologists and coaches we've talked to who have worked with older women tell us that weight lifting has become an especially popular activity. The upper extremities should be emphasized because that's where the greatest weakness lies for all women and especially for older women. If you've been primarily a sitter, abdominal exercises should also be something you'll concentrate your efforts on.

As often as you can, you should spend time doing flexibility exercises. These will help immeasurably to combat the musculoskeletal complaints you're otherwise likely to have. Feeling as though there's not enough oil lubricating the moving parts is definitely not a necessary part of growing older, as you'll find out after a short time in a good fitness program.

OVER FORTY-FIVE EXERCISES

*Those starred are especially recommended for women over sixty-five.

There is no reason why the physically fit woman of any age cannot use the exercise program outlined in Chapter 7. For those just starting out, however, this modified approach will be more appropriate, at least in the beginning.

SPECIFIC EXERCISE	AREA OF BODY WORKED	OBJECT AND PRACTICAL PURPOSE
*Head circles	Neck	This is to loosen the joints in the cervical spine and stretch the neck muscles. The object is to do a full range of motion.
Arm circles	Shoulder, upper arm	This is to loosen the shoulder joint and stretch the shoulder muscles. The object is to do a full range of motion.
Broomstick activities	Shoulder, upper arm	This is excellent for stretching the shoulder area and is a modification of the Towel exercise in Chapter 7.

*Arm crosses	Upper arm	This is good for stretching the triceps, the muscles on the back of the upper arm. The stretch should also be felt on the outer parts of the arms.
Extensor exercise	Forearm	This exercise stretches the muscles on the bottom of the forearm.
*Ball grip	Hand	This exercise will loosen the joints and stretch the muscles of the hand.
*Trunk rotation	Chest	This is good for loosening the muscles of the chest and trunk.
Side rock	Upper arm, trunk	This is excellent for stretching the upper body and the trunk.
Side kicks	Hip, thigh	The muscles in your upper legs will be stretched, and you should feel this down the outside of your leg.
High stepping	Thigh	This exercise is good for stretching the front area of the thighs.
Foot slide	Ankle, foot	This exercise stretches the muscles of the ankle and foot.
Stair stretch	Lower leg, Achilles tendon	You should feel this stretch in the lower leg region, specifically in the calf muscle and Achilles tendon.
Foot towel exercise	Foot	This is excellent for aching, tired feet.

Description of Suppleness Exercises

FOR THE NECK. *Head circles.* Standing straight with your hands on your hips and your feet shoulder-width apart, slowly rotate your head clockwise in a full circle, taking a count of ten to go completely around. An easy way to understand this maneuver is to picture the face of a clock in front of you and think of your nose as moving around that face, from twelve o'clock around to three, down to six, and back up to twelve. After doing a complete circle clockwise, repeat going counterclockwise. This exercise is a warm-up with some amount of stretching and is worthwhile only if done slowly. You may hear some cracking or popping, which

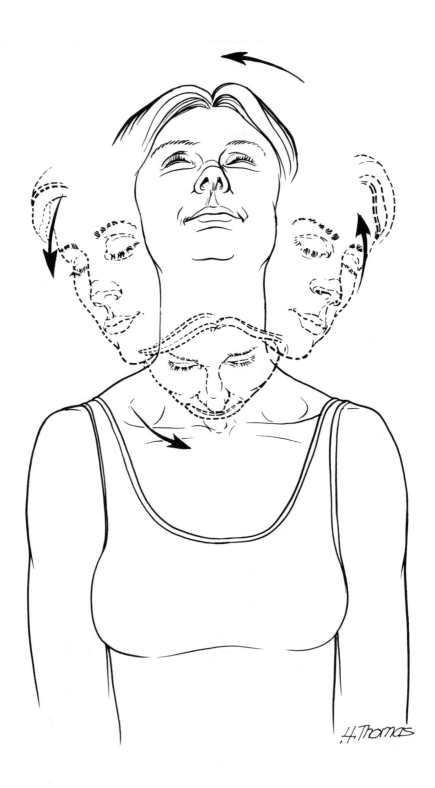

indicates that the joints of your spine are loosening up after being held in one position. It's a good idea to do some head circles after driving for a while or sitting at your desk.

FOR THE SHOULDER, UPPER ARM, CHEST. *Arm circles.* Standing with your elbows straight and your arms out to the side, make circles with your whole arm. Slowly start with small circles and then make them larger. Do two sets of ten, first clockwise and then counterclockwise.

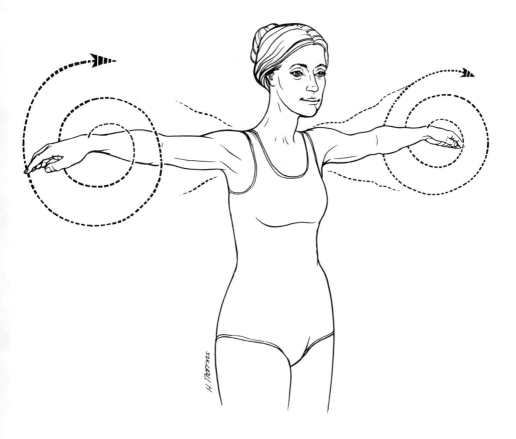

Broomstick activities. With your hands hold a broomstick overhead, straighten your arms and bend both shoulders to the right without moving your waist. Hold for a count of ten, and then repeat to the left, again holding for ten. Repeat five or six times.

Arm crosses. Bend your arms in front of you across your chest close to your body so that your right hand can touch your left elbow and left hand can touch right elbow. Slide your arms across your chest, right arm to the left and left arm to the right until your elbows meet and your forearms have extended beyond your shoulder. Hold for a count of ten. Then reverse the sliding movement with your elbows going outward so that your fingertips touch in the middle of your chest. Hold again for ten and repeat the whole sequence ten times.

FOR THE
FOREARM.

Extensor exercise. Hold your arm out in front of you, keeping your elbow straight. Fully extend your fingers and wrist and hold for a count of ten. Then with the help of your opposite hand flex your wrist down toward the floor at an angle as close as possible to ninety degrees. Hold. Then extend your wrist up and hold. Repeat, using the other arm. When your wrist is down, you'll feel the stretch on the top muscles of your arm, and when it's up you'll feel it on the bottom muscles.

FOR THE
HAND.

Ball grip. Place a soft rubber ball in your hand and then squeeze the ball rhythmically. Repeat ten times and then transfer the ball to the other hand and again squeeze it rhythmically ten times. This exercise can be repeated often.

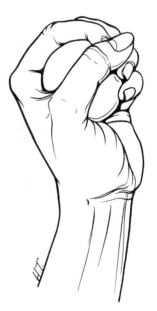

FOR THE
CHEST.

Trunk rotation. Start in a sitting position with your feet placed flat on the floor in front of you and your arms folded across your chest. With your neck and back straight, slowly twist at the waist, turning your shoulders and head as far as possible to the right. Hold for a count of ten and return to your starting position. Then repeat, turning your shoulders and head as far as possible to the left. Hold again for a count of ten. Repeat this sequence ten to fifteen times.

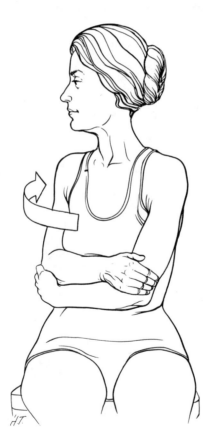

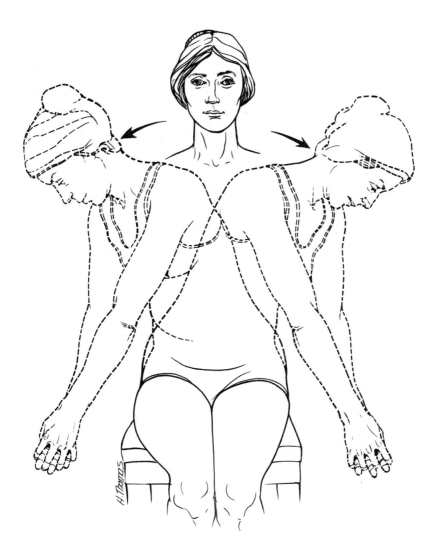

FOR THE
UPPER ARM
AND TRUNK.

Side rock. Sitting up straight in a chair, slowly bend your body to the right, reaching toward the floor with both hands and holding for a count of three. Return to your original upright position and then repeat, reaching toward the left. Repeat this ten to fifteen times.

289

FOR THE HIP
AND THIGH.

Side kick. Sit on a chair with your back and neck straight, your legs together, and your hands on your thighs. Then reach your left leg out to the left as far as you can and then return to the starting position. Then reach your right leg out to the right as far as you can. Return to the starting position and repeat these movements five to ten times with each leg.

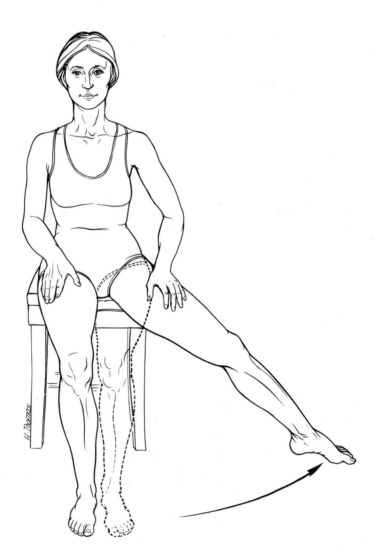

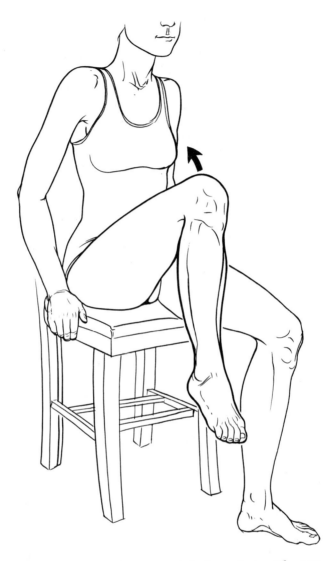

FOR THE
THIGH.

High stepping. Sitting upright in a chair with your hands resting on your thighs, lift your right knee up as high as possible, pointing your right toe downward. Return your right foot to the floor and lift the left knee up, bending the left toe downward. Return to the starting position and repeat the entire sequence ten times in a steady rhythm.

291

FOR THE
LOWER LEG
AND ACHILLES
TENDON.

Stair stretch. Stand on the edge of a step with your heels halfway off. Rise up on your toes and hold this position for a count of ten. Next, press your heels down below the step and hold again for ten. This second part can be done with one foot at a time.

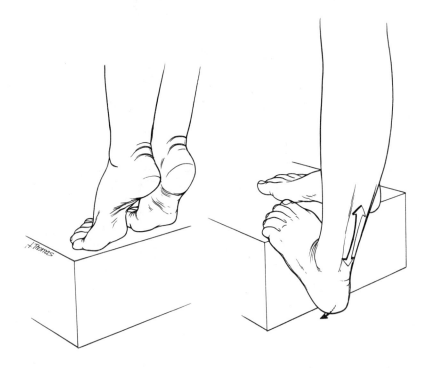

FOR THE
ANKLE
AND FOOT.

Foot slide. Sitting upright on a chair with your feet flat on the floor and your hands resting on your thighs, move your heels as far apart from each other as you can with your toes touching in a pigeon-toed position. Return to the first position and then move your toes out as far as you can with your heels together. Repeat ten times in each direction.

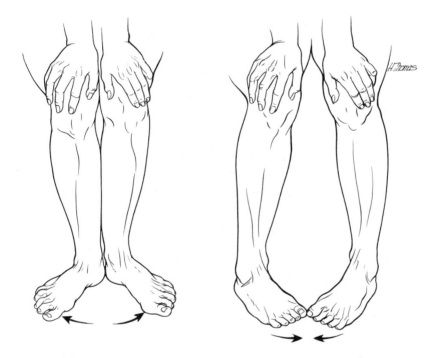

Foot towel exercise. Sit on a chair with your feet resting on a towel on the floor in front of you. Curling the toes on your right foot, try to grasp the towel. Then, relaxing your right foot, curl the toes of your left and grasp the towel. Repeat ten times with each foot.

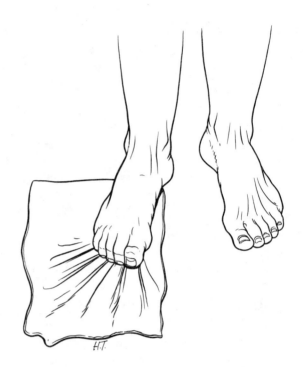

Stamina

Your stamina activities should start with a very gentle program of slow endurance activities. If you haven't been active in years, it will not take much exercise to raise your heart rate. Make sure you know what your resting pulse rate is (find this out by taking your pulse first thing in the morning). Then when you exercise, keep taking your pulse every five to ten minutes. What you want to do is keep your pulse rate up at your exercise rate which should be 60 to 75 percent of 220 minus your age. Try to keep this up for fifteen to twenty minutes of stamina exercises.

Suggested Activities

Walking in place. With your hands about waist-high lift one foot after another, trying to bring your knees up high so that they come up close to your hands. Do this in a slow, even rhythm, checking your pulse to make sure the beats per minute are not more than the exercise rate you've calculated.

Running in place. As your endurance improves, it may take more strenuous activity to get your pulse rate up to an exercise level. Running in place is similar to walking in place—just increase your pace and make sure you raise each knee as high as you can. You may feel more comfortable swinging your arms in rhythm to the leg movements.

Stationary bicycle. Use no resistance when you first start and then, as you become more fit, gradually increase the resistance.

Other activities could include: *Swimming, Walking, Golf.*

Strength Exercises

SPECIFIC EXERCISE	AREA OF BODY WORKED	OBJECT AND PRACTICAL PURPOSE
*Chin to opposite shoulder	Neck	The object is to strengthen the muscles around your neck. You should feel a pull on the side of your neck opposite the direction in which you're turning.
*Face isometrics	Face	This exercise should build up the small muscles in your face.
*Shoulder shrug	Shoulder	This is for the trapezius muscles on the top of your shoulder.
Cross-chest swings	Upper arm, shoulder, chest	This exercise will build up strength in the muscles that move your arm inward and outward.
Front lifts	Shoulder	This is for the muscles in the front of the shoulder.
Side lifts	Shoulder	This exercise will strengthen the muscles on the side of your shoulder.
Double arm benders	Upper arm	This is good for the biceps and triceps, the muscles in your upper arm.

295

Wrist curls and extensions	Forearm	The object of this exercise is to strengthen the extensor and flexor muscles in your forearm.
Forearm rotation	Forearm	This exercise builds up the muscles that turn your hand (both palms up and palms down).
*Finger exercise	Hand	This is good for the muscles in your fingers and hand.
*Sit-ups	Back	This strengthens your abdominal muscles, which help support your back.
Knee squeezes	Thigh, shoulder	This exercise strengthens the muscles on the inside and outside of the thigh. It can also help strengthen some muscles in your shoulder and arm.
*Lateral leg raises	Thigh, hip, abdomen	This exercise is for the muscles in the outer parts of your hips, thighs, and stomach.
Leg abduction	Thigh	This is for the outer muscles of the thigh.
Active bending	Thigh	The object is to build up strength in the quadriceps, which are the muscles in the front of your legs around your knees.
Hamstrings	Thigh	This exercise strengthens the hamstrings, which are the muscles in the backs of your legs.
Ankle isometrics	Ankle	This small group of exercises builds up strength in the muscles of your ankle. The outward exercise involves the peroneal muscles, the inward the posterior muscles. The last exercise strengthens the gastronemius muscles, which are the chief extensors of the foot at the ankle joint.

Description of Strength Exercises

FOR THE NECK. *Chin to opposite shoulder.* Start by looking straight ahead and then turn your head and neck slowly to the right, trying to touch your right shoulder with your shin. Hold for a count of ten and then slowly return your head to its original, straight forward position. Next, turn your head

and neck slowly to the left and try to touch your
left shoulder with your chin. Repeat once or twice
more.

Face isometrics. Smile broadly and hold for a count of five to ten. Then pucker up and hold that for five to ten seconds.

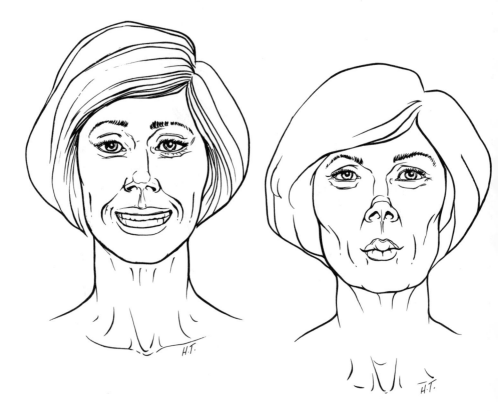

FOR THE
SHOULDER,
UPPER ARM,
CHEST.

Shoulder shrug. Shrug your shoulders up to your neck and hold for a count of five to ten. Slowly release. Repeat once or twice more.

Cross-chest swing. In the beginning of your strength-training program you can use one-pound

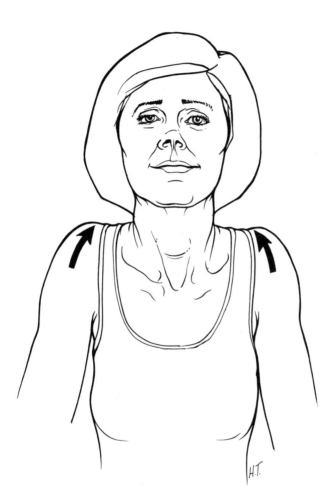

cans as weights. After a few weeks you might feel
able to increase the weight gradually, using
heavier cans, sandbags, or small dumbbells. Lie
on your back, holding a can in each hand. Extend
your arms to the side at shoulder level with your

palms facing up. Inhale, and as you exhale lift up the cans over your chest and cross your arms. Hold for a count of ten and then return your arms to their original position.

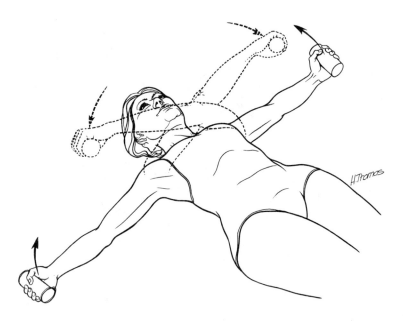

Front lift and *side lift*. Standing, lift your arm until you are holding the can straight out horizontally in front of you. Hold for a count of five and lower to your side. Then lift your arm straight to the side and hold for five. Repeat, using the other arm.

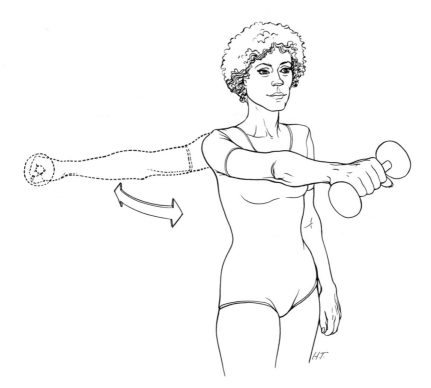

Double arm benders. Seated upright with a can in each hand, palms up and the backs of your hands resting on your thighs, stretch your arms straight out in front of you and lift them slowly to shoulder height. Lower them slowly. Next, reverse the position of your hands so that your palms are down. Again slowly raise the cans to shoulder height and then lower them.

301

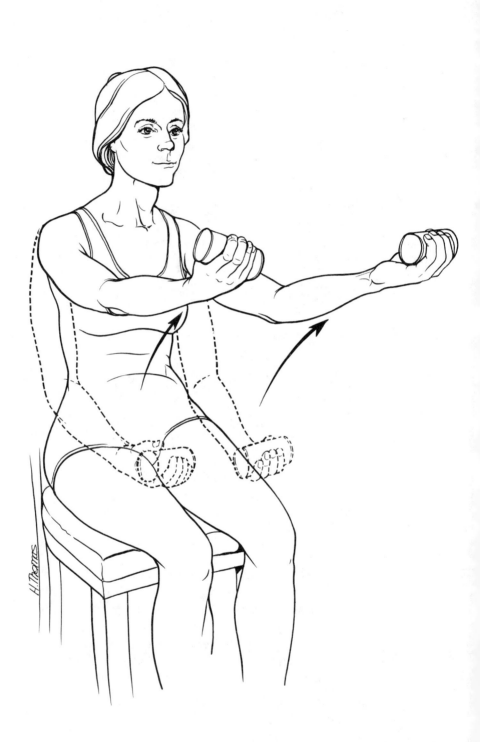

Wrist curl and extension. Sitting, with a weight in your right hand, place your right forearm (elbow to wrist) on your right thigh so that your right hand is past your knee, palm facing down. Keeping your forearm flat against your thigh, bend your wrist up as far as you can and hold for a count of five to ten. Release slowly and repeat with the left hand. You can also repeat this exercise with your palm facing up.

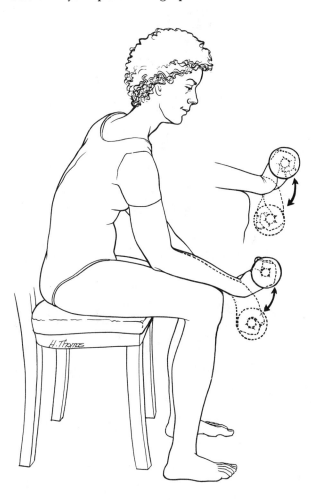

Forearm rotation. Sitting in a chair with the weight in your right hand, place your right forearm on your right thigh with your hand extending past your knee, your palm facing down. Keep your forearm flat against your knee and rotate your right hand clockwise, holding it for a count of five to ten and then counterclockwise and hold. Return your hand to its original position and again hold for a count of five to ten. Repeat, using your left hand.

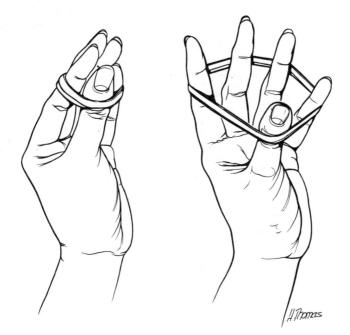

FOR THE HAND. *Finger exercise*. Place a fairly thick rubber band around all five fingers of one hand. Separate your fingers, stretching them out against the resistance of the band and hold for a count of ten. Repeat, using the other hand. Do three sets and if you find that it's too easy to separate your fingers, just add another rubber band.

305

FOR THE BACK. *Sit-ups*. This exercise strengthens abdominal muscles, which are essential for back strength. Lie on the floor on your back with your knees bent and the fronts of your feet hooked under some heavy object like a sofa (you might be more comfortable wearing heavy socks or using some padding between the tops of your feet and the underside of the restraining object). With your arms clasped behind your head, come up slowly, putting your right elbow to your left knee. Start by rolling your shoulders off the ground and then your upper chest. Hold for a count of ten and then let yourself back down slowly. Repeat this, putting your left elbow to your right knee, and hold for ten. After slowly letting yourself down, reach both elbows out to both knees, hold, and slowly lower yourself down. Perform as many as possible.

Note: Do not hold your breath while doing a sit-up, to avoid increased chest and blood pressure and subsequent fainting.

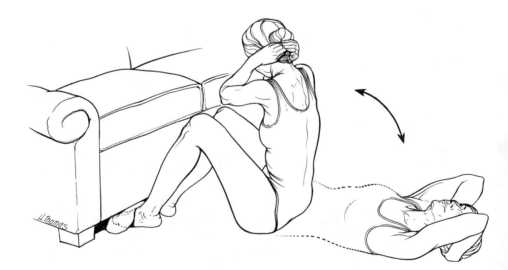

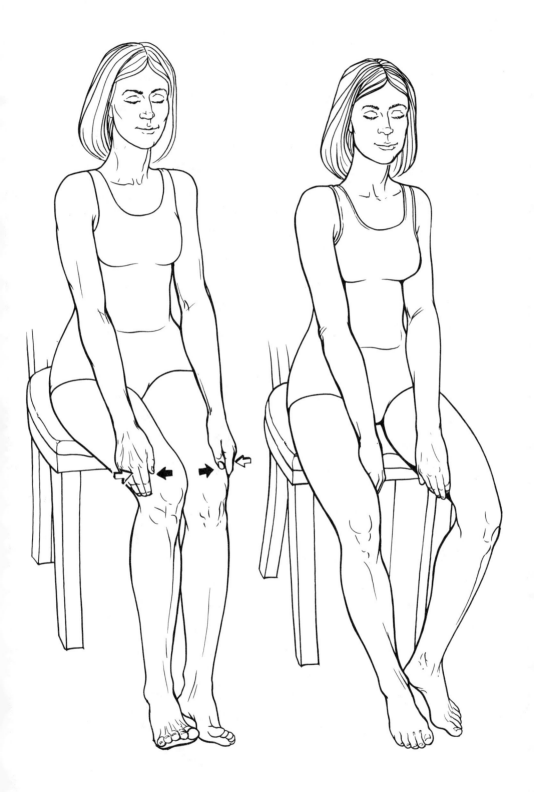

FOR THE
THIGH AND
SHOULDER.

Knee squeezes. Sit up straight with your feet flat on the floor and your knees and thighs close together. Place your hands firmly on the outsides of your thighs and try to force your knees outward against the resistance of your hands. Hold for a count of five to ten. Next, with your knees apart, place your hands on the insides of your knees and push outward while you try to force your knees inward against the resistance of your hands. Hold for a count of five to ten. Repeat the sequence, doing three sets.

H. Thomas

FOR THE
UPPER LEGS
AND SIDE
OF ABDOMEN.

Lateral leg raises. Lying on your side with your hip absolutely straight and a weight around your ankle, lift your leg slowly about two to three feet above the other. Hold for a count of ten and slowly lower it. Repeat, using your other leg. As you improve, you can add more weights.

In performing this exercise, be certain you never allow your hips to bend forward, since with the forward bend you would be compensating with another muscle.

FOR THE
THIGH.

Leg abduction. Sit in a chair with your legs straight out in front of you. Take a length of rubber tubing (an inner tube of a bicycle tire or rubber hosing will do) and wrap it around your thighs with each end tightly grasped in each of your hands. Then try to spread your legs apart against the resistance of the rubber tubing. Hold for a count of ten and repeat three times. Increasing the amount of tubing around your legs will make the exercise more difficult.

Active bending. For this and the next exercise the weight you use can be one or more cans in a pocketbook that has a handle. Sit on the edge of a table or desk with the weight on your ankle. Lift your leg slowly up in front of you until it has reached a full ninety degrees of extension. Hold for a count of ten and slowly lower your leg.

Hamstrings. Standing and holding on to the back of a chair for balance, with a weight attached to your ankle, bend your knee and lift your lower leg back as far as possible from your body. Hold for a count of ten before lowering it to a straight position. You can also do this exercise lying on your stomach.

FOR
LOWER LEGS
AND ANKLES.

Ankle isometrics. 1. Sitting on the edge of a table or desk, cross one ankle over the other. Try to move one ankle inward while pushing at it with

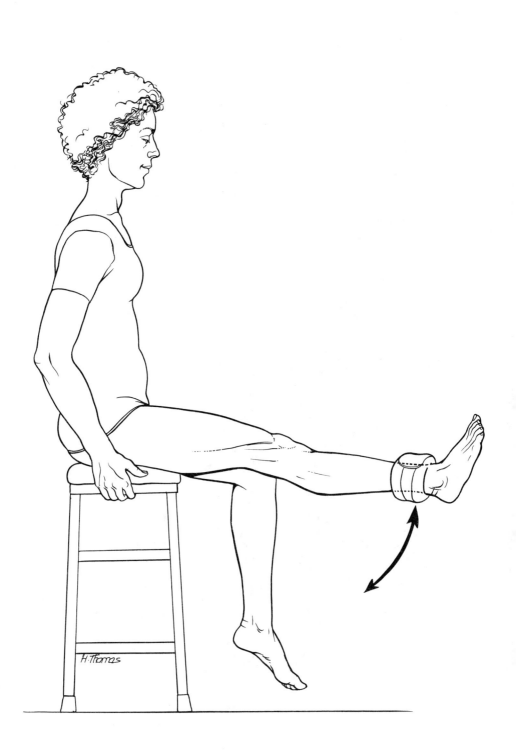

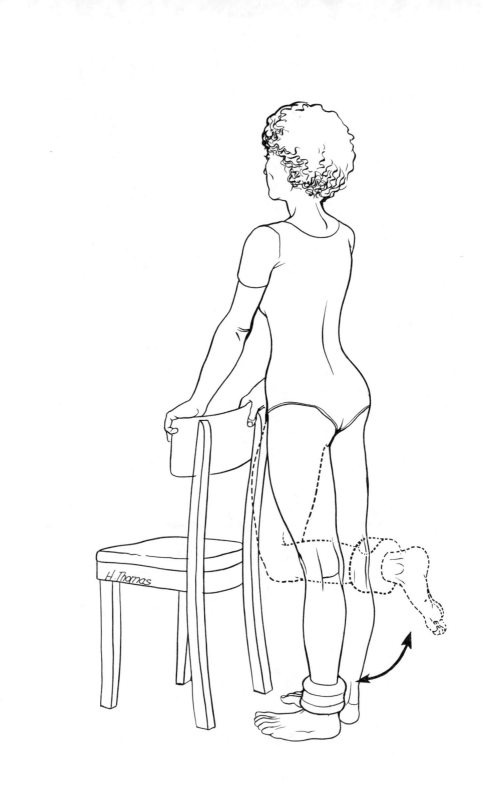

the other. Hold for a count of five to ten and then repeat, reversing ankles.

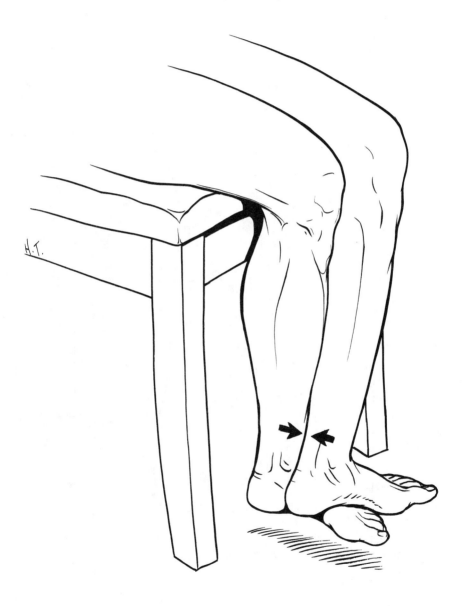

2. Sitting on a chair that is along the side of the wall, try to push your ankle that is closer to the wall outward against the wall. Then turn your chair around and now push the other ankle outward against the wall.

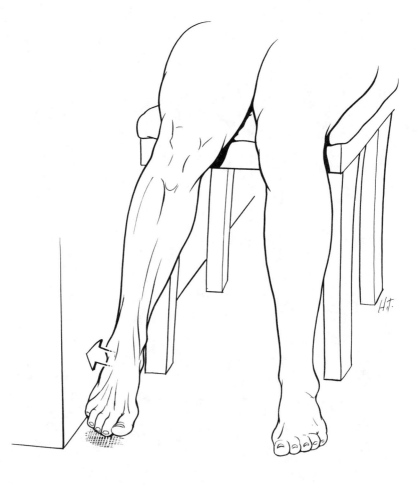

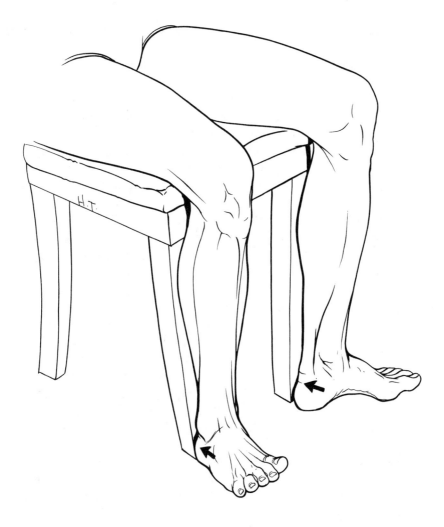

3. Sit on a chair and try to push your ankles backward against the chair legs.

As for the sports you might enjoy, once you get into shape, there will be few you shouldn't do. If you're over sixty and just starting to be active after years of doing little or nothing, you should avoid sports that require explosive speed or real quickness. The sports in this category, however, sports like basketball or hockey, will be unlikely ones for you to take up anyway. Bicycling, swimming, golf, or bowling are more appropriate and enjoyable sports for you, as are jogging and tennis. One coach we talked to has a beginners' tennis class for women who range in age from sixty-five to seventy-eight. These women come three times a week to practice their strokes, and all of them made considerable progress during the program's first year. As for jogging, an instructor in Nevada has been successfully training women, all of whom are over sixty. The oldest is eighty-eight and does at least half a mile at every session. All of the women have not only benefited mentally, showing great enthusiasm and spirit, but have made considerable aerobic improvement as well.

The older woman who has a more serious commitment to sports is now being offered a great deal in the way of competition, which, in turn, has spurred her interest. The United States Tennis Association runs senior tournaments with divisions up through seventy-five years old and older. Tennis and skiing both have established competition divided by age brackets and, more recently, running organizations and the PGA have been planning to do the same. Amateur golfers already have a Senior Women's Amateur Championship.

More and more older women who are swimmers have started taking advantage of the training and competitive events offered in the nationwide Masters swimming programs. Dr. Gail Dummer, Dr. David H. Clarke, and Dr. Paul Vaccaro at the University of Maryland have been testing a group of Masters swimmers who range in age from forty up to seventy-one and have found them in excellent condition with relatively low resting heart rates and quick recovery from the physical stress of strenuous activity. The women practice several times a week, usually for about an hour each session. They clearly enjoy both the challenge of competition and the sociability of the group. Many of them, retired from jobs that brought them into contact with people, find swimming and training in a group particularly enjoyable. When questioned about what other benefits they thought they were receiving from Masters swimming programs, they listed such specifics as reduction in tension, less depression, more energy, a sense of achievement, growth in self-confidence, deeper sleep, loss of excess weight, and better muscle tone.

Even if you're not involved in a sport, you can still supplement your exercising by becoming increasingly active in your daily life. Modify your behavior by walking when you used to ride. You can park your car a half mile from your destination or get off the bus several stops early and finish the rest of the way on foot. When you get to where you're going, walk upstairs instead of using the elevator.

You can replace coffee breaks and cocktail hours with exercise. In China and Japan, workers in factories and offices regularly leave their chairs or benches and go into some central area to stretch and exercise, often to music. These workers have been able to avoid many of the aches and pains that go along with repetitious movements or strictly sedentary posture. Older women, particularly in the People's Republic of China, are extremely involved in physical activity. In the factories they stretch, do calisthenics, and run in races; and in the village and city streets, early in the morning, they practice T'ai Chi, an exercise ritual. The fluidity of their movements and the firmness of their muscles make clear the benefits of their daily exercising.

Your exercise should also be part of your everyday life. When you travel, keep up your program even if it's more practical to switch to isometrics from weight lifting. When you're on a beach, try walking or jogging instead of sunbathing (which is an activity to be avoided in any case). When you're watching television, get up during commercials to run in place or stretch. You might especially like to exercise with a friend. One older woman told us that jogging with a neighbor has not only made exercising more enjoyable but has also kept her from turning over and going back to sleep on many chilly mornings. She's certain this also holds true for her neighbor.

317

Whichever activities you choose, your fitness program should be getting you feeling fit. If you have negative results—if you get insomnia instead of sleeping more soundly or feel persistent aches when you move instead of an improved comfort and ease of motion—then it's advisable for you to check out these symptoms with your doctor. It may be that you need to modify some activity. You should, with almost any physical condition or handicap you might have, benefit from the proper program. As you grow older, the rewards become even greater, far too significant for you to consider passing up.

13

Eating Right

One of the most widely discussed and equally widely misunderstood subjects today is nutrition. Diet book after diet book appears, each announcing a revolutionary theory that will reshape our figures while at the same time improve and insure our health. With each diet claiming different values for different foods and each theory contradicting the other, it's difficult to know just which nutrition plan to embark on. This becomes especially baffling for the woman, with her own special biological needs, and above all, the woman athlete, with her own distinct physical ones. Perhaps the wisest approach for the active woman is to get a better understanding of what does form the basis of any diet—nutrients. These are the essential nourishing ingredients that are traditionally classified as: water, minerals, vitamins, carbohydrates, fats, and proteins. Together these meet your body's need for energy, help build and repair tissue, and aid in regulating your body chemistry. Questions and controversy about diet often focus not only on which nutrients are included in a healthful regimen but also on the amount of each and the optimum balance among them.

The National Academy of Sciences periodically releases nutritional information known as Recommended Dietary Allowances or RDAs, which reflect some of the latest findings and theories. The 1980 shifts in nutrient balance favor starches and fiber-rich whole grains, beans, fruits, and vegetables as partial replacement for fats and refined sugar. The NAS recommends that healthy people eat more fish and lean meats such as veal and poultry instead of the meats high in saturated fats, beef and pork, and it suggests halving the intake of salt to prevent a prevalent condition, high blood pressure.

Another controversial subject addressed by the RDAs is that of megadoses of vitamins. Many people, particularly athletes, are under the mistaken impression that if vitamins are good for you, more vitamins are even better. There is no data at all to support the idea that massive doses of any vitamin improve athletic performance, and there is evidence that large amounts of some vitamins can be toxic. When taken in excess of ordinary dietary needs, the water-soluble vitamins such as thiamine or niacin cannot be stored in the body. They are generally excreted, making for unnecessarily expensive urine. Vitamin C in excess doses can precipitate kidney stones, interfere with certain diagnostic tests for diabetes, and produce significant stomach upset. Dr. Sally Short, nutrition expert and consultant for the United States Olympic teams, tells us that pregnant women taking massive doses of vitamin C have given birth to babies having a greater need of this vitamin. These infants, while on a normal diet, can actually get scurvy, a disease caused by a deficiency of vitamin C.

The fat-soluble vitamins—A, D, E, and K—are stored in the body fat, particularly the liver. Some nutrition experts believe that excessive vitamin E (and it is almost impossible to find a diet lacking sufficient amounts of this vitamin) can cause such undesirable side effects as headaches, nausea, fatigue, dizziness, and blurred vision. As for vitamin A, the margin of safety between the recommended level of intake and the level that is dangerous is extremely small: 5,000 international units (IUs) a day are considered beneficial and even as little more as 18,500 IUs a day can produce toxic reaction in susceptible individuals. Vitamin D in excessive doses can also cause toxicity to an extent that may be life-threatening. The toxic effects are increased by dehydration, a fact that points up a special caution for those involved in strenuous activity.

Minerals, too, are frequently taken in excess and can, like megadoses of vitamins, be not only unnecessary but also detrimental to your health. Too much phosphorus can interfere with your body's ability to use calcium, while excessive zinc can aggravate a copper deficiency. Dr. Short feels that when vitamins and minerals are taken hundreds or even thousands of times in excess of the recommended doses, they should no longer be considered within the realm of nutrition and might be more accurately described as drugs, requiring similar cautions and incurring similar risks.

Too many dieters are not aware that when they are restricting food intake, just taking vitamin pills even in the recommended amounts cannot assure them of proper doses. As Dr. Richard S. Rivlin, chief of nutrition at Memorial Sloan-Kettering Center and New York Hospital–Cornell Medical Center, points out, people who are, for example, on a 600-calorie diet and take vitamins in order to achieve normal nutritional status simply can't accomplish this through pills. To utilize vitamins, the body must have normal metabolism and produce normal amounts of enzymes, all in the proper combinations. If you are not in a normal metabolic state because of the excessively low calorie count of your food intake, the vitamins you may be counting on to make up for the food you're not eating will end up excreted in your urine.

If vitamins and minerals are taken in excess by many Americans, so is protein. The rationale behind the training table steak is the feeling that since strength comes from muscle and muscle comes from meat, eating more meat should make for more strength and muscle. In the average American diet, though, high-quality protein is adequately represented in sufficient amounts so that even the athlete who is intent on increasing strength is taking in enough. Excess protein can cause dehydration, loss of appetite, diarrhea, and can overtax your liver and kidneys. Besides these more immediate effects, a good deal of foods rich in protein, including the proverbial training table steak, also contain saturated fats that are potentially harmful to your cardiovascular system.

What you eat today can end up jeopardizing your health in years to come.

As for the specific benefits to the athlete, protein is an inefficient source of energy. Since the body does not store protein in the way that it stores fat, protein doesn't increase strength, and when it is excreted, it can cause dehydration for the athlete, who loses large amounts of water anyway through perspiration.

Increasing numbers of people have begun to realize that carbohydrates can make for a more efficient and certainly more economical source of energy. Whole-grain macaroni and pasta are now commonly recommended for athletes to use as easily digestible sources of energy, according to many of the coaches and trainers we've talked to. As for the competitive and amateur women athletes who have responded to our nutrition questionnaire, over 90 percent have described their diets as higher in carbohydrates and lower in protein than in previous years, with animal protein deemphasized the most.

Another dietary trend we've noticed among women athletes and those in fitness programs, particularly the younger women, is vegetarianism. Dr. Rivlin considers a vegetarian diet as having much to recommend it with its generally low-calorie, low-cholesterol content. Problems arise, though, because of a possible deficiency of vitamin B_{12}, which is derived only from animal sources, or of riboflavin (vitamin B_2) and calcium, which are present in meat and dairy products. The high fiber content of a vegetarian diet can also cause problems by binding such minerals as iron, copper, and zinc, keeping them from being absorbed into your system in adequate amounts. Dr. Rivlin suggests it is advisable for people who have been strict vegetarians for a long time to have regular blood tests to make sure vitamin B_{12}, zinc, and other metals are at a proper level. This is especially true for pregnant women since there have been problems in newborn babies whose mothers have been vegetarians over a long period of time.

The essential amino acids can be included in a vegetarian diet as long as a variety of vegetable products are eaten, including leaves, seeds, roots, and fruits. The quality of vegetable proteins is improved by combining those vegetables having high concentrations of some amino acids with those having the complementary ones. The overall quality of this diet will also improve if even small amounts of milk or eggs are eaten since these are high in B_{12} (a B_{12} deficiency can cause anemia and nerve symptoms). A vegetarian diet might contain prunes, dates, or prune juice for iron and mushrooms for niacin. From the growing numbers of good athletes who are vegetarians, it seems evident that with proper care and planning, this can be a nutritionally sound diet although it will require somewhat more attention than the traditional meat-based one.

Besides a new emphasis on carbohydrates and the growing popularity of a vegetarian diet, there has also been a concurrent reaction against food additives. Some of the attitudes advanced seem extreme, for as Dr. Short, who lives in Syracuse, New York, points out, she and her community would end up starving to death during the long and snowy winters if food were not preserved with additives. Those substances added to food that are not preservatives and simply offer some nonessential contribution such as coloring could be done away with, but a blanket statement against all additions to food is certainly unrealistic and unwise. The National Academy of Sciences finds additives acceptable when they improve or maintain nutritional value, enhance quality, and reduce waste. If, on the other hand, they disguise inferior processes, conceal spoilage, or in some other way are used to deceive the consumer, they are unacceptable. It is interesting to note that some additives are acceptable in some countries and banned in others, even though scientific evidence has been measured in all cases. This seems to bear out the idea that pressures from the population or from some group within it is responsible for the decision rather than any purely objective evaluation of scientific evidence. Since the issue involves a weighing of different risks, the final decision is a subjective opinion.

With a growing concern about fitness and diet, many women have been asking what special requirements they have. As athletes, both men and women frequently require additional calories because of greater energy requirements. Skiing at a high speed, for example, can use fifteen calories per minute, swimming can use five to ten, and running at ten miles per hour uses eighteen to twenty. Compare this to watching television, which requires one and a half to two calories per minute, and you can see the need for extra food intake.

The one special requirement all women in childbearing years have is for more iron. Iron is the number-one dietary deficiency in the United States and is especially prevalent among women, with two thirds of women in some studies having iron stores ranked as absent, trace, or marginal. When you stay within the 2,000 or so calories that are recommended for the average woman, it may be difficult to get enough iron in your diet, and so this is one area where the National Academy of Sciences recommends taking a supplement. Iron is lost in the menstrual blood, and when it is not replaced, some of the results can be shortness of breath, pallor, dizziness, and fatigue. Simply taking iron pills won't be enough if your calorie intake is too low, at a level inadequate to insure maximum blood production. A diet rich in iron is essential to all women, athletes or not, especially those using intrauterine devices, which often increase the amount of menstrual bleeding and so can cause more iron loss.

Important sources of iron include:

organ meats, such as liver
dried fruits, such as dates, prunes, and raisins
some vegetables, such as spinach, parsley, and asparagus
enriched bread, and cereals including bran
pork and beef

Vegetarians should be especially careful about getting enough iron since for some reason this mineral is more easily absorbed from animal sources than from vegetables. A small amount of vitamin C taken with meals is thought to help increase your absorption of iron from nonmeat sources.

Another special concern for women is the nutrient deficiencies that can be caused by birth control pills. Deficiencies in vitamin C, folic acid, riboflavin, and tryptophan (one of the essential amino acids) have been associated with the contraceptive pill. In general, the longer you've been on birth control pills and the more marginal your diet, the greater the likelihood of your having some nutritional deficiency.

There are particular nutritional needs for the pregnant woman and most often they can be met within the confines of a good basic diet. Iodine, found in seafood, is particularly important since it is an essential ingredient in thyroxin, the hormone produced by the thyroid gland, which controls brain and body development in the fetus. Folic acid, found in greens, mushrooms, and liver, is important for your blood cell production, and since levels can be low when you're pregnant, your diet should emphasize foods rich in folic acid. Despite your best efforts, your doctor may determine that you need supplements of folic acid as well as iodine and iron.

The demands for iron increase enormously when you're pregnant, as your blood volume increases as much as 40 percent. The amounts of iron-rich foods we've listed should be increased in your diet to aid hemoglobin formation for the larger amount of blood you must produce. If you're pregnant and a strict vegetarian, you may need to take supplements of B_{12}, which is not present in plants, along with increased amounts of such nutrients as iron, zinc, and chromium.

Does the woman athlete have dietary needs different from those of the sedentary woman? The only major difference lies in the energy requirements we've mentioned, requirements that can be as much as 25 percent above those of the less active woman. Of course, the intensity with which an exercise is pursued and the amount of time involved will influence the amount of energy required, so that just an occasional game of racquetball or a few laps across a pool won't be enough to alter your needs. If you are truly active, exercising enough to get your pulse rate up for a sustained period of time on a regular schedule, you'll be needing the additional calories to supply more fuel for your body.

Some sports with high energy costs include long-distance swimming, running, skiing, skating, gymnastics and tumbling, mountain climbing, and soccer. Sports with single efforts or of short duration, such as javelin throwing or diving, make lower energy demands, as do some less strenuous activities, such as archery, golf, and fencing. Your diet should be based on the energy requirements of the sport or activity as you participate in it. That is, if you walk at a pace of three miles per hour, your calorie expenditure per minute will be from three to five, while if your speed is up to ten miles per hour, you can quadruple the calories you burn. Skiing at moderate speed can burn only ten calories, while at maximum speed the count can almost double. Take these factors into consideration when you plan how much you need to eat, making sure that you decrease caloric intake when you are not exercising. It's important to eat sensibly since you are building up habits that will stay with you years after you retire from strenuous sports. We've all seen too many former athletes who still eat (or look as if they do) as if the big game were only hours off. We also know that coronary heart disease is not uncommon among former athletes who no longer exercise.

What should you eat if you're a serious athlete? There just isn't one special food that will insure success, despite the myths that tout royal honey or wheat germ or kelp. Fats and carbohydrates are the primary fuels; fats furnish more energy per unit, but carbohydrates are used more efficiently by your body. Proteins are less efficient, as we've mentioned, but if you believe you'll win your event if you eat a sirloin steak the day before, then the psychological value of that steak can make it an appropriate food for you.

Which brings us to the pregame meal. As Dr. Short points out, pregame meals are simply not all that important. By the time of competition, the athlete is either in good nutritional status or is not, and no extra vitamins or minerals can give any last-minute help. If you've reached the point where you're about to run a race or play a match, you probably know just what foods are going to agree with you and which ones tend to give you trouble. The athletes we've talked to describe extremely individual pregame menus, but the one thing they all agree on is the high level of nervous tension, which makes easily digestible foods all the more important. The American women's cross-country team in the 1980 race in Paris suffered from various minor but annoying stomach complaints that most of them recognized as a reaction to the psychological stress set off by the competition. When someone suggested that the unfamiliarity of some French foods might be responsible, some of the women on the French team assured us that while their meals consisted of their own native foods, they, too, had the same finicky stomach ailments. Grete Waitz orders a hamburger and drinks a glass of wine before the New York Marathon, while someone else decides on a bowl of cereal with milk and fruit. As long as the caloric intake is enough so that you won't feel weak or uncomfortable during competition, it doesn't much matter which of your own favorite foods you've chosen. Just be sure this meal is eaten two and a half to three hours before so that there is no food left in your stomach when you start to participate. As for foods to avoid, most athletes have learned to stay away from those that produce gas, such as broccoli or onions, or fried foods, which remain in the stomach longer.

Some coaches favor liquid pregame meals as easily digestible, while others find these don't really stick with the competitor, leaving her hungry and dissatisfied. Liquid meals can also be fairly expensive and can cause cramping and diarrhea. Since it's most important that your pregame meal be something you're personally comfortable with, the strangeness of a liquid meal can make it a poor choice. It would be better for you to experiment with these products before the tension of the big event intensifies your stomach disorders.

The liquid that is important to your performance and, even more crucial, essential to your health, is water. Don't depend on thirst to clue you in on when you need fluid. It's quite possible to be in need of hydration and yet not feel it, so be sure you have several glasses of water before competition. Most other liquids are less satisfactory: whole milk, because of its high fat content, takes longer to absorb; caffeine drinks can increase tension and elevate heart rate; and electrolyte drinks are usually highly sugared and so can draw fluid into the gastrointestinal tract, causing cramps and even dehydration. In sustained activity such as long-distance running there should be frequent fluid intake to replace the water lost in sweat. The American College of Sports Medicine recommends water stations provided at two- to two-and-a-half-mile intervals for all races of ten miles or more.

With the growth of interest in long-distance events such as the marathon, there's been more concentration on the specific needs of the endurance athlete. In the long-distance event even the best trained can't run on an aerobic, or oxygen, system alone. Energy, if it doesn't come from aerobic metabolism, must come from what's stored in your body. One source is glycogen, a carbohydrate stored in your liver and muscles that can be tapped when you're involved in activity that calls for heavy exertion or exertion over a period of time. The more glycogen you have on tap, the longer your system can run. In the early 1970s two Swedish physiologists, Karlsson and Saltin, published their findings that glycogen stores can be increased through a special diet regimen. In the first phase of the diet, what you eat is mostly proteins and fats, your daily carbohydrate intake limited to 100 grams. During this phase your glycogen stores will be depleted. Then you switch to a diet high in carbohydrates and low in salt and high-residue (fibrous) foods, this diet to be maintained up to the day of competition. Now you are resupplying your muscles with glycogen in an amount that may have increased from the 1.75 grams per 100 grams of muscle tissue while on your normal diet to as high as 4.7 grams after carbohydrate depleting. Since there is no long-range data available on the effects of this diet regimen, we would advise using this method infrequently, only for the most important events.

One mineral that even the marathoner competing in warm weather generally doesn't need in additional amounts is salt. Over the years the American diet has grown more and more salty, frequently supplying too much of it for general health. In most cases when you perspire a great deal, what needs to be replaced is water, not salt. Taking on concentrated amounts of salt—for example, swallowing a salt tablet—can draw water out of your cells in order to dilute the salt and can end up leaving your muscle cells so dehydrated that muscle fibers cannot work properly. Taking in additional salt is rarely necessary, but when it is, in situations where you've lost more than four quarts of sweat, which is represented by eight pounds of your body weight, it should come in the form of lightly salted liquids so that large amounts of water are also ingested.

The other often unnecessary addition to an athlete's diet is sugar. The "quick energy" value of sugar is not so quick after all. It takes twenty minutes of workout before you get any energy value out of a sugar snack, so that if the event you're in is short, such as a sprint, or if your part in it calls for only ten minutes or so of hard work, such as in a baseball game, the sugar is not going to do you any good. For cross-country track or Channel swimming, though, the addition of small amounts of sugar can help. Large amounts are best avoided by everyone in any sport because of resulting stomach and intestinal cramps and nausea.

Besides salt and sugar, the modern American diet reflects an increased consumption of alcohol, a fluid that competitive athletes should for the most part avoid. Alcohol does end up as glucose, but it's a slow process that is costly in calories. Alcohol is also dehydrating and acts as a depressant to your nervous system, giving athletes two more reasons not to drink any but the smallest amount while in training or competition.

The basic diet that is beneficial for the woman athlete is equally appropriate for girls. Most young people have an easier time expending calories and so usually don't require restrictive diets as long as they remain active. Decreasing calories drastically while you're growing can stunt growth, and so it is doubly important for girls who need to lose weight to do so under medical supervision. As for what weight is proper, the National Academy of Sciences offers some guidelines on heights, weights, and calorie requirements for girls who are moderately active.

Age	Weight	Height	Calories
10–12 years	77 pounds	4'8"	2,250
12–14	97	5'1"	2,300
14–16	114	5'2"	2,400
16–18	119	5'3"	2,300
18–22	128	5'4"	2,000

Younger girls require more calories in proportion to their weight than older girls, with a moderately active ten- to twelve-year-old needing twenty-nine calories per pound to maintain her desirable weight while an eighteen- to twenty-two-year-old needs ten calories less for weight maintenance.

Your basic metabolic rate—the number of calories you need at rest for the regular functions of your internal organs—declines as you get older. It's been estimated that every decade over the age of twenty-one your energy requirements will diminish by 2 percent. The American Heart Association strongly recommends that, along with keeping your weight down, you restrict your intake of cholesterol and saturated fats, since these are associated with coronary vascular disease. The following foods should be eaten in moderation:

eggs (especially yolks)
shellfish
organ meat
fatty red meats such as beef, pork, and lamb
fatty luncheon meats such as sausage and salami
whole milk, cream, butter, and soft cheeses

Instead, as much as possible try substituting vegetable oils, skim milk, margarine, poultry, fish, and veal. While there is some question as to how beneficial a diet low in cholesterol will be once you have a heart disease, Dr. Rivlin finds that the bulk of evidence favors watching your cholesterol count, which can be increased and decreased by adjusting your diet.

For the older woman who is a competitor, the basic well-balanced diet is satisfactory as long as there are lots of fluids and frequent small amounts of carbohydrates taken in during endurance events. Glycogen loading for men and women over forty as well as for the younger athlete should be done with a doctor's approval since there is some suspicion that this fairly drastic diet might be bad for the cardiac muscle. Older athletes may also develop an intolerance for sugar. If you suspect this is a problem for you, you should not eat large amounts of carbohydrate at one sitting close to the time of competition so that you avoid the abdominal discomfort you would otherwise be likely to get.

For the older and younger woman or man, and even for the child and infant, the growing American problem is obesity. Dr. Rivlin finds the blame starting with the idealized chubby baby who cannot melt away fat or think away habits of overeating when the time comes to turn into the idealized slender adult. There are many causes for overweight among children, including familial patterns. Whether genetic or environmental in origin or a combination of the two, obesity clearly can run in families, with some studies showing that when one parent is overweight, as many as 40 percent of the children are overweight as well, and when both parents are obese, the percentage of obese children jumps to as high as 80 percent. One of the causes of obesity in children that Dr. Rivlin has noted is inactivity. The overweight child is often more sedentary and less enthusiastic about sports and exercise. It is here, at the youngest ages, that physical activity should be encouraged. Drug therapy using hormones as a cure for obesity is generally unsuccessful and potentially harmful. Abnormal weight gain is rarely caused by hormonal disturbances. Other drugs to suppress your appetite stop being effective after a few weeks, forcing you to take more and more of them. Besides dangerous or otherwise undesirable side effects, they can also be habit forming. As for the diet pills you can buy without prescription, Dr. Sally Short rates them as generally ineffective since their main ingredient is simply caffeine. Clearly, physical activity is the safer effective alternative.

How else do you deal with obesity? Besides becoming more active, you may have to change your eating habits. Behavior modification programs, in which you examine what you've been doing all along and attempt to learn new habits, seem to work well for many dieters. One young woman who lost twenty-five pounds during a year at college and never put them back on told us that the first thing she learned was that she was so busy staving off hunger with frequent snacks that she never really experienced what it was to be hungry. Another member of a behavior modification program, a young mother who worked at home as a free-lance editor, reported that her major discovery about herself was that, although she ate extremely small amounts at meals, she consumed more than half her total calories after dinner when she did most of her work accompanied by boxes of cookies and candies. With behavior modification you not only keep track of what you're eating, you also keep track of the fact that you *are* eating. You always eat in one place so that you're aware that eating is what you're doing. Eating slowly, writing down everything you consume, and examining what emotions seem to go along with your heightened appetite are some of the methods used to change your eating pattern.

As for what you actually eat, you should try to get on a sensible regimen that you can remain on without endangering your health. Because of this, even if your calorie intake is lower, your diet should include all the nutrients. In order for you to stay on the diet, it should be palatable for you and satisfying enough so that you're not always feeling starved. If you travel or eat out a lot, your diet has to be adaptable.

New diets seem to appear daily and few of them come close to satisfying the biological, psychological, or practical demands of the dieter. Before you start on any, you should examine what they offer and, more importantly, what they omit.

SIX CURRENT METHODS FOR WEIGHT REDUCTION

Atkins Diet. This diet is high in fat and low in carbohydrates. The dieter, starting her regimen by cutting out almost all carbohydrates and eating instead large amounts of fat and protein, goes into a state of ketosis in which ketones, chemicals left when fats are burned in the body, become abundant in the blood and urine. The large amounts of fat in this diet can be dangerous for your heart and arteries, and ketosis is a highly risky state for pregnant women or anyone with kidney disease. For the athlete this diet can be particularly bad since it can produce fatigue and dehydration and is suspected of contributing to heartbeat irregularities (arrhythmia).

Fasting. Fasting is, of course, starving yourself. While there's probably no great harm in not eating for a day or two if you're in good health, longer periods without nutrients produce risks. For the athlete the decrease in physical performance—in muscle strength and coordination—along with the loss of body protein,

332

which can come from your muscles, and the dizziness that comes from a lowered blood sugar will certainly have a detrimental effect on training and exercising. For many fasters, strenuous activity can be dangerous.

Important minerals such as potassium, sodium, calcium, and magnesium are depleted during fasting, and a strain is put on your liver and kidneys. As with the Atkins diet, you go into a state of ketosis with its attendant problems. Clearly, this is not a regimen you can safely stay on long enough for it to make much difference in your weight.

Pritikin Diet. This is a well-rounded but extreme diet that omits cholesterol, salt, sugar, coffee, tea, and soft drinks, and is low in fat and protein. Most of the calories come from vegetables. An exercise program is recommended along with this regimen, which some people with hypertension, diabetes, heart disease, and other afflictions claim has helped them. It is often difficult to evaluate these claims objectively.

The Pritikin diet does require a tremendous change in eating habits, with copiously large amounts of vegetables. The 10 percent fat allowed is not very palatable, and few people can maintain such a regimen. This diet demands a great deal of dedication and adaptability.

Scarsdale Diet. This is a fourteen-day diet in which you eat the same breakfast and then have various combinations of protein and carbohydrate for lunch and dinner. The diet allows too little calcium to make it well rounded and includes too much red meat. It also neglects to specify quantities, a poor idea when dealing with people who tend to overeat in the first place. On this diet, as on the Atkins and Stillman diets, a good deal of what you lose is fluid, making this diet a particularly poor idea for the athlete.

Stillman Diet. On this regimen you can eat lean meats, poultry, fish, eggs, and low-fat cheeses. What is not allowed is bread, whole-milk products, anything with sugar, and alcohol. You are required to drink eight glasses of water a day in addition to diet soda, black coffee, and tea.

With such an emphasis on protein, and with carbohydrates and fats held at such a minimum, this diet lacks balance and can lead

333

to a dangerous rise in blood cholesterol. The dieter is encouraged to take supplements to make up for insufficient amounts of many important vitamins and minerals. For anyone pregnant or with liver or kidney trouble, this diet can be dangerous.

The Diet Clubs. Weight Watchers is the largest of the commercial clubs and has recently added an exercise program called PEP-STEP in which you walk briskly or climb stairs, gradually increasing the amount until you reach a maintenance level. Meetings start with weighing in, followed by an open discussion. The diets offered are well balanced and varied, with 25 percent of the daily calories in the form of protein, 40 percent carbohydrate, and 35 percent fat. The social support of the group is a crucial element for success.

Overeaters Anonymous is a nonprofit organization closely patterned after Alcoholics Anonymous. The emphasis is on behavior control, with members sharing experiences and insights with one another. There is a strong expression of spiritual belief, which is helpful to some dieters but off-putting to others. Special diets are offered but the real emphasis is on learning to deal with compulsive overeating.

For some women, particularly the young and active, there can be quite a different problem about weight—trying to put it on instead of take it off. Dr. Rivlin has noticed that patients with anorexia nervosa, a predominantly female psychiatric condition, often get up and walk around between courses or even between swallows of food. Both he and Dr. Short have advised seriously underweight patients to try slowing down, eating at a more leisurely pace and relaxing more completely during meals. In addition, Dr. Rivlin suggests tempting light eaters into consuming more by offering them varieties of food instead of plates full of large amounts of one thing. He has also found that 1,000 calories a day can be picked up with high-calorie fortified supplements given between meals. Besides diet suggestions, prompt diagnosis and treatment under the guidance of psychiatrists can be essential for those suspected of being anoretic. Anorexia nervosa is a serious psychiatric disorder with a significant mortality rate of about 5 percent overall and requires close attention.

As for the thin woman who is not suffering from anorexia nervosa and is otherwise in good health, she might consider herself fortunate since, as a rule, thin people live longer than fat people. As long as your diet is well balanced, total fitness for you if you are thin can be somewhat closer than it is for a person who is similar to you in other ways but is overweight.

14

Questions
and Answers

Selected from the Ones Most Frequently Asked

The questions, answered by Dr. John Marshall, were asked by women and men, adults and children, experienced athletes, novices, and those just starting to think about fitness.

Q. *At what age can my children start taking lessons in tennis? Skiing?*

A. Your children can start very young, probably at age six or seven, although you should keep in mind that children of this age have short attention spans. If an instructor can hold their attention, it's quite possible for young children to learn some of the fundamentals of the sport. Stay away from intensive lessons, which can destroy your children's interest. I've seen quality tennis players who were burnt out as teen-agers because of the strong competitive lessons they had as youngsters. I've also seen this in our international ski program where fifteen- and sixteen-year-olds drop out because they're tired of the rigorous

336

discipline of competition, training, and lessons they've had over the years. A better idea for young skiers is the teaching technique of free skiing, being taken down a slope to get the feel of the snow, of compensating for bumps, of learning about speed, coordination, and stability, and generally starting to feel at home on skis. Later on, as teen-agers, they can begin the actual technical training.

Nancy Greene, a former gold medalist from Canada, is convinced that too many lessons and too much training at a young age discourage interest in skiing. Her own teaching technique is to have youngsters run slalom gates, that is, learn to turn around poles. All competition is eliminated. The youngsters she teaches this way look relaxed, clearly enjoying maneuvering their way down a slope. At the same time they're becoming comfortable with the terrain, which is the best possible preparation for the more formal training ahead for those who want to go into competitive skiing.

Q. *Is it better for children to participate in many sports or should they stick to one or two?*

A. I think the best thing is to participate in many, developing good body coordination and fundamental sports skills, such as throwing, running, and being agile. Just by playing basketball or soccer or any of the racquet sports, your children will be improving their reaction time, their coordination, their body balance, and their leg movements. A variety of sports can be more fun for children when they're beginning. Later on, as they mature, they can bring to a favorite sport the basic skills they've developed in the several they've been playing.

Q. *How can I tell if my children are old enough to benefit from formal instruction in any sport?*

A. If your children can maintain a certain amount of concentration and continue to have fun along with a desire to participate, there's no age that's too young for formal instruction. Problems arise when children are forced into lessons with a rigid teacher who fails to adapt to children's changes of mood, limited attention span, and their attitude, which can be quite different from that of an adult. The right kind of coach can teach your children some of the proper techniques so that they can develop good habits.

Q. *Do you have to spend more time warming up for some sports than for others?*

A. The sports that particularly require good warm-ups are the running sports, which, because they are so repetitive, utilize the same muscles all of the time, and the explosive sports, such as basketball and hockey, where you must change direction quickly. If your muscles are tight, they are susceptible to tearing. A thorough warm-up greatly diminishes this possibility.

Q. *Can you catch a cold by sweating during exercise on a cold day?*

A. No. Sweating in cold weather is no different from sweating in warm weather—both serve to rid your body of excess heat. What is important is not to cool off too rapidly so that you lose too much body heat.

Q. *I used to be a ballet dancer. Will I be better at some sports because of my training and if so, which ones?*

A. As a ballet dancer you would have excellent flexibility and be good at patterned movements. You've had experience with executing good functional positions, keeping your body weight well distributed over your feet as you come down from a jump or start and stop a movement. All this is what we call movement dynamics, which is the essence of good sports technique. Your experience and training in dance should help you in many sports, including tennis, basketball, and volleyball.

Q. *What does it mean when you say you've pulled a muscle?*

A. When a muscle pulls, the muscle fibers themselves are torn apart. As your muscle contracts, it becomes hard and tense. If it is then forcibly stretched beyond its physiological limit, it will tear. An example of this is what we call a tennis leg. This happens when you're playing, pushing your toe up and down and contracting and releasing your calf muscle. If you take a step while the muscle is contracted and you forcibly push your toe upward very quickly, you end up stretching your muscle when it isn't relaxed, and you may well be tearing it.

Muscle pulls happen when your muscles are tired after a

period of play or when you're not in good shape so that your muscles stay contracted most of the time. Warm-ups will help, as will learning not only how to strengthen your muscles but how to relax them as well. We know from skill training that the more skilled you are, the more you are able to relax muscles. Many professional athletes have told me that one of their greatest assets is the ability to relax even in the heat of competition. In a sport like football, for example, where plays last for only a few seconds, there is time in between to relax completely. This is the way athletes are able to sustain what looks like tremendous levels of physical activity.

Q. *What is a stitch in the side?*

A. A stitch in the side is the diaphragmatic spasm or cramp and can happen from breathing very rapidly. Getting over a stitch in the side requires bending over and trying to get your abdomen to relax. Concentrating on shaking out your arms and fingers can help, as can breathing deeply from your stomach. Stomach breathing takes over for the diaphragm, pushing air out of the chest by moving abdominal contents up against the diaphragm. The abdomen is doing the work of breathing now, allowing the diaphragm to relax and recover from the spasm.

Q. *What is a shin splint?*

A. A shin splint is a soreness or mild chronic strain in the front of your leg. It happens when your calf muscle is tight so that the muscles on the front of your leg, the toe extensors and ankle extensors, compensate by overpulling as they lift and elevate your leg. Shin splints usually occur after prolonged repetitive running and can be relieved by stretching out your heel cords, warming up, shortening your stride, trying to land on your heels and push off with your toes, wearing good running shoes and sometimes by using orthotics, which are inserts in your shoes that place your foot in a good weight-bearing position.

Q. *What is a cramp?*

A. A cramp is caused by a lack of blood supply locally in a muscle and occurs when a muscle is fatigued. What happens is that when lactic acid, a waste product, is not carried away by the blood, it accumulates and puts the muscle into a state of contraction from which it is unable to relax. Gentle rubbing and then some passive stretching will help, as will keeping yourself warm. The inability of a muscle to contract synchronously and relax is a sign that you need physiological conditioning as well as skill development.

Q. *What is a stress fracture?*

A. A stress fracture is usually a partial crack in the bone. It is often due to new or unusual stresses, such as those caused by running long distances on hard surfaces. The bone, in an effort to grow strong enough to meet the new demands made on it, first softens. Small amounts of weaknesses may cause a fracture when this preparation for strengthening bone exceeds the speed of repair.

The treatment for most stress fractures is usually not a cast but instead simply the discontinuation of the stressful activity to allow your bone to heal. Without rest, the fracture can progress and worsen. A good way to prevent stress fractures altogether is to develop a good balance and change your running technique so that your weight is redistributed over the bones of your legs and feet. Always work up gradually to changes in distance.

Q. *Every time I run any distance, I end up with leg cramps. How can I prevent this?*

A. You should try running shorter distances, perhaps faster, after a good warm-up and stretching before you even start. Learn to run landing on your heels and be sure you are relaxing when you exercise. Strength training will also help.

Q. *I've been told I should only exercise in a warm room. Is this true?*

A. It's really better *not* to exercise in a warm room, and if you have a choice, choose a room where you will be very cool. In a cool room you can rapidly increase your body heat through activity whereas in a warm room, the room temperature itself increases your body heat and can cause a loss of fluids and salts through excessive sweating.

As long as there are no abrupt changes in temperature and you are exercising intensively enough to elevate your body heat, the cooler the room the better. Just make sure you wear clothing that is warm enough when you start, yet not too warm once you've raised your body heat.

Q. *I always put on a sweat shirt or sweater after I play tennis. Is this necessary?*

A. Not really. What is important is to make sure you don't cool off too fast. After a good workout, you'll be hot and sweaty no matter where you are, even on a mountain where it's twenty degrees below zero. Then, when you start to cool, you should put on a shirt or sweater so that you don't get chilled. The best rule is to keep yourself reasonably cool so that you don't oversweat and soak your clothes. Then make sure you remain reasonably warm afterward, staying warm until you get inside.

Q. *Is it bad to exercise outdoors in cold weather?*

A. It's actually very good. Exercising in cold weather just takes some adaptation. It's best to dress lightly and in cotton clothes, which breathe. You may be surprised at just how light your clothing can be as long as you have your hands and head covered and your legs reasonably warm. After about five to eight minutes of exercise you'll be warm and sweaty. Most people tend to overdress for skiing, running, or other outdoor sports. They end up sweating too much so that, when they stand for periods, they cool off quickly and get a chill from their wet clothes.

Besides wearing the proper clothing, the other caution for cold-weather exercise has to do with your state of health. If you have cardiac or pulmonary disease, you tend to get fluid in your lungs. The cold air can sometimes irritate the lungs and let them collect a little more fluid. You should be aware of this and check with your doctor.

Q. *Is it true that it's too much of a shock to your system to take a cold shower or jump into a cold swimming pool after exercising?*

A. I would not recommend it if you're not in reasonably good shape, that is, if you can't withstand rapid pulse rises, heavy exercise, or sudden temperature changes. I would say that, in general, this type of occasional self-flagellation has no particular value. After exercise your muscles can be tense, and a warm shower can offer some relief. Jumping into a cold swimming pool can be invigorating, but I don't recommend it right after exercise. Cooling off and generally relaxing your body would be a lot better for you.

Q. *Are saunas good for you?*

A. Saunas are excellent for you if you use them properly. First, the temperature must be extremely high, 200 degrees Fahrenheit or even higher. Next, the heat must be dry with the clear pine walls absorbing moisture. Even when you pour water on the rocks, the moisture in the air never gets higher than about 20 percent, which is still quite dry. The object of the sauna is to get your skin temperature higher than the temperature of the core of your body. Usually it's the other way round, with your body temperature 98.6 but your skin much lower. When your skin is warmer, circulation increases to bring blood to the tiny vessels on the surface, which are usually not used. Small sweat glands will open, cleansing pores in areas like the skin on your legs, axilla, and groin where you ordinarily don't perspire. Stay in the sauna as long as you can, which is usually fifteen to twenty minutes depending on your tolerance for heat. If you feel you're not in good shape, stay in only three to five minutes. Then come out and take a tepid shower, scrubbing yourself with a brush and soap. Next, return to the sauna, again for as long as you can. This time, after you come out and scrub yourself in a tepid shower, turn the water icy cold.

Saunas may be good for you by increasing the circulation of blood to the surface of your skin. If at any time in a sauna you feel faint, dizzy, or have a rapid pulse, you should leave. However, if you feel no ill effects, be sure you stay in long enough. I've seen people just walk in a sauna, get warm, and then leave to take a shower. This does little more good than sitting in the sun on a hot day—it may be soothing, but it has little to do with fitness.

Q. *Are steam rooms good for fitness?*

A. The temperature in a steam room is a good deal lower than in a sauna, only around 120 degrees. The warm temperature is soothing, especially if you feel tight and sore after exercise. The warm, moist air is also good for mild upper respiratory congestion and postnasal drip, not unlike the old remedy of putting your head under a towel that's draped over a tea kettle on the stove. A steam room can be an agreeable adjunct to activity but not very much more. I think that a steam room is more pleasant than it is beneficial.

Q. *I've been told by a tennis coach that it's more important to stretch after exercise than before. Is this true?*

A. It can be more important after repetitive activity such as running in which certain of your muscles tend to get stiffer. In good movement sports where there is more variety of motion, it is not quite so important. After exercise, when your muscles are warm, it's a lot easier to stretch well. Stretching a cold muscle is really not effective and can be painful.

Q. *In my calisthenics class I've noticed that women have an easier time touching their toes than do men. Why is this so?*

A. Women are indeed more flexible. They not only have an inherent trait for flexibility, but many of the activities in which they've traditionally participated, such as yoga and dance, have helped increase their adaptive flexibility.

Q. *In discussing training, what is meant by "aerobic" and "anaerobic"?*

A. The aerobic system uses oxygen for fuel. This process involves the complete breakdown of carbohydrates such as glucose, as well as fats and proteins, into carbon dioxide and water, with the concurrent release of large amounts of energy to allow your body to perform. Generally, in exercise, when we talk about total fitness, we're talking about the ability to utilize oxygen, which is what the aerobic capacity is, along with the other components of fitness, which are strength, flexibility, coordination, and quickness.

The anaerobic system, unlike the aerobic, does not require oxygen. Instead, it involves the incomplete breakdown of carbohydrates, turning them into lactic acid, with a concurrent release of energy, although the amount of energy released is smaller than on the aerobic system. The lactic acid released in

343

the anaerobic system, when accumulated in large amounts, will cause muscular fatigue.

The anaerobic system is used in exercise of short duration, such as sprints, while the aerobic system is used in activities of longer duration, such as long-distance swimming. During such prolonged activity, the anaerobic system is also involved, but only at the very beginning of the activity, during the first few minutes. After that you move on to the aerobic system, your major energy system for endurance activities. However, after a certain amount of exercise—the amount differs from person to person depending on her state of fitness—you will reach what is called the "anaerobic threshold." This is when you are no longer able to run your energy system on oxygen and must instead use your body stores, that is, glycogen (the glucose stored in your muscles). Naturally you have a limited amount of glycogen. When it depletes and as lactic acid is formed, as it is during the anaerobic process, you will go into muscle fatigue.

Q. *I've been told never to bounce when I stretch. Do you agree?*

A. Bouncing is basically not a part of stretching. What you should be doing is stretching very slowly and gently up to the point where it begins to feel uncomfortable and then stop. Contracting the same muscle and trying to stretch it again allows for synchronous relaxation of the muscle. Still, you may find it comfortable to start to bounce a bit when you're trying to warm that muscle up. Don't keep on bouncing indefinitely because, when you bounce, your muscle starts contracting before it's fully relaxed and stretched, so you won't be getting as much improvement as you will when your exercise is slow and steady.

Q. *Are there special problems of overexertion for women who are underweight?*

A. No, I really don't know of any. Most women who are normally underweight are usually in excellent shape. They exercise regularly and have body fat below average for women—14 to 16 percent of body weight in the form of body fat. If they exercise to the point of losing large amounts of body weight, the only special problem might be becoming amenorrheic from excessive exercise. This problem, though, is a transient one

344

and has nothing to do with fertility or permanent menstrual problems.

Q. *Do stretching exercises make a difference before jogging?*

A. Yes, they do. But I think you should have warmed up first so that your muscles *can* be stretched. I like to run about a half mile to three quarters of a mile and then do some stretching, even in the middle of a run. The best and most effective stretch that I get is after a run.

Stretch slowly and for a significant period of time—at least ten to fifteen minutes.

Q. *Are there advantages and disadvantages in stopping for short rest periods in any sport?*

A. There are certainly advantages in resting intermittently during a heavy workout so that you can recycle, get your pulse rate down, get down from the level where you are burning body stores for energy and start burning just the oxygen you're breathing. It is possible to relax this way, however, without stopping. If you know how to relax, you will be able to play a lot longer. For example, in skiing, the less skilled you are, the more you have to keep your abdominal muscles in a state of contraction as you make turns to the left and the right all the way down the hill. A skilled skier, on the other hand, works her abdominal muscles only in an explosive burst. These bursts can develop a much higher tension in the muscles and so are much more effective in propelling you into quick, well-balanced, and efficient maneuvers.

The relaxation the skilled skier has developed is just momentary. Actually, stopping or short rests occur in the middle. You may have noticed that you tend to shift your weight from one leg after you feel a burning sensation in your muscle and then return to the first leg as you continue. This maneuver has given you a short period of rest, but it's long enough for your muscle to relax.

Q. *Is it bad to exercise without wearing socks?*

A. Yes, it usually is. With a bare foot there is friction between the shoe and the skin. Socks provide a cushion, giving a surface that both prevents blistering and absorbs sweat.

Q. *My wife always wears two pairs of socks when she plays tennis. Is this a good idea?*

A. Two pairs of socks is usually not a good idea unless they're very thin socks and stick to the skin. Usually with two pairs, there's too much slip and not enough friction and contact between the foot and the shoe, the shoe and the surface. Your wife may lack the traction she needs for starts, turns, and cuts.

Q. *My daughter has had a recent knee injury. Can a brace help? Can it prevent recurrence of injury?*

A. I would say that 90 percent of the knee braces worn are not necessary or are inappropriate for the particular condition. There are basically only two kinds of braces that should be used for the knee: one for the kneecap and one to stabilize a loose knee. The huge cumbersome braces that keep kneecaps in a completely stable condition will only make the knee sore. Braces can help but they have to be appropriately designed. Just choosing to wear a standard knee brace after a knee injury is not a recommended procedure. It is imperative that a proper diagnosis be made by your doctor.

Q. *Do large muscles always indicate strength?*

A. No. There are some people with large bulky muscles who are not strong at all. One woman tennis player, a top athlete, has good-sized muscles but is not particularly strong. She has to train constantly to keep her muscles in good tone and strength.

Q. *Is it a bad idea to exercise in the rain?*

A. No. The rain is cooling and can feel very comfortable. When you are exercising and generating body heat, the rain will cool you off by convection. Your body is cooled when you breathe and sweat, moisture evaporating from the surface of your skin. Rain can increase that evaporation process, helping you get cool when you feel hot. The only problem with exercising in the rain is that when your clothes get wet, you may cool down too rapidly once you stop your activity. Rapid changes in temperature and humidity can chill your body or add stress, making you more susceptible to infections. Whether or not you should exercise in the rain, therefore, should be governed by the temperature.

346

Q. *I've been told that exercising on concrete or asphalt is a mistake. Do you agree?*

A. I don't agree. I don't think that running for long distances on hard surfaces is a bad thing for the knee. The normal knee does not wear out. It is a tremendous structure that can take phenomenal forces for long periods. The entire human body, in fact, can do extraordinary things, far beyond what you would normally expect. However, I do see a number of degenerative changes in the knees of runners, and they are usually due to some abnormality such as bowed legs, knock-knees, kneecap difficulties, old operations, or a long-standing condition of loose kneecaps.

Q. *Should a nearsighted person wear contact lenses or glasses when exercising?*

A. Shatter-proof glasses are far safer than contact lenses in most sports.

Q. *My friend is nearsighted, but she never wears glasses or lenses in sports. Should she?*

A. Nearsighted people need visual aids. Most sports require good hand-eye coordination and visual acuity. An exception might be running over a familiar trail. But just running down the street, avoiding pot holes, stepping on and off the curb, or maneuvering over uneven terrain would certainly require glasses.

Q. *Are there problems in wearing tight clothing when exercising?*

A. Yes. Tight clothing can restrict circulation, causing swelling if you wear tight bands around your arms and calves. An elastic band around your waist, if it drops down around the pelvis, can cause pressure on the nerve that goes down the front of your thigh. Socks around the little bone just below the knee on the outside can make for pain and numbness, actually causing you to have a foot you can't lift. I've seen all these conditions in healthy people, conditions that could have been avoided with more comfortable clothing.

Q. *What could happen if you drank an alcoholic beverage before you exercised? Or after?*

A. What happens is that you get some dilation of peripheral blood vessels. Anything more than just a beer should be avoided be-

347

fore exercise because of the metabolic effect in your stomach and liver. After exercise, beer can be beneficial because of its rehydration effect—it replaces lost liquid and salt and has proteins and carbohydrates that you may have lost.

Q. *Are there any sports you know of in which women do better than men?*

A. I think there are many sports where women have the potential to do better. Grete Waitz's time in the New York Marathon, 2 hours 27 minutes and 33 seconds, beat the majority of the men running. The improvement in women's running times in the past decade has been far greater proportionally than the improvement in men's times. In basketball, too, there have been tremendous changes and improvement. The whole game of women's basketball, in fact, has changed, with players now moving over the entire court instead of being restricted to one half. At the present time we haven't yet had the opportunity to see an accurate picture of either the capabilities or the limitations for the woman athlete. When women are matched to men size for size, lean body weight for lean body weight, and muscle fiber for muscle fiber, their performance level is extremely close to men's.

Q. *Do women have less stamina than men? If so, why?*

A. No, they don't. In fact, women have more stamina because of their larger fat stores. These good endurance capabilities allow them to exercise for longer periods of time, which is why they do so well in distance events like running and swimming.

Q. *How exactly do running and biking benefit your aerobic system?*

A. Running and biking, as well as swimming and rope jumping, improve your capacity to use oxygen. Biking brings you to greater aerobic efficiency without being a weight-bearing sport, a consideration if you are overweight or have joint problems. Running has the advantage of being simple to execute. The advantage of jumping rope is that it can be done indoors in a small place. Swimming is good because it involves your upper extremities, which many other activities do not. It is also not weight-bearing and can offer good condition if done for enough

348

time and intensity to get your pulse rate up high enough to give you good aerobic training.

Q. *What is a charley horse?*

A. A charley horse is a cramp in the muscle that occurs when your muscle runs out of enough blood to remove the buildup of lactic acid and goes into a tight knot. This condition often occurs in muscles that are fatigued or tense, and it calls for rest, massage, and gentle stretching to get the circulation back into the part that lost its blood supply.

It seems possible that the name comes from a condition in horses we call Monday-morning sickness. After a weekend of excessive exercise, horses leaving their stalls on Monday are often stiff in their muscles and tight in their joints. They are in similar condition to the marathoner, who may take close to two weeks to recover from a race if she hasn't been properly trained and conditioned.

Q. *Are there any sports to help firm the body?*

A. Many sports help firm the body. Firmness can occur in two ways. First, by losing superficial body fat so that your muscles become the prominent feature; this can occur in aerobic activities, which actually can burn body fat stores. Second, by strength training. Sports that improve strength are the explosive sports of hockey, field hockey, and lacrosse, as well as upper body sports such as gymnastics, volleyball, and basketball. There is also, of course, weight lifting in a gymnasium or at home, the most direct type of strength training, which is growing more and more acceptable for women.

Q. *Which sport is best for improving a woman's body?*

A. Probably the best sport for improving the body is one that involves the arms, abdomen, and legs. Such a sport could be skiing, gymnastics, basketball, or tennis. I should add that there is no one sport that's best for everyone. It all depends on the individual.

Q. *Someone told me that swimming a lot gives a woman large chest and shoulder muscles. What do you think?*

A. Swimming can firm the muscles but not change their size or bulk.

349

Q. *Do women develop "saddlebags" (those solidified fleshy areas around the hips) by horseback riding?*

A. No. If women do develop this kind of shape when riding horseback, it means that they're basically not in good general condition. They've acquired body fat in the thighs and abdomen, the usual places for excess body fat. Localized accumulated fat or muscle in this area is simply a natural repository for the overweight that comes from a high caloric diet and a lack of exercise, not from riding a horse or any other particular activity.

You put on fat where fat tends to accumulate, not where you might choose to put it on. By the same token, you cannot take off fat from any localized spot on your body you choose, no matter what part of you some special exercising machine shakes up. You can only reduce your entire body, the weight coming off in the areas where it is in excess. Some people accumulate more fat in certain parts of their bodies than others, which is why weight loss proceeds differently for different people.

Q. *My daughter plays a lot of basketball, and I've been warned that her arms can get stretched so that they end up longer than they would have otherwise been. Is this true?*

A. This is a complete myth. There is just no way we can increase bone length. There have been ways that have been tried for stimulating the growth of bones but none have worked consistently. There are many congenital conditions in which one limb or both are too short, and for years we've tried to find ways to get bones longer. So far, we've found it impossible to do.

Q. *Is there a team sport particularly good for my two daughters, eight and ten years old?*

A. Good team sports for this age are soccer, team swimming, basketball, and field hockey.

Q. *What team sports can be played with the opposite sex?*

A. Almost all sports except football. However, you should make sure that players are evenly matched according to physical capabilities.

Q. *My daughter's skating instructor tells me that expensive ice skates will make all the difference. Is this true?*

A. While skates are not the whole answer, there is no question that a good fit and good support from firm leather is best for the foot.

Q. *I've noticed in squash and tennis that the best of women and girls can't compare to the best of men and boys. Is it strength that makes the difference? If not, what does?*

A. Squash is an extremely fast explosive sport that requires lateral movements, tremendous quickness, and intense concentration. There are some girls and women who are excellent squash players and, not surprisingly, these players have had the same kind of preparation that men of equal caliber have had. Most girls and women, though, have not participated in sports that develop the skills called for in squash, those which call for lateral, forward, and backward movements as well as quick stops and starts. As for squash itself, only very recently have many private clubs—in some locales the only facilities for squash—admitted women to their courts. And so it really is much too early to pass judgment on the quality of women players.

Tennis is a different case. Women's tennis has been developing to the extent that we now see many thirteen- and fourteen-year-old girls who are average recreational players able to compete well against men of even regional ranking. The skill level of girls who start training early may well outstrip the skill level of many men. The average man may be stronger and have some more innate quickness than the average woman, but what counts for even more is the level of skill, which comes from preparation and training. The more enthusiasm for women's tennis, the earlier and better the training will be and the more experience gained from practice and competition. The increasingly excellent performances make clear that the physiological differences between men and women are no handicap in the racquet sports.

Q. *The girls in my class, ages thirteen to fourteen, are less competent than the boys are in the same sports. Why is this true?*

A. I think the reason there is a difference in performance is not only because of physiological factors but also because of a change in sports habits as girls get older. We've tested children at the Concordia College Racquet Club in Bronxville and found

351

that changes between boys and girls start even younger than thirteen, somewhere around the age of eleven. Girls this age are usually not involved in throwing sports such as baseball and basketball, and we've found the largest disparity between boys and girls lies in arm strength. More girls, however, are still involved in running sports at eleven, and their leg strength is quite close to the leg strength of the boys. This seems to support my feeling that adaptive differences—those differences you develop because of activity—are an important part of the reason the girls in your class don't do as well as the boys in sports.

Q. *Can athletics make females sterile?*

A. Absolutely not. There is no evidence that sterility is produced by participation in sports. Even when there has been an absence of menstrual periods, there have been pregnancies reported. Menstrual periods that diminish or disappear during intense training remit when training slows down.

Q. *Is it true that, because of their shoulders, girls can't throw as well as boys can?*

A. As we've noted before, girls just don't throw as they get older. They stop throwing sports at ages eleven to twelve and then, if they do remain active, their sports tend to involve running or skating. If they do anything at this age and when older that involves the upper arm, it is the racquet sports, which don't train the arm the way baseball and basketball do. It is this lack of utilization rather than anything to do with shoulder structure that keeps girls from throwing well.

Q. *The girls and women in my tennis club can't serve as well as the boys and men. Is it because of the female shoulder structure? Or is it due to some other reason?*

A. Serving is a very synchronous motion that takes repetitive practice to execute. It involves external rotation, leading with the shoulder and following through with the elbow, wrist, and then the body. Boys practice this motion all the time in the throwing sports so that moving on to executing a tennis serve seems natural. For girls and women, on the other hand, the throwing motion called for in serving a tennis ball can be extremely awkward simply because it's unfamiliar.

352

Q. *Is it true that prepubescent girls are better coordinated than boys of the same age?*

A. No. In fact, in our testing we've shown that from the ages of seven to eleven there are great similarities in all activities—vertical jumps, speed, endurance; upper body, lower body, and abdominal strength, and so on. Some girls may seem somewhat better coordinated because they have the advantage of being slightly more flexible.

Q. *Have you any tips for increasing concentration in sports that call for strategy?*

A. Proper preparation can help your concentration. In tennis, for example, we use drills, hitting balls at you so that you're forced to concentrate on them. We also suggest that before a match you keep an image in mind of the types of movements you will be making and the exact strokes you'll be using. In golf you can do the same, visualizing yourself hitting the ball squarely with a full swing so that there are no jerks or twists.

Q. *I have been told never to swim right before playing tennis. Do you agree with this advice and can you explain the reasons for it?*

A. I would agree. If you're swimming in cold water, your muscles can tighten and stiffen after you come out. Another reason is that swimming involves such a different form of motion from tennis, utilizing the upper arms in rotary movement and kicking in relatively slow, repetitive rhythm. Tennis, on the other hand, involves quick, explosive types of forward, backward, and lateral moves along with twisting motions of the abdomen and trunk. When you go right from the pool or lake onto the court, the transition in muscle movement may be hard for you to make.

Q. *Are there sports that shouldn't be done in combinations because one will have an adverse effect on your performance in the other?*

A. Most sports actually complement each other. Sports that mostly involve the upper extremities, such as golf or tennis, would go well with sports which utilize the lower extremities, such as running. If you're a more serious competitor, you might choose a sport to augment another by using the same movements. For example, some of the women on the United States ski team also play soccer, both fast sports that help build balance and coordination while intensifying strength in the trunk and lower extremities.

Q. *My grandmother and mother both have varicose veins. Since I've been told this condition can be hereditary, should I stay away from sports that involve running?*

A. Just the opposite. Keeping active is one of the best things you can do to help avoid varicose veins. Exercising your legs will increase the movement in your circulatory system so that your blood won't stay in your lower extremities, swelling and dilating the veins in your legs.

Q. *Is there any exercise that can help a woman who already has varicose veins?*

A. An excellent exercise for anyone with varicose veins is the bicycle exercise—lying on your back with your legs up, moving them rhythmically in a bicycling motion. When you aren't exercising, for example, when you're lying in bed, elevate your legs as much as possible. And try to remember to avoid crossing your legs.

Q. *Do you think all women have to work on being fit or are some just naturally in good physical shape?*

A. I think everyone has to work on being fit. The day we are born, we begin to adapt to our environment, and it's not always one that promotes the best of our bodies' capabilities. This means that even our inherent talents can decline. Then, too, while some of us have naturally better endurance, others greater strength, and still others more flexibility, none of us have all these natural gifts. Since fitness is made up of these three components, we have to develop what we don't have, as well as improve what we do, in order to achieve total fitness.

15

The
Changing World

Most of this book is about physical fitness in the United States. Still, all over the world we can see a similar concern—although it takes different forms in different countries. In the Orient, particularly in the People's Republic of China, the concern with fitness has become above all a matter of assuring the health and efficiency of workers. Exercise there is an integral part of life, with university students traditionally beginning each day in group calisthenics and men and women, even the most elderly, lining the streets of towns and cities to practice the ancient Chinese disciplines of T'ai Chi or shadow boxing.

Today, in addition, these concepts of group exercise have been extended into factories, farms, and offices, with modifications to suit the particular demands of specific occupations. One orthopedist in Shanghai, Dr. Shung Yuan Min, has been working out, over the years, groups of exercise routines to counter most of the stresses ordinarily produced by various factory tasks. One important focus has been workers in the textile industry—who by the way are mostly women—and who must use their fingers and thumbs in repetitive motion for hours, often developing arthritis in the joints of their hands. After only a short period of undergoing Dr. Shung's exercise regimen, the arthritis in many cases has been improved dramatically. The entire scope of exercises has recently been categorized into eighteen series of actions, each focusing specifically on the arms, legs, neck, back, or shoulders. Dr. Shung's research is continuing in the rice paddies and fields, where other forms of physical strain can be seen. The regimens he is evolving as a result of these efforts have been set forth in pamphlets and distributed throughout the densely populated section of China around Shanghai province.

Halfway around the globe in Scandinavia, where exercise has also traditionally played a significant role in daily life, there is a continual search for new developments in the study of the human body. Kinesiology clinics, where the mechanics of movement are examined, are not uncommon these days in Sweden, Norway, and Denmark, and these clinics are generally run by men and women who have both an M.D. and a Ph.D. in physical education. The idea is to bring together medicine and exercise, allowing one to serve the other, and the results are found in the excellent programs for different age groups. With all the body systems studied, the cardiopulmonary and respiratory as well as the musculoskeletal, it becomes possible to evolve realistic norms for the various activities as well as to determine, on an individual level, the amount of exercise that is, on the one hand, well within the bounds of safety while, on the other, vigorous enough to be beneficial.

In other countries involvement with fitness has focused on developing proficiency in sport, determining the amount and kind of physical preparation and training needed to produce the best athletic performance. At the French National Sports Institute (I.N.S.) on the outskirts of Paris the men and women athletes not only work at perfecting their skills but also at the same time are studied by coaches and doctors to see how they respond to various exercise regimens. In these studies, one of the directors of sports medicine at the institute, Dr. Parrier, has just begun to use a new computer that he hopes will help lower injury rates. Getting the recorded observations of coaches and trainers, monitoring the respiratory processes of the athletes, and meeting regularly with other doctors, including cardiologists, gynecologists, and psychiatrists, he is accumulating relevant facts to feed into the computer, and he is optimistic that in a few years the I.N.S. athletes will not only suffer fewer injuries but also be able to break new records of performance.

In Australia, where tennis and squash are by far the most popular sports, the emphasis is on developing the special skills and strengths that are particularly applicable to racquet sports. To this end Joe Dunnage, a committed squash player and enthusiastic teacher, has evolved a training program that requires sprints, quick turns, and various cardiopulmonary exercises. Dunnage's program is worked out in steps, each slightly more strenuous than the one before, and he has found that those players who devote themselves to this program make remarkable strides, some of them now entering the top national ranks.

And along with the rest of the world, what are we now discovering? As are the Chinese, we, too, are aware that exercise has an important place in the office and factory, and consequently we are developing many work-related fitness regimens. Corporate exercise programs are being instituted to reduce the numbers of workers on sick leave, and these programs have helped counter some of the mental lethargy and physical stiffness that accompanies those tasks that are basically repetitive. At the moment such programs exist only in a few of the larger companies, but if we learn from China, we will see how this can be done even in small factories. From Scandinavia, on the other hand, we've gotten much of our information on the cardiopulmonary system of the athlete, and like France and the rest of Europe, we've come to recognize the special importance of sports medicine.

Today the new emphasis in the United States, as in many countries throughout the world, is on the exercise needs of women. Growing numbers of women are entering the labor force and going into new occupations, ones that require large amounts of strength and endurance. Women are becoming firefighters and have to prove themselves capable of lifting and carrying heavy loads;

they're driving eighteen-wheel tractor trucks and consequently need arm, shoulder, and back strength as well as flexibility; and they are working at construction sites, where they have to maintain a strenuous level of activity over a sustained period of time. Looking at these and other jobs and assessing their requirements, it is clear that becoming physically fit and staying that way is an important aspect of equal opportunity.

Equal opportunity for women these days is extending as well into American sports. Now that girls who enjoy sports are getting more exposure, better coaching, and greater social acceptance, the women's performance levels are rising and will continue to. Think of basketball in the United States. With a million youngsters in New York City alone to choose from in this popular sport, it's no wonder the skill level is high. If many of those players end up being female, women's basketball has got to reflect the rich pool of talent by becoming a game of greater and greater skill.

These new areas of sports and fitness for women are especially encouraging to observe, and instructive as well, since they give us a good indication of what we can look forward to in the future. Looking around us, we can pick up clues, and a clear one was at a sporting event where only a few years ago no females would have been among the players. It was an ice hockey game organized in a suburban town for a team of fourth- through sixth-grade boys playing against a team made up of girls from the seventh through twelfth grades. Although the girls were older and a good deal bigger, both teams were fairly evenly matched in skill because these girls had started to take up the sport only recently. Of the entire group of boys and girls, the most skillful was a small slender girl in the seventh grade who could skate backward better than anyone there. This little girl sailed through with the puck, handling her hockey stick like a professional. Only recently she might have been limited to taking up figure skating if she liked maneuvering on ice, or field hockey if what she wanted was a fast team sport with puck and goal. And so, until now this girl would have never had the chance to find out whether or not she had any real talent for ice hockey. Today, however, if things go on the way they have—with the town's ice hockey league alive, active, and well

358

supported by the community—when this girl reaches high school, she's likely to become one of the finest of her age in the sport. She'll find out, just like the girls starting out in soccer and other fields recently opened to females, that there are whole new areas where girls and women can show their ability and excel.

Index